STEVIE CHALMERS
THE WINNING TOUCH
MY AUTOBIOGRAPHY

STEVIE CHALMERS
THE WINNING TOUCH
MY AUTOBIOGRAPHY

hachette
SCOTLAND

Copyright © 2012 Stevie Chalmers

The right of Stevie Chalmers to be identified as the Author of the Work
has been asserted by him in accordance with the
Copyright, Designs and Patents Act 1988.

First published in 2012
by HACHETTE SCOTLAND, an imprint of Hachette UK

1

Apart from any use permitted under UK copyright law, this publication
may only be reproduced, stored, or transmitted, in any form, or by
any means, with prior permission in writing of the publishers or,
in the case of reprographic production, in accordance with the terms
of licences issued by the Copyright Licensing Agency.

Every effort has been made to fulfil requirements with regard to
reproducing copyright material. The author and publisher will be glad
to rectify any omissions at the earliest opportunity.

Cataloguing in Publication Data is available from the British Library

Hardback ISBN 978 0 7553 6322 3

Typeset in Minion Pro by Avon DataSet Ltd,
Bidford-on-Avon, Warwickshire

Printed and bound by CPI Group (UK) Ltd, Croydon, CR0 4YY

Hachette's policy is to use papers that are natural, renewable and
recyclable products and made from wood grown in sustainable forests.
The logging and manufacturing processes are expected to conform
to the environmental regulations of the country of origin.

HACHETTE SCOTLAND
An Hachette UK Company
338 Euston Road
London NW1 3BH

www.hachettescotland.co.uk
www.hachette.co.uk

To David and Margaret, my mother and father; David junior, Betty, Jim and Maureen, my sisters and brothers; mum and dad Brackenridge; Jimmy Johnstone, Bobby Murdoch, Ronnie Simpson, Willie O'Neil, Jock Stein and all the backroom staff; all of whom have been a great influence in my life.

ACKNOWLEDGEMENTS

A big thank you to my wife, Sadie, and all the family: Stephen & Maria; Carol & Gerard; Paul; Ann & Kevin; Martin; Clare & George.

Also to all my grandchildren: Stephen, Chris, Vicki, Martin, Natalie, Paul, Michael, Scott & baby Jack. Life would be very dull without you all! Also to my extended family – the Lisbon Lions and wives.

A huge thanks to Graham McColl for his patience throughout the writing of this book. Apologies to anyone I have omitted, and heartfelt thanks to you all.

Picture Credits

The publishers would like to thank the following for providing the photographs included in this book (page references refer to the picture section):

Author's collection pages 1 (top and middle), 2 (all pictures), 5 (inset and bottom), page 7 (all), page 8 (middle and bottom); *Celtic View* page 8 (top); Express Syndication pages 3 (middle right), 5 (middle); *Glasgow Herald* page 1 (bottom); Mirrorpix page 6 (bottom); Popperfoto/Getty Images page 5 (top); *Scottish Daily Express*/Express Syndication page 3 (middle left and bottom); *Scottish Daily Record* pages 4 (bottom), 6 (top and middle); SMG/Press Association Images page 4 (top); D.C Thomson & Co. page 3 (top); Topfoto page 4 (middle).

While every effort has been made to trace and acknowledge all the copyright holders, the publishers would like to apologise should there have been any errors or omissions. If notified, the publishers will be pleased to rectify these at the earliest opportunity.

CONTENTS

	Prologue – Fighting for My Life	1
1	A Born Footballer	7
2	A Rub of the Green	27
3	Travels and Travails	45
4	Into the Blue	59
5	The Stein Scene	75
6	Forward Motion	95
7	Out of the Blue	117
8	Matching the Masters	135
9	The Winning Touch	151
10	Descending from the Summit	169
11	Reaching the Right Conclusion	197
12	Up Until Now	213
	Postscript – Stevie Chalmers: In Their Own Words	229
	Facts and Figures	245
	Stevie Chalmers: Career Statistics	249
	Index	271

PROLOGUE – FIGHTING FOR MY LIFE

Even when the ambulance screeched to a halt outside our house and the orderlies came panting up the stairs to my bedroom, I still didn't think there was anything seriously wrong. I was a young and very fit man, one so active in sport that, at 20 years old, I was still trying to decide whether I ought to pursue a career in top-level football or in professional golf. It was unfathomable to me that there could be any serious problem with my health. But that illusion was soon utterly destroyed.

I was rushed from my home in Balornock to Belvidere Hospital, a stone's throw from Celtic Park. It had long been a private ambition of mine for there to be a special place reserved for me at Parkhead, but not in a hospital ward for the terminally ill. The chance to enter Paradise had just drawn a good deal closer but not in the way I wished.

I had been playing Junior football for Kirkintilloch Rob Roy, happily awaiting my chance of being snapped up by a senior professional club, when I became ill. It had seemed, initially, to be nothing more than a mild feeling of not being quite right in myself but, just to err on the side of caution, the doctor came out to see me at home – house-calls were common during the late

1950s – and once he examined me he immediately knew I needed specialist attention and had me whisked into hospital straightaway. At the Belvidere they diagnosed me with TBM – tuberculosis meningitis – an extremely rare condition. When they told me, I didn't know what it was exactly or what it meant for me – although I knew it was serious. I know now that it means that tuberculosis bacteria have entered the fluid surrounding the brain and spinal cord.

I was given intensive treatment, including lumbar punctures, on a regular basis – three or four times a week. It was a difficult process. I had to kneel on the bed with the top of my head flat down on the mattress so that my back was fully extended. A nurse would then hold me firmly in place to keep me as still as possible with my spine in position while a doctor went into action with a syringe that had a needle several inches long and drained fluid from my spine. All the while I was aware that if the nurse were to let me slip, the needle could get stuck in my spine – not too nice a prospect. It was hard to go through treatment like that but I still didn't feel, in my early days on the ward, that things were too serious for me.

It was only after I had been in the ward for a few weeks that the reality of my situation struck me fully. Too many of my fellow patients were passing away for me to hide from the truth any longer. There were, in that ward, some people slightly younger than myself, some children, who had been stricken with polio, and older people who had contracted tuberculosis. Often I witnessed members of the medical staff gathering anxiously around somebody's bed before the curtain was drawn solemnly all the way round. Then the lifeless body of the patient in question would be wheeled out of the ward. It was not a very pleasant or

PROLOGUE – FIGHTING FOR MY LIFE

encouraging sight. It also seemed ominous that I had been set down in ward 13. And so, from being impatient to be released from that old hospital, it soon got to the stage where I was happy simply still to be alive.

Not that things were particularly dramatic most of the time; in fact, it was generally tedious in the extreme. I had been ordered to remain in bed permanently and the only things I could do to pass the time were read books or magazines or chat to someone in a nearby bed. Twice a day my poor mother would travel from Balornock on tramcars and buses to see me at the Belvidere and I always looked forward to her visits. The nurses were as attentive as they could be but they were kept extremely busy attending to the needs of the patients, while the doctors were kept busy too, fighting these terrible diseases that were claiming the lives of so many people.

My greatest emotion soon became extreme frustration, because I was prevented from going outside the ward to walk about. If you were in that hospital, then, ominously, you were not allowed out at all. It was as if we were condemned, cut off from society. This was exceptionally hard on a young sportsman whose entire life had been based on athletic activity. I wasn't allowed to do very much at all but, when nobody was looking, I would put my legs over the side of the bed and get them moving – I didn't want to get stiff – and if anyone came along I would quickly have to get my legs back up on to the bed and under the sheets. I could feel my fitness gradually dwindling away.

I do, though, feel that the high levels of good health and strength that I had built up before I became ill helped me endure both the illness and the severity of the necessary treatment. Seeing those other poor people succumb to their various conditions encouraged me to fight even harder to make sure I left the ward alive and well. I never thought I was in the same danger as those other people, though clearly I was. I am convinced that my positive mental attitude and refusal to give in to the seemingly inevitable, allied to my well-developed physical strength, helped me through the entire experience.

I was inside that hospital for six dreary months – I spent my 21st birthday in the Belvidere – but eventually it appeared as though I was clear of the illness and I was transferred to a nursing home in a place called Touch, near Stirling. I spent six weeks there in a big, old house, convalescing in a quiet atmosphere. They encouraged you to walk around the grounds but at first I wasn't strong enough to do so. Once I was able to walk, I soon became frustrated because you couldn't walk very far. The best thing about it was that you could talk to the other patients, get to know them and feel that you were easing your way back towards some sort of normality. I felt my health returning very gradually and it was nice to sit in that rural retreat, breathing in good, fresh air and being able to look up at the trees and the open sky.

My recovery was so dramatic that once I had returned home, Dr Peter McKenzie, a physician who specialised in infectious diseases, and the man who had overseen my progress in his role as the head consultant at Belvidere Hospital, invited me to visit him at his impressive home in High Cambuslang, where he and his wife were kind enough to give me dinner. He had set up a tripod and a motion camera to film me, and once it was running he stood behind it and asked me questions about how things had gone. He was going to Canada and the United States of America to see people who had particular new medicines and he was taking the film of me with him to show it to student doctors and nurses who would be dealing with the same disease. This film was to show how quickly and how well I had recovered from a normally fatal condition. I was his star patient, as it were.

It had been a fight for life and the closeness of my brush with mortality was only brought home to me fully when I was informed that the reason Dr McKenzie had picked me out to film was because, at that stage, I was the first of his patients to walk out of Belvidere Hospital alive. That is how close I came to feeling the hand of death on my shoulder.

CHAPTER ONE

A BORN FOOTBALLER

The jet fighter screeched off the runway and had only just cleared the land and soared into the air when the pilot tilted it 90 degrees on to its side. That had a dramatic effect on me, given that I was the passenger in this streamlined two-seater as we travelled from Suffolk to Scotland. It did not help that I had a serious fear of flying, even though I happened to be in the Royal Air Force at the time. I suddenly wondered why I had opted for this means of transport home when there were perfectly good trains running up and down from England to Glasgow; even hitching a lift began to look much more appealing. Nervousness was affecting me so much that I was moved to ask the pilot, via the microphone on my headset, what would happen if my ejector button would not work. He responded that he would simply tip the plane on its side, ping open the Perspex hatch and tip me out. That only added to my misgivings.

My stomach was lurching in every direction possible but things improved slightly when I heard the pilot check in with control and tell them that he was over Carlisle and that we'd be in Glasgow in five minutes. He was as good as his word and as we approached the runway at Abbotsinch, I was looking forward to landing and, finally, being set down gently on the ground and enjoying a return to sanity. Just as those comforting thoughts were floating around inside my head, the pilot suddenly corkscrewed the craft downwards to make the most dramatic landing possible. When we came to a rest, I disentangled myself from the straps that had been holding me in place and attempted to lurch out of the aeroplane. However, I was unable to do so before vomiting violently and copiously inside the aircraft. It was the only flight I took in my two-year stint in the air arm of our services.

Life was not always so fast for me as a young man. I spent the best part of a decade after leaving school attempting to become a professional footballer and it was a slow and sometimes tortuous process, not helped of course by my debilitating illness, which had been preceded by that enforced stint of National Service in the RAF. Both experiences were serious delaying factors in my achieving my ultimate ambition. Not that I ever became dispirited. As long as I could see a way of playing football and feel that I was improving, I was happy. The only time I could not play, perform and improve was, of course, during my joust with serious illness but even then, despite the grave nature of my affliction, I never once doubted that I would one day be back on the football field.

I always had a strong belief, allied to a powerful determination, that I would make it as a professional. Indeed, I think it was written in the stars from the moment I was born that I would become a footballer. My father had been a player and, given that I worshipped him, I was driven, naturally, to emulate him. He had played alongside Jimmy McGrory at Clydebank during the early 1920s and Mr McGrory would go on to become Celtic's greatest ever goalscorer, so I was regaled with tales of the great man from the earliest age possible. I was also the baby of our family and that meant that my father made time to take me on long walks, on which we were inevitably accompanied by a ball.

As well as being the youngest, I was also the first genuine Glaswegian in the family. This meant two things: firstly, it earned me the family nickname of 'The Glaswegian' and secondly, it made me extra-lucky in that as I was growing up I would have close to hand a demanding, football-crazy, inner-city environment in which I would thrive. David and Margaret, my parents, and David junior, Betty, Jim and Maureen – my older brothers and sisters – had all been born in Hamilton, Lanarkshire. My parents uprooted the family in the early 1930s, as a necessity to pursue better opportunities for work, and moved to Glasgow. They secured a tenement flat in James Nisbet Street, on the edge of Garngad, close to Alexandra Parade and the Glasgow Royal Infirmary. I was born on 26 December 1935, in the Royal Maternity Hospital, otherwise known to people in the west of Scotland as 'The Rottenrow', a rather ugly and threatening moniker for a hospital, but which was derived quite innocently from its address at Rottenrow, Montrose Street.

School meant only one thing for me – and that was football. Once I had departed toddlerhood and had started formal education, football dominated my thoughts almost completely, morning until night. It was at school, much more than in the street, that my enjoyment of the game mushroomed. It helped that in our local environment in the very heart of Glasgow a lot of boys were obsessed with football; so there was a good, competitive atmosphere, even in bounce games in the playground, which could only be extremely healthy in terms of nurturing the talents of a young footballer. I attended St Mungo's Primary

School in Glebe Street and my sister would take me there, then go to the secondary school and then meet me again after school to take me home, at which point my only thoughts were where, when and how I was going to find another game of football. Brother Gabriel, a Marist Brother, was both headmaster and in charge of the football team at St Mungo's and I got on very well with him.

One of my earliest memories is of being in the bomb shelter adjacent to our tenement when Adolf Hitler's Luftwaffe was dropping its bombs on Glasgow. For all that those circumstances were scary, I was able to adapt even that to a footballing purpose – using the shelters for practice by heading a ball against their walls time and again.

Our tenement was quite cramped but I was too young to realise that. Nor were the people in our family unhappy with it, because we didn't know anything else. We didn't live in luxury and nor did any of the people up our close. They were the same kind of people as us, just working people; no one had a swanky job, people just worked to keep themselves going.

We looked out of our window on to Alexandra Parade, which was just along from us, and on to a canal. My father always had a rope hanging up inside the flat so that if someone fell into the canal, this rope could be used to try to get them out. On occasion, he would hear people shouting for help, throw the rope down to their potential rescuers and they would use it to save the life of the unfortunate person in the canal. It was a fairly frequent occurrence in the Glasgow of that time for people, quite often children, to fall into a canal, and not everyone was able to swim. I couldn't swim and I avoided the canal studiously – the lingering effect of all that is that I have been frightened of water ever since.

A BORN FOOTBALLER

A better childhood memory is of wintertime and my father making me a sledge, on which I'd be up and down the hill at the back of the house incessantly.

I was ten years old when we moved a short distance away to Balornock. We had a new, semi-detached house that was considerably more spacious than the tenement and had a garden at the front and back. Best of all, it backed on to a golf course, Littlehill Golf Club, a public course, but one good enough, at one time, to have been used as a qualifying course for the Open Championship. When we first moved, I didn't know a golf stick from a cricket bat. I had no lessons – I simply picked up the game. My friend Benny Friel and I would pick up old clubs from the Barras market in the centre of Glasgow – the first set I had had hickory shafts – and I soon discovered I had a talent for the sport. I'd watch older people who were good at golf, and who played in competitions, and follow what they did, and Benny and I would use the course legally, paying our green fees, to try to put our ideas into practice. Sometimes, though, we decided to dispense with the formality of paying for a round – there was a wooden fence at the bottom of our garden that we could jump over and we would skip on to the course to play a few holes. The greenkeeper would sometimes see us, blow his whistle and give chase. Once the golf club had become wise to our exclusive, alternative entrance to the course, they put up railings that were bolted down. It wasn't long, however, until we found a way to loosen the bolts and get out on to the golf course again.

Once I reached the right age for secondary school, I began attending St Roch's, which is in Royston or, if you prefer, Garngad.

People were more likely to call it Garngad than Royston. Royston was the fancy name for the area. St Roch's was always associated in my mind with good football teams, in much the same way as St Mungo's. That was what school was all about for me – the chance to play for a good football team. I had little thought for lessons. At St Roch's we'd go up to the ash parks at Cowlairs to play our home games. We'd also go to Glennconner Park, just off Royston Road, to play and it had ash parks as well. We did not have the luxury of grass parks. Glasgow Green, which was always teeming with people playing football, also had a host of ash parks. If you wanted to play football on grass, you had to head for Ayrshire. It wasn't really a question of liking or disliking playing on ash – that was what we had, so we didn't know anything else.

My father was a very quiet man, whose life was regulated by the necessity of working extremely hard to provide for his family. On the walks we took together he would talk away to me and I'd talk to him, and the main subject of conversation would, of course, be football. He also stressed to me the importance of avoiding trouble and I've never been in trouble in my life.

My father had played football to a very good level, initially for a club called Cadzow St Anne's in Hamilton from around 1916, and then for a club in Glasgow called St Anthony's, which is where he got a Junior international cap for Scotland in 1921. Following that game, against Ireland at Celtic Park, he got the chance to go to Clydebank, who were then a senior club, and he played for them during the first half of the 1920s, when they yo-yoed between the top flight and the Second Division. He scored 23 goals in his time with them as a more than useful midfield player.

His footballing days were well behind him by the time I was born but he was an invaluable source of help and advice to me and a rock-like presence around the home. It helped that he wasn't much of a drinker, although I do remember that he and my mother would go to a club down in Kilmacolm, an isolated, rather upmarket little town that sits way out in the countryside a few miles inland from Port Glasgow. I don't quite know why they would go away down there; maybe they knew somebody at the club. Given that they didn't drive, they would have taken the bus and it would have been quite a journey. They were probably only attending a dance hall or just going for a refreshment but the reason I remember them doing it is that it was quite quirky in comparison to the general regularity of their lives.

As with most working people, my parents made the most of simple pleasures. Dad liked a wee bet on the coupon and used to stand at the sideboard and write out his line and then walk away down the road in Balornock to where the bookie's runner stood. Gambling was actually illegal at the time but everyone knew that the bookie's runner would stand on a particular corner at a certain time and would take bets. He used to go down there and place his wee lines like that – it would be a shilling on one thing, sixpence on another. He would also often take me back to Hamilton to see his family and my mother's relations, all of whom still lived in the town. Coming to the big city for work must have been a bit of a wrench for my parents. My dad used to leave the house at six o'clock in the morning and take a tramcar from Castle Street out to Glasgow Cross and from there out past Celtic Park on the Auchenshuggle tram to its terminus way out in the East End where he worked in a factory as a moulder. Like my father, my mother was a fairly quiet individual, and for her, too, working consumed much of her time. She had been in a bakery in Hamilton, making rolls and cakes, and did various other jobs to help us all. My parents were, more than anything else, very careful people.

I enjoyed schools football, winning competitions and medals, and I was chosen for a Glasgow Select team several times. We once went down to Vale of Leven to face a Dunbartonshire Select – I'd only have been ten or eleven – and I don't remember the score but I remember that I had to go to Bridgeton railway station, walking all the way as there was no other transport available to me, to meet a whole lot of new people and go down to deepest Loch Lomond-side with them. It was an interesting experience – quite a journey for the time – but for me, more than anything else, it was all about playing. More than representing Glasgow, or participating in an interesting journey, it was the chance of another game that meant the most to me and I never passed up the chance to play.

On leaving school, at 14 years of age, I had one sole ambition: to become a professional footballer. In those days, though, clubs were much less organised in terms of taking on young players. The normal route was to play for a Junior club – in the semi-professional level below the senior game – and hope that you did well enough to be spotted by a scout from a major club. I took a job in a tool-shop to earn some money but I was always sure that this was just a temporary measure. When not working, I was constantly at the Brunswick Club, a local institution for youngsters in Balornock, where we could play table tennis, badminton, five-a-sides and other sports.

The Brunswick had been built by German prisoners of war and was situated right in the middle of the housing scheme. The

A BORN FOOTBALLER

club was run by a man named Dunky Stewart and I got on very well with him. I've always had the facility to get along with people. People in the houses near to the club would open it up at night and their stewardship meant that it didn't get vandalised. It was the perfect community facility. I played for the club's youth team. I was tempted away briefly when Dougie Gray, a famous former Rangers player, started up a team in Govan and I played a few times with them. Mr Gray was a lovely man and very kind to me and wanted to put something back into the game for youngsters. He tried to be helpful and he never raised his voice but, unfortunately, his team never quite got off the ground and I returned to the Brunswick Club. It was while I was playing for them, aged 17, in 1953, that I was asked to join Rob Roy, a Junior football club based in Kirkintilloch, in Dunbartonshire.

Rob Roy suited me fine because I could get to Kirkintilloch from my home quite easily. The club gave you your bus fare – one and six – and that was it. I never thought about money at that stage – I was just happy to be playing. It was a well-organised club and its ground, Adamslie Park, had a beautiful playing surface, a nice grass pitch at a time when almost everywhere else I had played previously was ash. We played in front of good crowds too. During the 1950s football was booming and sizeable numbers of people followed every game at senior and Junior level.

At that time young players who had signed for senior clubs were then sent out to Junior clubs like Rob Roy as a part of a process to toughen them up for the rigours of seriously competitive football. I suppose the football at Junior level was pretty rough at times but I don't think it was deliberate – I think it was because that was all we knew as players at that level. Even though I was never a footballer who relied on hard tackling or extreme physical strength, I was quite happy to be in the middle of all that rough and tumble. I wanted to experience it. As a footballer, you need to learn that side of the game and how to handle it. A lot of players signed for Celtic and Rangers and were then sent out to these Junior clubs, but a number of them failed to benefit from it because they had the wrong attitude. They thought, 'I'm not going to get injured here. I have signed for Celtic.' I didn't like that attitude. I wanted to win. All my life I've been a winner, whether it was at table tennis, badminton, football, running, golf . . . I wanted to win. I think it kept me more professional. I badly wanted to win, even as a Junior footballer.

I also liked playing Junior football because it meant you were part of high-profile football, as the wider public in Scotland then understood it. There was not so much English or European football in the press at that time – and only a minuscule amount on television – so if you did well in a Junior match you might see a snippet mentioning you in one of the newspapers, alongside all the news of the senior Scottish game. You always wanted a mention in the papers and the more mentions you got the more it attracted attention. The better you played, the more chance you had to progress to the higher level. We habitually finished close to the bottom of the Central League Championship at Rob Roy but it was an enjoyable team in which to play even if it did not quite fulfil my desire to be part of a team that was winning regularly.

The people who ran Rob Roy owned a company called Watson's, which sold office furniture, and they found me a job in their Glasgow warehouse. I tried to get an apprenticeship as a joiner through them, as a fallback in case things didn't work out with the football, but the company didn't really make things as such. Instead, you were assembling ready-made furniture, such as tables and chairs. You had just to put the pieces into place and send them out. That was Watson's. It wasn't great but I was so into football that I put my concerns about that aside and concentrated on improving my game. For me, any job was only a means of marking time until I got into a football club and became as good as I could, so I didn't push too hard for the apprenticeship. My burning desire to become a professional footballer overrode everything else.

I was playing away happily at Rob Roy, feeling that I was making progress in learning the game, when I got my papers to go on National Service. In the 1950s, every young man was compelled to do it, but it was a hammer blow to me because I saw it as a seriously damaging interruption of my fledgling football career. I immediately asked the officials at Rob Roy what I could do to avoid it. They made enquiries and came back to me and said that the only way I could miss it was to go underground, down into the mines. I said, 'OK, I'll be going into National Service.' That was in 1954, when I was 18, and the beginning of a two-year stretch that would claim the remainder of my late teens and take me into my twenties. At that stage it seemed like an eternity. It was especially irritating in that I had become a bit sharper, stronger and fitter since I had been at Rob Roy. Every game was a lesson. It was like serving your time in an apprenticeship. For someone who wanted to play football, performing National Service was nothing more than a complete nuisance.

When you received your call-up papers you were asked whether you wished to serve in the army, air force or navy. You might not always be given your choice but you could make the request. I opted to join the RAF because that was what my brother Davie had done. The fact that I had a terror of flying in an aeroplane never came into it; the issue was never raised.

I was based at RAF Stradishall, in Suffolk. It was tough, petty and cruel at times but it did have its merits. It enabled you to make friends from all over Britain and it taught you lessons that would remain with you for life. They were quite hard on you in the training. As well as marching and square bashing, you had to have your shoes bulled up to a fine shine. Just as you had them looking perfect, you would be made to walk through mud and sheeps' muck and when you were finished you would be forced back into a hut with the sergeant yelling at you to get your boots clean. He would tell you he'd be back in 20 minutes and when he returned he would have with him a big sword or a big stick, just to frighten you. I hated National Service for things like that. Sometimes, you would get into bed at night and would be dropping off to sleep, when a bell would ring and you would have to get up and go and participate in an exercise, such as running from point to point with a heavy pack on your back. Funnily enough, even though I was in the RAF I only ever sat in one plane and that was the one in which I 'enjoyed' that turbulent journey home to Glasgow. Even then, I had only been hitching a lift. I was grounded, never near the planes. I had pals who did work on them, who were involved in maintenance, but once I had settled in at Stradishall, I was largely carrying out office work.

Thanks to football, I was actually more fortunate than many of my contemporaries in the RAF. If you are in the forces and you are an athlete, they do very well by you and I was soon enjoying the perks of performing for the RAF Stradishall football team. You would often be excused exercises if you were playing football the following day and as I settled into military life I found that I could spend a lot of time playing sport and being let off lightly in terms of drills and square bashing. That was one way in which National Service was lightened for me. Another was through our weekend evenings out. The nearest place to us was a little village called Haverhill, six miles away, and that's where we'd go on a Saturday night. We'd take the bus at about half past six and go out for a few drinks and dancing. This was where all the boys went. The girls would come from all over the place because the troops were in town.

We were typical young men – all looking for women. One night, I went to the dancing and I met up with a girl called Grace, whom I quickly nicknamed 'the Swede'. I saw her a couple of times but I quickly came to understand that she was far too nice a girl for me, given that all I was interested in was running about and enjoying myself. She was a country person, a lovely girl, and one evening I said to Jim Beeson, one of my pals, from Sunderland, 'I'm going to set you up with a woman tonight.' He quickly agreed, so we went into the village, to the dancing, and I fixed him up with Grace. He went out with her for quite a while and they are together to this day as man and wife.

I played for RAF Stradishall all the time and at weekends began playing for Newmarket Town, a local club that played at a slightly higher level. Newmarket is a town more regularly associated with its famous racecourse than with football and the football club even appeared to acknowledge that fact: they were nicknamed 'The Jockeys'. I played 32 games for them during the 1954–55 season and scored 13 goals, mostly from the inside-left position. I also played inside-right and on the left wing. I made a low-key debut in English football, for Newmarket away to Maldon in the Essex and Suffolk Border League, and scored twice in an 8-3 victory. That season I also took part in the FA Cup, albeit briefly, losing 3-0 to Somersham. The club finished seventh bottom of the league, in which we played against clubs such as Ipswich Town Reserves and Colchester United Reserves as well as numerous small-town outfits.

I was coming off the park at Newmarket Town one afternoon when this Englishman behind me started muttering, 'you little Scotch *******.' I turned round to confront him, hackles up, only to be greeted by a big smile and an outstretched hand. This was Alan May, who was standing there with his wife Eve. They had no children and at weekends would invite me round for dinner. I think they knew how much a youngster away from home would be missing his home comforts. Alan was a joiner who had built his own house and he and Eve became great friends of mine.

For all that I enjoyed some aspects of National Service, and Suffolk was a beautiful place in which to be based, I was pleased finally to be discharged and in 1956 I was back at Kirkintilloch Rob Roy, where I signed up happily for the coming season in the summer of that year. It was later on that year that I took ill, a matter noted in the *Kirkintilloch Herald*, which reported that, 'Rob Roy officials were rocked when Steven [sic] Chalmers, the young Auchinairn boy who Rob Roy discovered while playing for Brunswick Youth Club in Springburn, may have to quit for health reasons. Steven's Rob Roy appearances were curtailed due to National Service but he played for them while on leave.'

Even that early brush with mortality at the Belvidere Hospital had a positive effect on me. Once I was discharged from the nursing home in Touch, I was more determined than ever to embrace life, to make the most of my talents and to do all I could to become a professional footballer. It felt good to be free of confinement and to be able to get my body moving properly again and in the summer of 1957 I did everything to rebuild and improve on the fitness that I had almost completely lost. I surprised myself with the distances I ran on the roads. I'd go from the Brunswick Club in Balornock to the end of Wallacewell Road, turn up towards Robroyston Hospital, then left towards Lenzie, as far as the monument to William Wallace, down towards Auchinairn, almost to Springburn Road, left through Stobhill Hospital and back to the Brunswick Club. If I saw a bus coming along behind me, I would race it to a pole, 80 or 100 yards away, to try and work on my sprinting. It's the type of work you would do as a footballer only if there were no games to play. It was my equivalent of pre-season training, a means of building myself up to full fitness. It was good to feel the strength in my legs steadily returning.

In tandem with road running, I was constantly at the Brunswick Club. I worked like the blazes up there on getting fit and I got back my strength and fitness slowly but steadily through that club – playing table tennis, five-a-sides and anything else that might improve my reactions and speed.

It was during this time that I met a girl named Sadie at the Saturday-night dancing at St Paul's Hall behind St Mungo's Chapel in Townhead, Glasgow. We'd often go there to hear Jimmy Boyle's band. I went there one night with four pals and we all saw Sadie home that night after the dancing, as we did for weeks afterwards. Once I began going out with Sadie, in the first flush of romance, I would visit her at her house in Springburn and then run home in my everyday clothes to top up my fitness. Sadie and I were both not long out of hospital – Sadie had come out of hospital in August 1957 after having successfully battled tuberculosis.

Once I felt ready to play football again, my next task was to find a club that would take me. Rob Roy didn't seem to want me – perhaps they were concerned about what I would be like as a player after such a debilitating illness, or even concerned about the effects on my health of playing football. Maybe they just believed that I could not possibly play football again after being out of the game for the best part of a year. I continued to play for Brunswick and one day I was approached by someone from Ashfield. Unlike Rob Roy, who often struggled in the Central League, Ashfield were the premier Junior club in the Glasgow area and frequently won competitions.

I was excited at the prospect of joining Ashfield, I knew a bit about them. I knew they had a few Glaswegians in the side and that they were a team with a bit more venom and bite, but what I liked best was that this was a team full of players who wanted to win. I already knew a few of them, given that their Saracen Park base was fairly close to Balornock. One of them was Willie Brackenridge, a goalkeeper I had known since schooldays at St Roch's. En route to Saracen Park, from my home in Balornock, I would make a point of passing slowly by Willie's house in Springburn to make sure that we would hook up and walk down to the football ground together. By happy coincidence, Willie was Sadie's brother and that association helped me to get to know Sadie even better. My friendship with Willie allowed me to visit her home that bit more frequently.

I enjoyed Ashfield. I felt good there and I felt I made progress. As had been the case at Rob Roy, I played at inside-forward, on the right, and Neil Duffy, who was a smashing player, was the inside-left. I always say he was a better player than I was. He appeared slightly too small for the liking of some scouts, but perhaps because I played with him I could see how skilful he was. Scouts can't see everything from the touchline, and although Neil Duffy went on to play for St Johnstone and Partick Thistle, I am sure he could have performed at an even higher level.

Having had to wait patiently for a major opportunity, life suddenly began to speed up immeasurably for me. Things had gone well enough at Ashfield during the 1958–59 season for me to be awarded a Junior international cap, playing for Scotland against Ireland at Firhill, Partick Thistle's ground, on 24 January 1959. I was proud of my father and my aim had been to emulate him and what he had done in football. I wanted to be as good as him and this was a big step towards that: winning a Junior cap, and against Ireland too, the same opponents he had faced back in the early 1920s. I scored once in a 5-0 victory and that evening proposed marriage to Sadie – on her 21st birthday. My good fortune held firm when she said 'Yes'.

Junior internationals were a focal point for major clubs wishing to scrutinise the better players in that level of football and it was perhaps no coincidence that within days Celtic got in touch to ask me to sign. Twelve days after that appearance for Scotland I met Jimmy McGrory, the Celtic manager, and Jock Stein, the reserve team coach, on Thursday 5 February 1959. We met at Green's Playhouse on Renfield Street, Glasgow, and I signed for the club as a part-time player, with the initial agreement being that I would continue to feature for Ashfield on a Saturday. Mr McGrory was a lovely man – you couldn't say a thing against him as a human being – and Celtic had a brief burst of success under him, winning the League and Cup Double in 1954. If you looked closely, you also noticed that the influence of Jock Stein, as centre-back and captain, had been paramount in that achievement. Stein had been forced to retire from playing a couple of years later and his influence was now being felt at the club in his role as coach – witness his presence at my signing. He didn't say an awful lot on that day – I got the feeling he was sizing me up as a person very carefully.

I wore the Hoops for the first time when I played for Celtic's third eleven against Albion Rovers on 24 February 1959. We won 5-2 and I scored two goals. I must have done quite well because I was 'called up' a couple of weeks later. That meant I had to leave Ashfield entirely and join Celtic as a full-time player. The following day I played for Celtic's second eleven against Dunfermline in a 3-3 draw. I recorded in my diary for 7 March that I 'had a poor game' but, nonetheless, on the Monday afterwards I went in to Celtic Park to begin a daily routine as a full-time footballer with Celtic.

My father's help had been vitally important in moulding me as a player. As a boy, if I hit the ball the wrong way he would correct me, gently. Once I began playing Junior football, then, after a game, he would maybe tell me I had been too greedy. When I went to Celtic he was a lot less likely to offer me advice. I think he felt that he ought to retreat a bit, given that he had never reached that level himself, and that there were people at the club who might be better placed to give me advice on how to play at the highest level. It was interesting that we had both won a single Junior cap. I had aimed to emulate him and now, in getting to Celtic, I had gone further than him. But I never felt superior to him, I still owed him so much and I knew that without his input and advice way back when I was a boy, it was unlikely I would ever have attained my ambition of becoming a player at Celtic Park.

I don't know who spotted me for Celtic but in the years to come I would never be short of a whole host of people – from Jimmy Boyle, the bandleader, to many others – who would be happy to tell me that they had been the one who had put in the right word that had convinced Celtic that they ought to sign me. The decisive factor was probably that Junior international more than anything else but after a long and tortuous journey I had finally arrived at my ultimate destination. It was great, finally, to be at Celtic, but things inside the club were far from paradisiacal, as I would soon discover.

CHAPTER TWO

A RUB OF THE GREEN

The Celtic I joined in 1959 was a big club with a big support but one that was run like a small business with particularly eccentric owners. On matchdays, it was rumoured among the players and supporters Desmond White, the club secretary, used to walk up the stairs to the directors' box just before kick-off, take a quick glance out over the stand and across the three expansive terraces and mutter the first crowd figure that came into his head, and that figure would usually be a modest one. He'd look out and say, '23,000 today' and that would be recorded as the official attendance. Out on the terraces, they'd be jammed in, people would be struggling to move, but Desmond would see only a run-of-the-mill crowd. This rumour was a running joke among the playing staff but I don't believe that it was at all true – Desmond White seemed to me to be too much of a sensible accountant and businessman ever to have been involved in doing something as daft as that. It does, though, give a flavour of how the club was seen by the players and fans at the time.

On the night I made my debut for Celtic, even the Desmond of that mythical story would have had difficulty in reducing the size of the crowd, given the small number of supporters who were inside the ground. The few thousand who had turned up for the match with Airdrieonians on that Tuesday afternoon – Celtic

Park did not yet have floodlights – of 10 March 1959 had plenty of room in which to roam around should they become restless. And they did indeed become restless. Our opponents were having a good season – they had been a point behind league leaders Rangers at New Year, although they had fallen back slightly after that. Celtic, in contrast, were in a desperate condition, winding down the latest in an unbroken series of mediocre seasons, in each of which the club's chances of the championship had evaporated quickly. As if to confirm the wisdom of those who had stayed away that day, we were beaten 2-1, the team's ninth league defeat of the season. It was typical of those rather unpredictable, inconsistent times at Celtic that although I had been promoted to the first team with almost indecent haste – only four days after joining the club as a full-time player – that Airdrie match would not only be the first but also the last game for me in the Celtic first team for that season.

The fact that the crowd was so small that afternoon had no effect on me at all. I was used to playing in front of small crowds. The one major difference I noticed in comparison to playing for Ashfield was that as a player you got far more protection in League football than in the Junior game. I really felt a difference in that. I was excited to be playing but not overexcited, very happy and quite surprised at being named in the team for that game. Once the game got underway and pre-match nerves and awe at my Celtic debut had dissipated, I quickly became enormously conscious of us not playing well as a team. It was a strange debut – I hadn't even been at Celtic Park long enough to know all of my teammates' names. Also, in circumstances such as those at Celtic at the time, where the team was drifting and there was a lack of guidance at managerial level, it was possible to wonder whether there was someone playing alongside you who might be concerned that his own place in the team might be under threat if a new player, in this case me, were to come in and do well. He might be thinking, 'I'm maybe going to lose my place here if I help this guy too much and make him look good . . .' and duly do his utmost not to help. But I don't know whether that was the case or not. I was just so proud to be playing for Celtic at last. I had always been a great Celtic follower – I can remember coming off the field at Ashfield one day in October 1957 and hearing the announcer broadcast the result of the League Cup final over the tannoy: 'Rangers 1 Celtic 7 . . . I'll repeat that . . .' I walked off the park with a big, cheery face that day.

Funnily enough, a fellow who had been at RAF Stradishall shortly before me, called Jim Sharkey, was Airdrie's star man in my debut match. I never met him at the camp but everyone kept saying Sharkey had been there. He was a kind of hardman: he'd been in the cookhouse, where, if you said a word out of place they would throw tatties at you. Shortly after leaving the RAF he had joined Celtic and now that he had moved on to Airdrie our paths had crossed again.

As a professional you always know whether you have played well or not. You can cut through any hype or the opinions of those not so closely involved. After that match with Airdrie I didn't feel I had done well enough to be brought back into the team again. I was right, although things were so erratic at Celtic during that era that it was impossible to know exactly who had come to the decision to leave me on the sidelines or why it had been made.

I've got every respect for the smaller clubs in Scotland and what they do but there is no way that Airdrieonians should ever have come to Glasgow and beaten Celtic at Parkhead. It's different when you go to Airdrie – up against their fans in a tight little ground, you would expect the going to be a lot tougher. I'm a bad loser and I certainly did not like losing on my debut but Celtic had developed a bad habit of losing frequently at that time and it was one they were struggling to kick. They had lost both of their matches against Falkirk that season – a Falkirk side that would end up being relegated. Celtic had also been ushered out of the two cup competitions that season by Partick Thistle and St Mirren.

I'm not sure whether my father was at the Airdrie match or not. Sometimes he would go along to a match in which I was playing and wouldn't tell me. Even afterwards he wouldn't tell me he had been there. What he would do was watch how I had played and then a week or two afterwards he would mention, quite casually, something about my game and it would be clear from what he was saying that he had seen me play in a particular match. I'd make the connection between what he was saying and what I had done in the match in question. But he would still not tell me he had been to watch.

I was absolutely delighted to sign full-time with Celtic, and even though I had joined a club that was fast developing a reputation for consistent inconsistency, that did nothing to detract from my pleasure at being at Celtic Park. For any footballer it is a huge leap forward to go full-time. When you are part-time you maybe work hard but it's only for two nights a week. When you're full-time, you can feel yourself becoming fitter, faster and stronger, on a daily basis, and fitness is key to everything you are able to do as a professional footballer. A lot of people didn't want to do fitness work but they were the kind of people who wouldn't be able to finish a match. My immediate intention was to put everything I could into the football and that's what I did. I had always been devoted to the game and now that I was a full-time professional I was determined to make the best of every advantage I had.

It suited me to have gone full-time really quickly. In getting the opportunity to run about for five or six days a week and concentrate on the game I loved, I had achieved my earliest ambition and I loved it every bit as much as I had expected. It makes the game so much easier if you are very fit. However, I don't think I realised just how fit I could get and just what that would add to my game.

I got £20 for signing for Celtic, which even back in the late 1950s was not a great deal of money. Shortly before I signed, St Johnstone had enquired whether I would like to join them. On offer from the Perth club was a sum of more than £100, which was big money for a small club. Newcastle United and Nottingham Forest also showed an interest in me. But I was happy instead to join the club that I had supported since boyhood. It just shows you how that feeling for Celtic grips you when you've gone through your life wanting to get to that club.

It's a funny thing, but it was not until my second game for Celtic, which took place six months after my debut, that I felt as if I had truly arrived. A lot of that was because it was an away match, against Fife side Raith Rovers at Starks Park, Kirkcaldy in September 1959. When the team had to travel the players would meet at Ferrari's restaurant in Buchanan Street for a late breakfast, and then it would be on to a Cotter's bus and off to the venue in question. For me to be involved in all that, with several of the players who had been my heroes during my boyhood, made it feel like a more complete experience, as if I were part of things much more than simply having turned up at Celtic Park to discover I was in the team, as had been the case for the match with Airdrie. Travelling on the bus alongside several Celtic greats of the 1950s, such as Bobby Evans, Bertie Peacock and Neilly Mochan, with them all having me on about different things and having a great laugh, albeit at my expense, made me feel great. It made me feel as though I was among people who really wanted me to be there. I also scored two goals, which always helps, in a 3-0 win. I enjoyed that game a lot more than my debut. I felt as though I was much more integrated into the scene, and the team. It felt, to me, like my real start at Celtic Park.

There were 13,000 at Starks Park that day to see us face a Raith team that featured a young man named Jim Baxter. There was always a fair atmosphere at busy grounds for games against the medium-sized Scottish clubs, not least because the only way to see the action was to be present on the day. Television cameras were rarely to be seen at football; and would largely be found only at the bigger matches, such as the latter stages of the Scottish Cup and internationals. For people in a town such as Kirkcaldy, at a time when few people owned a motorcar, the only chance to see the bigger clubs, such as Celtic, would be when they came to town.

It was good to play in tight little grounds such as Starks Park, with its eccentric, L-shaped main stand that stretches only halfway along one touchline, but I soon discovered that I liked the really big crowds best, the tens of thousands that could be crammed into the Edinburgh clubs' grounds or that were to be found at Hampden Park for cup finals. At the smaller places, there was a different challenge, with a densely packed local crowd pitted squarely against you. You could pick out individual calls better in those matches, given that the crowd was closer to the pitch. I remember one incident from the early 1960s that took place on a visit to Airdrie's Broomfield Park. One of the Celtic players was waiting to take a corner-kick when a mince pie flew on to the turf alongside him, followed quickly by a shout from the terracing in our player's direction, 'That's two puddings on the park now!' A comment such as that can be very funny when you hear it up close during a pause in a match.

I was on the wing for that Raith Rovers match – it would be some time into my career before I was regarded as a central goalscorer. It wasn't particularly easy to score goals from the wing. With the old leather ball, it was hard to curl it – it was hard enough to get the ball all the way across to the centre-forward, never mind cutting inside and getting enough power and accuracy on a shot to beat a goalkeeper. A favourite trick of managers at that time was to leave the ball in the bath all night to make it heavier for the match the following day. I enjoyed playing on the wing, but the fact is I simply enjoyed playing football and through playing in different positions I developed a better insight into the game as a whole.

I had very rarely been played as a centre-forward in any of my teams even though I had the knack of scoring goals right through my schooldays, into my stints with my two Junior clubs and continuing through my early days at Celtic. At Ashfield Juniors I had been mostly known as a midfield man. I usually played right-half. At Celtic, it's possible that the people on the managerial and administrative side – Jimmy McGrory and Bob Kelly, the chairman – thought, from watching me in earlier matches, that I tended to tire towards the end of matches and so opted to put me on the wing. The thinking at the time was that if you were outside-right or outside-left you weren't doing as much work, that you were just remaining up the park and when you got the ball, sprinting quickly down towards the goal line to put in a cross. The idea would be to put me out on the wing to build up my match fitness and stamina. I wasn't a big, strong fellow – but I was a good runner – so it may have looked as though I would fit in best as a winger.

Up to the time I joined Celtic, my ambition had been to emulate my father's achievements as a footballer and so I had wanted to play where he had played. He had been a midfield player, a No. 8, an inside-right. Emulating him made me happy and I enjoyed playing at inside-forward when selected there. That was another position in which I often featured for Celtic during those early years, even though I wasn't particularly well designed for it because you have to do a lot of tackling in that position, and that was never one of my strengths.

Despite my experience in playing in different positions, it had never been my ambition to be a centre-forward. I wanted Bobby Murdoch's position – inside-right – and I wanted to play the way he played. I was cute enough, though, to know that I would not displace Bobby Murdoch in the team because of my poor tackling. I was a forward who wanted to push up and score goals. If an attack broke down, the inside-forward was expected to get back – the wingers and the centre-forward were the players in the team least expected to tackle.

Mr McGrory and Mr Kelly should be bracketed together in terms of team selection at Celtic because while Mr McGrory was the manager, he did not say much to the team or appear to have much influence on it. On the day of a match, he simply stood at the door as you were leaving the dressing room to go out for kick-off, gave you a wee pat on the back and dispensed advice such as, 'Get up that wing and get the ball across!' Everyone knew that it was really Mr Kelly who was selecting the team.

Mr McGrory would not don a tracksuit – I never saw him in one – and he had very few dealings with the players. He would not take you aside and give you advice on how to play the game. You'd be in the snooker room or playing table tennis before the match and you'd get a shout to go into the dressing room, where Mr McGrory would read the team out. If you weren't playing, it would be back to the table tennis or whatever.

Bob Kelly certainly had the best of intentions – he was a man who desperately wanted the best for the team and the club. He was not a man after the money; he was 100 per cent Celtic. Desmond White, in contrast, dealt with the money side of things and was always looking to maximise the amount of income that the club was generating. Jimmy McGrory would have been in the board meetings, but I don't know how much influence he would have had on Bob Kelly or on the selection of the team. He would be there noting down the team once it had been chosen. Jimmy Steele, the masseur, would actually be around at Bob Kelly's Friday-night team selection meetings and on the Saturday morning the players would kid him on, asking him for the line-up or if they were in the team. We managed to extract as much humour from the situation as we could.

Although Bob Kelly was heavily involved in selecting the team, I don't think he knew much about football. He didn't look like a footballer. He did not look physically strong and he too didn't come out and talk very much at all to the players. He tended to sit back, in the background, but he had a considerable influence on the club. He didn't, for example, want players at the club who had a bad record; people who had perhaps been in trouble with the police or who had a disciplinary problem on the field of play. Bob Kelly loved players such as Alec Byrne because Alec and his wife had a big, young family. He always spoke to me in a very friendly fashion and I got on very well with him. That may have been because Dr Fitzsimmons, the club's medical man, was very friendly with Mr Kelly and I played a lot of golf with Dr Fitzsimmons. So he may have put in a good word for me.

It may also have helped that my father had known Jimmy McGrory, and so the manager would have known what kind of player my father had been and what kind of a man he was. It's like putting in poor seeds or bad seeds – it always helps to know something about someone's background.

When I had been at Celtic for a while I got a car – it was actually more like a van – and one foggy evening, after visiting Sadie at home, I was getting in the car to go home and realised that I was going to have some difficulty because of the poor visibility. Suddenly, Johnny Kelly, a fellow professional who had joined Celtic shortly after me, materialised out of the gloom and walked in front of the car all the way to guide me home. It was very kind of him. I was ready for bed when I got home, but for Johnny the night was just beginning. He was to make only three appearances for the club before Bob Kelly moved him on to Morton.

Despite the quirks to be found in the managerial and directorial infrastructure at Celtic Park, I still wandered around in something close to a state of amazement and wonder during my early months at the club. When I first joined Celtic, I couldn't believe that I was going in with my heroes: players such as Bobby Evans, Willie Fernie, Bertie Peacock and Charlie Tully, all of whom I had admired from afar. Tully was the closest thing to a 1950s superstar – there was always a press frenzy around him. Initially, I was always thinking how good those players were compared to me – but I was gradually getting there by building up experience and fitness. If one of them was chosen for the team instead of me, I could accept it and understand it. I would still want to be in the team but I was always aware that for me it was a case of building myself up towards becoming a fully fledged Celtic player.

For all that these players were true Celtic greats, it was clear that they were reaching the latter days of their careers and as the club eased into the 1960s the names of those more senior players began to disappear from the side as Bob Kelly sought to reduce the age of the team. To do so, he would simply throw young players into the side whether they were ready for it or not. It wasn't easy playing in those young Celtic teams and we knew that the supporters weren't happy. When the ground's full, the crowd's behind you and you're facing a European team up at Celtic Park on a dark, atmospheric night, you've got everything going for you. If the ground is almost empty, you're playing a small team and things aren't going well, you don't enjoy it, and during the early 1960s there was a good deal of the latter at Celtic Park. Professional footballers are not impervious to the situation around them. I always, unwaveringly, felt as though we had to work hard to try to keep the supporters happy no matter how critical or unsupportive they might be as we toiled through this match or that. It's essential as a footballer to do all you can to keep the fans content because life is hard when they are unhappy.

Although the fans were on our backs, there was no one more critical of my own performances than me. My diary entries from the time show that even though the team might have won and even if I had scored a goal or two, I was capable of assessing clearly and rationally how well I had done. 'Saturday 26 September 1959, played first team against Clyde 1-1 – had a poor game'; '3 October 1959, played against Arbroath, won 5-0, scored two goals, had a fair game'; '10 October, Aberdeen, drew 1-1, had a poor game'; '12 October, played Wolverhampton to open the floodlights, had a poor game, Wolves won 2-0'; '16 October, back in second eleven – played in first league game under lights at Celtic Park, beat Third Lanark 2-1, scored two goals – had a fair game'; '24 October, back in first team, had a fair game – beat Motherwell 5-1'; '7 November, Ayr beat us 3-2, had a good game'; '14 November, Dunfermline, won 4-2 – had a poor game'; '21 November, 2-2 v Stirling, had a fair game'; '28 November, Partick, got beaten 3-1, had a poor game'; '5 December, Dundee, lost 3-2 – scored one goal, had a poor game'; 12 December, travelling reserve first team v Airdrie'. It is interesting to me that I could score and still be frank enough with myself to realise I had played poorly or that we could lose and I could decide that I had played well. Being honest with yourself is vital in professional football.

Following my second appearance in the first team, in that game at Raith Rovers, I steadily established myself as a first-team player and I had scored seven goals in 13 league appearances for the club by early April 1960, when we faced Rangers at Hampden Park in a Scottish Cup semi-final that would be watched by 80,000 people. It was my first taste of the Old Firm fixture, and I loved it.

I did like the bigger games and the big crowds and that meant I was always going to enjoy the Old Firm games as much as I enjoyed other major games, even though there was and still is too much trouble surrounding those matches. You would be playing away and you would suddenly see a flurry of movement on the terrace and people being hauled out of the crowd by the police. It was quite a distraction. Not only that but the referees in those matches were often biased against Celtic – it was so blatant to see when you were on the field of play – and did not give us the decisions that should have gone our way. It was quite noticeable as far as I was concerned. I would like to be able to give you all the instances of that happening but there are too many of them for me to be able to recount them all here.

I didn't think the football in Old Firm matches was particularly good. They were more about being quick to the ball and moving it on quickly and trying not to lose. They were always very tight, tense games and they were a wee bit tougher, in terms of the strength of the tackling, than most matches. You had a vast crowd of blue on one side of the ground and a vast crowd of green on the other side and the atmosphere was vile. Some of the shouts that you heard were dreadful. The crowd's chants as a whole were not pleasant. The Rangers players themselves were no worse in terms of backchat than those from other teams. Then again, they had plenty of reason to be happy as they were finding that the important decisions were going their way. That biased refereeing in itself would lead to a lot of trouble in the crowd.

For all that I found too weighty the baggage with which the Old Firm match came laden, I still managed to open the scoring that day, meeting John Colrain's corner-kick with a nice, looping header that curved high into the air and over Georgie Niven, the Rangers goalkeeper. One newspaper reporter described it as 'cheeky' and although I never tried to make a fool of any of my opponents, I suppose that goal was a little bit cheeky, in the sense that it was audacious. I was quite far out and I sent the ball in an arc out of the keeper's reach. It probably looked a bit daring, a bit confident, on my part, as it went into the far corner. It put us 1-0 ahead at half-time but Jimmy Millar equalised for Rangers and at the end the deadlock remained.

The replay was set for Hampden, four days later, on 6 April 1960. Beforehand, I received a very nice letter from Dr McKenzie, the physician who had supervised my recovery at the Belvidere. It read:

> Belvidere Hospital,
> London Road, Glasgow E1,
> 4 April 1960
> Mr Stephen Chalmers,
> c/o Celtic Football Club,
> Parkhead,
> Glasgow E1
>
> Dear Stephen,
> Allow me to congratulate you on your wonderful performance on Saturday. I can assure you I was very proud to read of your great success, as you are undoubtedly a triumph of modern medicine. Had your illness occurred only 10 years ago, Celtic would not have had their right winger there to score such a brilliant goal.

Even as a Rangers supporter I will be delighted to see you collect a Scottish Cup medal.
The very best of luck to you.

With kindest regards,
Yours sincerely,
Peter McKenzie
Consultant Physician

Sadly, despite Dr McKenzie's magnanimous good wishes, we didn't get to the final, as we collapsed to a 4-1 defeat in the replay.

Becoming a footballer enabled me to get married and settle down. Sadie and I were married on 18 June 1960 at St Aloysius Church in Springburn. We had to share the ceremony with another bride and groom because we had to get married in the close season and by the time we arranged it all the dates had been booked. We had our honeymoon in a caravan in Maidens, the fishing village a couple of miles north of Turnberry, on the Ayrshire coast. In our early days as a married couple we lived in a tenement flat in Dennistoun, only a couple of blocks away from Bertie Peacock. He would pick me up at ten past nine every morning and drive me down to Celtic Park for training. Bertie was such a nice fellow and his advice to me was to take my time and not rush into things or be overeager. If you said to him that your pay of £10 a week wasn't a lot of money, he would tell you, in his beautiful, steady Irish brogue, that you had to be very nice about things and see it this way and see it that way and not rock the boat and just enjoy life for what it was.

Every season I just hoped for the best, and the best that could happen would be that Celtic signed me on again. It's a funny thing but in my entire time at Celtic I never had more than a one-year contract. Every year, I had to wait and see if I would be offered another year. When the time came to have my contract renewed, I would just be shouted into the manager's office and they would give me one more year. Being on a one-year contract was unusual, even at that time. There were other players on longer contracts and I have to admit that I wasn't happy with it, exactly, because you never know what sort of situation you are going to be in at the end of the season.

My wages at Celtic were never great but I was satisfied with my life. Also, being a footballer meant that once we had children I was there at home in the afternoons after training, which was very enjoyable and meant that, unlike a lot of young fathers, I could watch very closely their progress as they grew. Our flat in Dennistoun was rented and my brother Jim lived downstairs. There were a lot of good properties in Dennistoun and we had what was called a single end: one room that served as bedroom, kitchen and living room, with a toilet outside. We furnished it beautifully and were very proud of it. It was an area of choice for young, newly married people. When I wasn't playing with the children, I would play golf in the afternoons, which was almost as enjoyable. It was good to be doing something that would add a little bit to my fitness. It also meant I wasn't running around up the town in the fashion in which some footballers with time on their hands after training would be tempted to do. That could lead to problems with alcohol and gambling but I was never tempted down those well-trodden but still dangerous paths.

We had great neighbours. We also had other neighbours, whose teenage boys would start to play their Rangers records as soon as we pulled up outside in our car – the kind of thing kids do – but even they would also help Sadie up and down the stairs with her pram once Stephen was born in April 1961. Once we became a family we had to move because we needed more space, and so we flitted to Easterhouse, where Carol was born in June 1962 and Paul in October 1963. We found great neighbours there too, especially Mrs Gardner, who was next door to us and who was particularly notable because she used to bring us plates of delicious, steaming-hot pancakes.

At Celtic we were on what might be described as the minimum wage for players at a top, well-supported professional British club, although it has to be said that we were still earning considerably more than the majority of the British working population. The directors of the club knew how badly most of us wanted to play for Celtic so they were able to employ, let's say, pay restraint on our behalf. Of course, they were right. I was in heaven. It was what I had wanted all my days and I was getting more enjoyment and satisfaction from playing football, even in a bad Celtic team, than I would ever have had anywhere else, even though we were certainly never cosseted at Celtic Park. After a game, we would simply be given a quick cup of tea and then it was straight back home. Nor, as the early 1960s progressed, was there any sign that our thirst for trophies would be quenched. That would lead to restlessness among some of my fellow Celts – and I would also have to weigh up my love of Celtic against being at a club where mismanagement and supporter discontent had quickly become as much a part of the club as the wearing of the green and white hoops.

CHAPTER THREE

TRAVELS AND TRAVAILS

Travelling abroad with Celtic in European competition was never to my taste and Portugal was one destination that I had particular reason to dislike. It was not that I had an aversion to playing against the Continental clubs – quite the opposite. I enjoyed immensely the challenge presented by taking on teams that had quite different styles of play to our own. The difficulty for me was that I was a bad traveller. I always took travel-sickness pills because I didn't like flying at all, but even when we had landed my concerns were far from over. Going by road was just as tricky. On buses, I used to take a seat as near the front of the bus as possible. The boys would all be up the back having a laugh at me but if you were sitting at the back there was more bounce in the seats and that was bad for my travel sickness. The pills would help and Dr Fitzsimmons would always travel with us when we went abroad, but neither medicine nor the medicine man could entirely eradicate my feelings of queasiness and uneasiness at voyaging abroad. Still, I knew that travelling was a growing requirement in modern football and that I had to put up with it.

One trip that proved doubly debilitating for me was a visit to Portugal in September 1964, for an Inter-Cities Fairs Cup match with Leixoes, a club from a small town near Porto. We were based in Vila do Conde – which, once I had settled down after the journey, I could appreciate was a beautiful seaside town for a match that would be played on a tight pitch that had been baked hard by the sun. The temperature on the day was 88 degrees in the shade and Bob Rooney, our physio, distributed salt tablets to help us cope with the draining conditions. We discovered that even though our opponents represented a modest-sized Portuguese club they were being paid £30 a week – three times our weekly wage – and were on a bonus considerably larger than ours for winning the match. They owed their good standard of living to the largesse of their club president, Francisco Malnomenes, who, pre-match, after praising the individual talents of his players, added that 'our team will have to watch out for Celtic's great centre-forward threat – Stevie Chalmers.' It was nice to receive such a compliment, but would it mean I was a marked man? With the referee enjoying hospitality at the hands of the wealthy president of Leixoes, just how neutral might he be expected to be?

We did well in the match and were comfortably sailing along towards a 1-1 draw in the Estadio do Mar, a good result to take home from the first leg of the tie. In the last few minutes, I became involved in an incident with the Leixoes goalkeeper. I made a run and jumped for the ball and, like any player then and now, had to extend my arms to maintain my balance in the air. I made a slight connection with the goalie and he fell down and lay prone on the ground. He had dropped the ball and this was his way of covering up for it. He made the most of the incident but I was entirely unprepared for what happened next, when the referee instantaneously ordered me off the field of play. It was an almost hysterical overreaction to the goalkeeper's feigning of serious injury. It was the only dismissal I would suffer in my career . . . and

I didn't like it at all. I felt instant despair. I knew my father wouldn't like it and that my entire family would be displeased. When they heard about it, they would think that I had acted thuggishly, especially as they would not have seen the match back in Scotland.

In his report submitted on the day after the match, the French referee, Monsieur Jacques Barberac, remained stubbornly adamant that his decision-making, in dismissing not only me but also Ian Young, our full-back, had been correct. Young, he said, had been dismissed for 'deliberately kicking an opponent' and I had been sent off for 'unlawfully and violently charging an opponent'. He expanded further: 'At the beginning of the second half of the game, play became more robust for one reason and another. Near the touchline, at the centre of the field, facing the stand, a Portuguese player and a Scottish player were disputing possession of the ball. The Celtic player [Ian Young], with his right foot, and in the fashion of a scythe, deliberately kicked his opponent on the legs. The Portuguese player fell, got up quickly, and butted Young, like a bull. Players of both sides, defending their colleagues, argued and punched one another. It is for this reason that I ordered off the two players – Young and a Leixoes player.

'So far as the Celtic centre-forward, who was ordered off shortly before the end of the match, is concerned, the position is as follows. The game was always lively and heated. A long ball of medium height was kicked in the direction of the Portuguese goal. The goalkeeper jumped into the air and Chalmers charged him like a cannonball, causing the goalkeeper to be on the ground motionless for at least a minute. I made a sign to the player to leave, which he did, without discussion, knowing well what he had done and fearing violent reaction on the part of the Leixoes players.'

Perhaps the colourful imagery used by the referee in submitting this report was a fair reflection of a vivid imagination. In the face of all this, I wanted drastic action to be taken to clear my name and I must say that Celtic backed me to the hilt in this. Monsieur Barberac's refereeing had prompted the Inter-Cities Fairs Cup Committee to instigate an investigation into the match and on his return to Glasgow Desmond White, the club secretary, wrote a lengthy, carefully constructed and well-argued letter to Willie Allan, the secretary of the Scottish Football Association, to put forward the case for my dismissal to be rescinded. Some extracts from it show how strongly Celtic felt about the matter and that Desmond could produce a well-turned phrase just as easily as our referee had done in his report:

Celtic FC,
Celtic Park, Glasgow,
29 September 1964

Dear Mr Allan,
At the outset, we would like to make it clear that it is not our opinion that, in normal circumstances, the referee, Monsieur Barberac, is an incompetent official... It is our considered opinion, however, that his interpretation of the rules of football differs greatly from that prevailing in Scottish football... As the game progressed he began to lose his grip on the game and his decisions began to become more and more inconsistent. Finally, he appeared to lose control completely.

At the end, matters deteriorated to such an extent that two of our players were sent off in circumstances that were, in our opinion, quite unjust . . .

With reference to the second incident, in which Chalmers was involved, it was difficult to appreciate why the referee took the action that he did. Celtic had gained a corner-kick on the right wing. This was taken by Gallagher. He is accustomed to kicking the ball with his left foot and, as such, this normally results in the corner being an in-swinger, and, of course, Chalmers is well aware of this. We understand that he observed the goalkeeper was standing well to the left-hand side of his goal and when he saw that the corner-kick was going to be rather short he ran forward in an effort to head it in between the junction of the crossbar and the post. The goalkeeper also realised the position, however, and advanced towards the post and they collided in mid-air. In our opinion it was a simple accident . . . The goalkeeper appeared to be hurt but we think it only fair to comment that as soon as Chalmers was ordered from the field the goalkeeper made a speedy recovery. It is further to be advanced on Chalmers' behalf that as soon as he realised the goalkeeper appeared to be in pain, he went immediately to his assistance.

We are strongly of the opinion that a serious injustice has been done to our two players. Stephen Chalmers, who has been a senior for approximately seven years, has been cautioned only twice during that time. Both have exemplary characters and we feel in the circumstances outlined above that they are victims of

incomprehensible decisions by a referee who was, in the last resort, not a fit and proper person to have control of such an important game.
Yours sincerely,
Desmond White

The letter had the desired effect. It was the job of our own national football association to deal with disciplinary matters, even, quirkily enough, in European competition, and I was subsequently not suspended for the home tie with Leixoes, which took place a week after Mr White's letter had been despatched, and which we won 3-0, with me being in place to score the first two goals.

It was always enjoyable to be garlanded for hitting the net but I must say honestly that I didn't care who scored the goals. Certainly it was nice to score goals but if I scored three times and we lost I would not be happy at all. That 1964–65 season would see me score 26 goals and become the leading goalscorer at the club for the third season since I had joined, five years earlier, but I don't think I had it really too much on my mind in terms of trying to beat other people at the club to that distinction. I was more interested in scoring a goal that got us the points for winning a match rather than worrying that someone was scoring more goals than me.

Although I was scoring goals regularly, I must admit that during those years when Jimmy McGrory was manager I was a bit concerned about my future at the club. You would have to be concerned. You have a contract and you've got to make sure you do well enough to get another one, but Celtic were going through an extended bad spell and, by 1964, had failed to win a national competition since the League Cup in 1957. After five years at the club, I was still awaiting my first senior winner's medal. The club had had a bit of success in the 1950s with the team before us – the one featuring players such as Charlie Tully, Bertie Peacock and Bobby Evans – and they were trying to get us, a team composed largely of youngsters, to emulate them. But the team just wouldn't settle down and the situation was unstable. At the front of my mind I knew that I still had to work as hard as I could because if I did not do so I felt I might lose the chance to establish myself as a Celtic player. I couldn't let that chance to play for Celtic slip from my grasp. They were still, regardless of the condition they were in at that particular time, very much my team.

At that time, though, even if you were dedicated to improving yourself and your game and becoming a better player for the benefit of the club, you could still find yourself being made to feel as though you had done something wrong. I used to come into Celtic Park in the morning a bit earlier than most players. There was a wee gymnasium inside the stadium and I used to like hitting the ball off the wall-bars so that it would bounce off anywhere, forcing me to dash around, control the ball and return it with either foot. It was an exercise that sharpened up my skills. If it came back hard you controlled it first then returned it; if it came back more gently, you returned it first-time. It was simply my way of getting some practice with the ball and I knew that it would come in very handy on a matchday. I tried to make sure I didn't get caught doing it, though. There were people on the managerial side at that time who if they saw me practising like that would intervene, take the ball away from me, put it under lock and key, and then, as if I was a naughty schoolboy, tell me, 'You'll see enough of the ball on Saturday.' I was told to cut it out and get about the business of being a footballer... by lapping the park. It was hard, at that time, to get a hold of a ball to practise with.

Billy McNeill, who had been at the club for a number of years by that time, was starting to feel restless around 1964. The disorganisation at the club had left him disillusioned. I felt the same way as Billy about the way the club was going but I have to say that I did not want to leave Celtic at any time. It really never even crossed my mind. This was my club, the club I had dreamed of representing since I had been a child. I knew, though, within myself, that there were things that needed to be done to turn the club around.

I also felt that I should stay at Celtic because, for all that things were not quite right at the club, I still felt that to have a chance at Celtic was better than moving somewhere else. Things might not work out at the new destination in the way you wished, whereas, with Celtic, I knew the club and had this great feeling for it. That still counted for a lot. Also, by late 1964, we had been blessed with a very young family: four children – Stephen, Carol, Paul and Ann, who arrived in November 1964 – and all four were under the age of four. With them being so very young, I didn't want to move – and while we were not being paid very much at Celtic in comparison to footballers at other clubs, we were still earning a good living.

During the early 1960s, as Celtic players we felt awfully low at times and the supporters weren't supporting the team just as well as they could have done. It's great to hear the big crowds roaring but it's horrible hearing them boo you. They weren't wanting to cheer a bad team and we must have been a bad team. That would bring me down because I was getting the boos as much as anybody. It was a thing you had to try and fight through. When you got into the ground on a Monday morning and started training you felt right again and you were desperate to win for the supporters the next time out, even though they had been giving you some awful stick. You would never think that they could go and stuff themselves. You had to do everything to win them around and get their support back. It was their club and through their booing they were expressing their desperation to see something better.

It wasn't good to be losing to Rangers so frequently. Most of us were from the west of Scotland and we knew how the supporters would be suffering, getting stick from the Rangers' fans. That made us try harder to get victories against our city rivals. We were usually unsuccessful, but we would always be trying our best. Rangers were a more tightly knit team than us in the early 1960s. They had goalscorers such as centre-forward Jimmy Millar, a terrific man for putting the ball in the net, and he had a fine partnership with Ralph Brand. I think they got on well together and even lived close to each other through in Edinburgh.

We were more disjointed than Rangers at the time and we may subconsciously, I feel, have believed that they were indisputably the stronger team. Results tended to suggest that that belief was correct. When we beat them 3-0 in a league match in September 1964, it was our first victory over them in 15 consecutive games. The previous season, 1963–64, had been particularly painful. We had lost all five matches in which we had faced Rangers, in League, League Cup and Scottish Cup, conceding 11 goals and scoring only once in the process. That goal had come from me, when I had nicked the ball past Billy

Ritchie, the Rangers goalkeeper, to open the scoring in our league encounter at Ibrox early in the season. A couple of minutes before half-time, with us still leading 1-0 and clearly the better team, Bobby Lennox sent over an excellent cross and I got my head to it only to see it come back off the post. A two-goal lead with us in the ascendancy would have made it hard for Rangers to recover, but after the interval they took the initiative and ended up winning 2-1. That was us all over in the early 1960s, hard-luck stories and near misses.

We found things equally testing in European competition. Following our aggregate victory over Leixoes in the Fairs Cup in the autumn of 1964 we were pitted against Barcelona. Not only did we lose 3-1 on aggregate but, even more painfully from my point of view, I got a bad injury during the second leg, a 0-0 draw at Celtic Park. I suffered a chipped bone, which was worse than a leg break. I had a lot of bother with that and the pain from it would recur throughout my career, especially during cold weather.

My first taste of European football had come two years earlier against another Spanish club, Valencia. Again this was in the Fairs Cup and it was a very hard game, as might have been expected given that Valencia were the holders. The terracing at their Mestalla stadium was very tight to the pitch – their supporters could have reached out and touched players on the touchline had they so wished – and the dramatic, vibrant surroundings were equalled by the impressively colourful means by which the home side went about defeating us 4-2. It was a match in which I felt as though we were well below the level required for that type of football. The bigger the crowd, the more I wanted to play in the game and there were 40,000 inside the

Mestalla that hot, sultry night. But for all the excitement that the occasion provided, I came to the conclusion that we were clearly the apprentices while the Spanish team's players were the master craftsmen. Their control of the ball was so much better than ours and they were exceptionally good at holding it. We were fit but had not been coached in those sorts of skills and would never receive any instruction in how to play the game. I would have loved to have been trying any methods that might have helped to make me a better player, with better control of the ball, but there did not seem to me to be enough coaching going on at Celtic. Training was more about attaining, maintaining and topping up physical fitness, which is vitally important, but not at the expense of honing skill. I always felt we should have been using the ball more.

During those dark days for the club, we reached two cup finals against Rangers. We lost the 1961 League Cup final 2-1 and the 1963 Scottish Cup final 3-0 in a replay after a 1-1 draw. On that evening at Hampden, with Rangers three goals ahead by half-time, it was dispiriting to see vast swathes of the Celtic support in the 120,000 crowd streaming for the exits soon after the second half had resumed and it became clear that we lacked the impetus to make even the slightest dent in Rangers' lead.

Perhaps the most telling setback for us during those times, though, was the semi-final of the 1964 European Cup-Winners' Cup, a tournament in which we had done very well, even though, ironically, it was one for which we had qualified through having lost that Scottish Cup final so disastrously to Rangers. With our rivals having won the league title, they went on to participate on the much grander stage offered by the European Cup. We had reached the semi-final stage by defeating good clubs in the shape of Basel, Dinamo Zagreb and Slovan Bratislava, scoring 16 goals and conceding just two.

We were paired with MTK from Budapest in the semi-finals. Hungarian football was strong and memories of their greatest international team of the mid-1950s, which had featured Ferenc Puskas, were relatively recent so we were expecting a testing encounter in the first leg at Celtic Park in mid-April 1964. Jimmy Johnstone darted in to put us ahead with a close-range shot shortly before half-time and I struck a sweet shot from the corner of the penalty area to put us 2-0 ahead. As the game wound to a close, I met a neat cross from Bobby Murdoch and pinged a header off a post and into the net to give us a 3-0 lead. It appeared so complete a victory, so absolutely sure to be a passport into the final in Brussels, that our supporters remained in their places at the end of the match and demanded noisily that we reappear from the dressing room, some of us in our stocking soles, and perform a lap of honour so that they could hail us properly.

It looked a near-unassailable lead, and it should have been too, but we went into the return in the Nepstadion with no clear plan as to how to protect our advantage and with only a very basic dressing-room pep talk from Bob Kelly, the chairman, to prepare us for the match to come. It proved a torrid evening. A match can be turned on its head in 90 minutes if one side knows entirely what its aims are and the other does not and after an hour the Hungarians were 3-0 ahead and the tie, overall, was level. When they got a fourth, there was no way back for us as we had flagged in the face of their energy, coordination and skill. We had been outmanoeuvred, outsmarted and outplayed. It seemed to sum us up during that era. Any time it appeared as though we were about to release the club from its long depression, we would sink surely, whether slowly or swiftly, back into it.

Although Celtic were failing to compete as consistently or as well as all of us at the club would have liked, there were still occasional humorous moments to brighten up our days. There is always talk about football players liking a drink and at that time Celtic were no exception to the rule. I remember Mr McGrory got a phone call one day to say that a particular player was in the pub and that he was steaming. The caller was outraged. 'What sort of a state is that for a Celtic player to be in?' Mr McGrory assured him that he would look into the matter and treat it with the utmost seriousness. He then went out to the park and the person in question was out on the field training. We never found out whether the caller wanted to get that particular player into trouble or to have a joke at Mr McGrory's expense, but whatever the reason we all had a good laugh about it.

Mr McGrory was a wonderful person, a man who was always very kind to me and for whom I had enormous affection, but I felt the same surge of excitement as everyone else at the club when I heard in January 1965 that Jock Stein would be leaving Hibernian and returning to Celtic as manager. Jock had left his post as Celtic's reserve-team coach in 1960 to become manager of Dunfermline Athletic and had proven himself to be entirely shrewd in everything he did for Dunfermline and, following that, Hibs. When he managed Dunfermline to victory over Celtic in the 1961 Scottish Cup final he would have known everything about our players and that would have been a big help to Dunfermline. Over those two matches – they won the cup after a replay – we had shown ourselves to have a better quality of individual player, as might have been expected, but we had been undone by Dunfermline's expert teamwork, and that owed itself to one man: Jock Stein. We did not have anyone of the same ilk at Celtic, someone who could get the measure of an opposing team and upset them through employing a similar depth of knowledge about the game. But now, on hearing the news of Jock Stein's appointment, we knew that we had, at last, acquired just such a man. We knew things would improve under Jock Stein – it was simply a question of how far and how fast.

CHAPTER FOUR

INTO THE BLUE

I managed to cram rather a lot into a short Scotland career that constituted only a handful of appearances in the national team's colours. I missed out in the cruellest fashion possible on what would have been the international match of my life or that of any other Scotsman, scored Scotland's first-ever goal against the world's premier international footballing nation and the reigning world champions, was singled out specifically to exchange jerseys with the most famous footballer in the world, found myself and my teammates booed off the park after winning a vital World Cup tie and was cold-shouldered by the Scottish selectors after making as good a start to my international career as could have been expected.

It was exactly what I ought to have anticipated when first called up by my country. Anyone hitching a ride with the Scotland team of the mid-1960s, when the nation's international vehicle for football was akin to a driverless juggernaut, would have found themselves attached to an entity that was capable of roaring off in any direction on the merest whim.

Despite all this, the experience as a whole was entirely magical, truly wonderful. Before being capped by my country, I had always thought that if I got picked I would be truly honoured and when it did eventually happen I felt marvellous. I'd love to think that although I only got five caps, I did my country proud. Having achieved one ambition, of playing in a Junior international, just like my father, I was utterly delighted to complement that by playing for the Scotland team at full international level. Some people have suggested that playing for Scotland must have been an inconvenience, a bit of a waste of time in comparison to playing for Celtic, but I never for one moment saw it as that. I had always been desperate to play for my country and was sure it would be a wonderful feeling and, although the experience would have its peaks and troughs, pulling on a Scotland shirt was always truly special. Never, not for one moment, was it ever anything less.

My only regret is that I did not pick up a few more caps than the five that came my way, but the problem was that there was no continuity about the Scotland team of the 1960s and team selections often appeared to be conjured up on a whim. The SFA representatives, who were heavily involved in choosing the team, kept their distance from us players and I don't think a lot of them knew one player from another. They would often dig up someone from the most obscure club and pitch them into the team. I think the manager must have had some involvement in team selection but it was impossible to know, as a player, just how much influence he possessed.

I had appeared to be on the verge of a full international cap for several years before it actually happened. During the early 1960s, I was selected to represent the Scottish League against the English League, which was enough to bring me out in a cold sweat. Not through nerves or overanxiety but because, within days of being notified of that prospective honour and becoming very excited about it, I subsequently spent a fortnight in bed, in a fever, soaking the sheets. I had been given a flu jab to protect me for the winter – an injection that contained the actual flu bug to act as a repellent – and it had simply floored me. I missed out on a match in which I had really wanted to play because when you have the chance of being involved in a game against a top-class team you want to see how you stand up with the other players.

In fact, I was called up several times to play for the Scottish League but was unable to join the squad for various reasons. I was particularly annoyed to miss out on a trip to Rome in 1960 to face the Italian League. Then, in 1961, I made it into the Scotland international squad for the vital World Cup play-off against Czechoslovakia in Brussels. I knew on that occasion that I was there principally as a squad member and that the chances of playing in the match were very slim indeed; and so it proved.

Something of a hiatus followed in terms of my international prospects – even though I was managing to score a lot of goals in a struggling Celtic team. I would have thought that if I was displaying a talent for scoring goals in a misfiring side, it might have made me look very much like a prospective cap. When the international call did come, it was indeed Celtic's up-and-down form of the first half of the 1960s that indirectly helped me. During the autumn of 1964, Celtic travelled to the modest Bayview Stadium, in Methil, Fife, to face East Fife, a side mid-ranking even in the Second Division, in a League Cup quarter-final. Our 2-0 defeat in that match was one of the most shocking setbacks in the club's history. It was a defeat that rocked any belief that the club was making progress during that period – and the only relief for Celtic was that this was a two-legged tie. It meant that we had to bring extra fire to our play in the return, in front of a busy Celtic

Park crowd, with the fans drawn almost fatalistically to the match. Those Celtic supporters were, in turn, anxious about our progress, curious about the extent of this East Fife side's previously hidden talents and at how the game might go, and, on the night, furiously demanding that there would be no further humiliation of their club and that we repair the damage with alacrity.

We did get things right in the return, winning 6-0 against a side that was revealed to be as limited as might have been thought. I scored five of the goals and a potential humiliation for the club was transformed into a personal triumph for me, with the press suggesting that I ought to be considered for an international call-up.

I was delighted that their prognosis was proven correct when I was named in the squad to face Wales in a Home International in October 1964, but it does suggest that the SFA's selection process was considerably flawed. I had, after all, been scoring goals regularly throughout the first half of the 1960s – and regularly against opposition of a much higher calibre than East Fife – so it seemed almost whimsical that it had now been decided that the time was right for me to show what I could do for the national team. The process of choosing a Scotland squad at the time was in the hands of a group of selectors, SFA committee men. It was then, in theory, up to the manager to choose the starting eleven, though the selectors were renowned for their interference.

With momentum building behind my name, it had helped that, following the win over East Fife and on the Saturday before the selectors were due to meet, I had whipped a right-footed shot across Sandy Davie, the Dundee United goalkeeper, to give Celtic the equaliser in a 1-1 draw at Celtic Park. As more and more soccer scribes piled on to the bandwagon that had been set in motion to win me a cap, press reports stressed my tenacity and graft in that match with United and one fearless reporter even went so far as to suggest that I had been solely responsible for Celtic securing a point. It is interesting how the press get hold of an idea and then make it fit; make it work to suit their purposes. Although I was doing well and enjoying a good patch, I always saw football as a team effort and believed it ludicrous to suggest that any result could be attributed to the efforts of just one player.

However, I was desperate to win my first cap and this time the cards were falling in my favour, not least because Scotland desperately needed someone new at centre-forward. Alan Gilzean, who had become established as the first-choice man in that position for Scotland and who was an exceptionally talented player, had handed in a transfer request to Dundee during the summer of 1964 and had consequently not played for their team all season so, although fit and training on his own, he could not realistically be considered for the national team. That's what managers do – drop a player who has put in a transfer request. With a press campaign building behind me, the selectors appeared to have been backed into a corner – if they had decided not to pick me, a scorer of 15 goals only a month or so into the season, there would have been an outcry, and they knew it.

Adding some spice to the stew was the fact that just as the SFA were about to announce the team to play Wales – at that time the starting eleven would be named several days in advance – I was also due to arrive back from Portugal, where I had been sent off in the Inter-Cities Fairs Cup against Leixoes. That put the SFA in a slightly uncomfortable position. They dealt very strictly with disciplined players during that era and if I was about to incur a suspension in a European club competition, it would not look good for me to be named simultaneously in a Scotland team. Another quirk of those times was that it was in the gift of the SFA rather than UEFA to decide whether I ought to be suspended for my doings in Portugal and, having weighed up the evidence carefully, they decided I did not. Perhaps my case against the fairness of my dismissal – strong as it was – was assisted by Scotland's desperate requirement for a centre-forward? The SFA, after all, were not renowned for their liberal attitude towards players who had incurred the displeasure of a referee.

The match with Wales was viewed as being crucial to Scotland's efforts to reach the 1966 World Cup finals, which were, of course, to be held in England. With the qualifying matches for that tournament on the horizon, Scotland, hosting Finland at Hampden in the opener two weeks later, needed to hone a team to try to get past the mighty Italy who were favourites in our qualification group. So, along with representing my country – a boyhood dream in itself – this match was also, as I saw it, an open invitation for me to establish myself in a Scotland team that could be together for the succeeding two years and that, if successful in qualification, would participate in a World Cup being held almost in our own backyard.

It proved a rather tricky audition. We arrived at our base in Porthcawl only a day before the match, leaving little time for training. That was not ideal but, counterbalancing that, I was not at all apprehensive about playing alongside big names such as Denis Law, who was in such devastating form that he would be named the European Footballer of the Year for 1964, and Jim Baxter, who was already recognised as being one of the greatest midfield players ever fielded by Scotland. The team all made it good for me by being helpful. They all wanted to do well for their country and that meant fostering a good atmosphere among the squad.

Ian McColl was the Scottish manager and I must admit I found him very friendly, which was something that I hadn't particularly expected because he was very much a Rangers man. Prior to becoming Scotland manager in 1960 he had been, as a midfield player, one of the stalwarts of the powerful Rangers teams that had dominated Scottish football during the post-war years. He had actually still been a Rangers player when appointed as Scotland manager but he came over very well in his dealings with me. I'd say he was a real gentleman. I enjoyed dealing with him and we got on very well. There was no suggestion at all from him that because the selectors had chosen me that he was not sure about me. I felt I had his backing, entirely. I think he had a tough job too. Even though he was manager, people such as Baxter and Law were bigger names than him and that can put a manager on the back foot a bit. If he feels his players have more sway with the board, or, in this case, the selectors, than he has, it can make him feel less able to exert authority and discipline because if it comes to a choice between the big name being retained or the manager being asked to move on, there is usually a fairly predictable outcome. The manager probably feels he has to ease back a bit, not confront the big-name players and allow them a degree of leeway that they might not be given if he was their manager at club level and had more control over their futures.

When I played for Scotland, I was very surprised at how little detail went into planning for games. The managers merely told us to play the way we played for our clubs. They emphasised that quite a bit. The argument went that if you had been picked for the national team on the basis of your club form then it made sense for you to carry on playing like that in international matches. I've always thought it hard for international managers. They haven't the time to work with you the way the manager has at your club, where they're working with you every week, know inside out what you can do and how to get the best out of you. It must be a lot harder for someone taking on a national team that is an assembly of big names, some of them quite assertive characters, and the manager is maybe not as big a name as some of the players. The manager maybe has to wonder if he even knows as much about the game as those players.

For the match at Ninian Park in Cardiff, I was pitted directly against John Charles, the great, gigantic centre-half who was good enough to have played for Juventus and Roma at a time when few British players were transferred abroad. Facing up to him was like gazing up the side of a mountain. He was a lovely big fellow, very much the dominant centre-half, very certain in what he was doing. He had also played as a prolific centre-forward at the highest level; not just in Britain but in Italy, where he scored with astonishing regularity. I had always admired John Charles for the way he played the game in such a fair manner – he was not once booked or sent off in his entire career despite playing in two positions in which the action is at its most rugged. I was keen to face him, but despite his nickname of 'The Gentle Giant' and his deserved reputation for fair play, I still decided that it would be best if I kept out of his way. He was such a huge man that I didn't want to bounce off him.

I couldn't see very much wrong with the way he was going about his business that day as he settled the defence around him but I decided to wait until after the match to get to know him better and spent my time darting here and there, trying to free myself from his attentions as much as possible. As a player, I always wanted to move about and keep others on the move. I was never a lazy player – I always thought hard about my positioning. I like players who work hard off the ball. Having been a player like that myself, I can appreciate what they are doing. The things you do off the ball are as important as what you do when it's at your feet.

It was hard playing against the Welsh in their own country, but I must have been doing something right because I scored a goal – and a good one at that. That was the reason I had been selected for the team – to put the ball in the net – and that was what I did. The goal came from a breakaway; I got myself clear of the Welsh defence and then sent the ball across Gary Sprake, the Wales goalkeeper, and into the net.

Despite that fantastic moment for me, we lost 3-2, with the team's performance scrutinised severely and critically in the days after the match. We had been the more accomplished team but Jim Baxter and Denis Law, the stars of the side, were criticised in the press for playing the game too slowly and for indulging in too much trickery at the expense of directness. Ian McColl, the manager, was told off by the critics for failing to ensure there was more urgency in the team. Fortunately for me, I escaped blame, not least because I had scored one of our goals. Indeed, one of the principal criticisms of the others was that they had failed to use the ball cleverly enough to exploit my pace in driving through the middle of the Welsh defence.

I was oblivious to all the negativity. I was just delighted to have one Scottish cap and a Scottish jersey and I really enjoyed my first experience of playing for my country. I didn't think I could complain too much about them not supplying enough ammunition for me because it was new for me to be playing with people such as those and, equally, it was new for them to adjust to my style of play. That was something the press failed to consider. I felt I got a fair amount of the ball so I had no complaints and I never felt that Jim or Denis slackened their game in any way. It may have looked different from the terraces or the stands but it is important to understand that we were flung together as a team, given one training session and then expected to gel in the match. There were no fewer than four debutants in the Scotland team that day: centre-half Ron Yeats, Spurs' outside-right Jimmy Robertson, Jimmy Johnstone and me. Several others in the team were as good as newcomers too. The only players who had enjoyed an extensive run in the team were Jim Baxter, Denis Law and Alex Hamilton, an exceptionally fine full-back who played for Dundee. Nowadays the Scotland manger has a chance to see all his players and work with them over several days. We didn't have quite so much preparation, and that's an understatement.

Two days after our defeat in Wales, the squad was announced for the next international match, with Finland, the opening World Cup qualifier, and I was pleased to find that I had retained my place. We went down to Largs to prepare for the game and training was quite light because we had only a couple of days together before the match.

One thing that I would say about the Scottish squads in which I was involved was that while we may not always have been together for too long before matches, we were still always quite tightly bound. Everyone made sure that everyone else was involved and felt part of things. Everyone made sure we got together as a team, on and off the park. It was never cliquish, certainly as far as I could see. I roomed with Denis Law and Denis would kid on, 'Hey you, my boots need brought down . . .' It was all just joking and keeping everyone together. Denis was actually very good to me – at the end of each trip he would generously make a point of thanking me in front of everyone else, for having been such a good butler to him.

I did well in the match against Finland. Denis Law opened the scoring after only a couple of minutes. Later on in the first half, I met a cross from Davie Gibson and scored with a header from the heart of the penalty area that slipped past Martti Halme, the Finnish goalkeeper, who dived full-length but could not prevent the ball eluding the outstretched fingertips of his right hand. Davie Gibson got a third for us shortly before the break to put the game all but beyond the Finns. At 3-0 up, it looked as though we had the chance to double the scoreline against a team that had fielded only one full-time player. But Jim Baxter, who was our playmaker but always colourfully unconventional, started swaggering in style, indulging in tricks and casual play and, as a result, much of the urgency was released from our play. We were never in danger of defeat but midway through the second half the Finns punished our lassitude by scoring and although we were not exactly hanging on by the end, the concession of that goal took some of the shine off of our performance, especially from the point of view of the huge crowd, who wanted to see us going all out for further goals. It finished 3-1 and we had done our work and secured full points towards qualification, but we were booed off the field of play because of the low-key manner in which we had allowed the second half to proceed.

That rudely healthy burst of crowd disapproval mattered little to me when I retained my place in the Scotland Select for the next match, a friendly against Tottenham Hotspur, scheduled for November 1964 at White Hart Lane in London. The match was to raise funds for the dependants of the wonderfully talented former Falkirk, Spurs and Scotland midfield player John White. He had died, tragically, the previous summer at the age of 27, having been struck by lightning while sheltering from stormy weather on a golf course. I was keenly anticipating my participation in such a notable match but collected a niggling injury in Celtic's encounter with St Johnstone in Perth on the Saturday before and had to withdraw from the game. It was the third time I had missed a really important Scotland match through illness or injury. I had been kicked behind my right knee and had to remain at Celtic Park for treatment. The injury had cleared in time for me to return to the Celtic team for the following weekend's game with Dundee, but long after the pain from the injury had subsided, its effect on my Scotland career would be hurting me.

Shortly before the World Cup qualifier with Finland, Alan Gilzean had re-signed for Dundee on a short-term contract, but on the understanding that he was still seeking a transfer from the club. He scored twice for the Scotland Select against Tottenham and played superbly, having an involvement in several of the other goals in the 6-2 victory. The Scottish press felt that defeating a fine Spurs side so handsomely, even in a match that was not recognised as a full international, was one of Scotland's best performances for years. A couple of months previously they had thought Scotland to be short of goalscorers; now they saw the Scottish team as being over-endowed with talent in that department. Alan Gilzean and Denis Law were back in favour with the sportswriters, enormously so, and Willie Wallace, then a Heart of Midlothian player, also found that his star was in the ascendancy. One writer in a populist newspaper suggested that these were the forwards that would and should take Scotland into the future, leaving little room for me, even though I had done nothing to deserve exile. This journalist used all of his analytical powers to say of this new situation, 'Tough on Stevie Chalmers? I know – but that's football!'

A week after the Spurs game, the next Scotland team to face Northern Ireland in a Home International was selected, and what a surprise, it chimed with the opinions of the press. Willie Wallace, Alan Gilzean and Denis Law were all named in the team. It was unfair for me to be jilted summarily in such a fashion even in the face of such a glittering cast of compatriots. I had scored in my first two appearances for the team so I had done little to merit the omission. Within days of his appearance for Scotland against Spurs, Alan Gilzean had been signed by the London club and for the rest of Scotland's World Cup qualifying matches he would be the regular fixture at centre-forward.

Being left out of the Scotland squad was, as that callous pressman had written, 'tough' on me but life was busy enough for me not to dwell too much on the entire affair. Ann, our fourth child, was born the week after the match against Tottenham and 24 hours after she arrived in the world I had to fly out to Spain to face Barcelona in the first leg of our Fairs Cup tie against the Catalans. I could not concern myself too much with missing out on further

Scotland recognition; I could only hope that one day I would get a recall. I thought Alan Gilzean was a magnificent player and an excellent goalscorer so there was no disgrace in losing out to him, but I definitely deserved a further chance to consolidate on the good beginning I had made to my Scotland career and to get a chance to establish myself in a Scotland team. Despite my disappointment, my desire to represent my country remained undimmed.

When Ian McColl left the post of Scotland manager and Jock Stein took over from him, on a part-time basis, during the second half of 1965, my chances of further Scotland caps may have seemed, from the outside, to have brightened considerably, but Jock would overlook me for Scotland entirely during that period. His tenure as manager of Scotland did not actually increase my chances of selection at all. I have to say that in all the years I played under him as Celtic manager, I did not find him to be the most supportive of people. Jock never interfered with my international career – he simply did not select me to play for Scotland when he had the chance to do so.

I think if anybody gets their chance to represent their country, nothing should stop them. It is such a great honour. But managers of football clubs, particularly the major clubs, are often less enthusiastic about the whole thing because their players might get injured in an international and the clubs, which pay the bulk of their wages, would then suffer, sometimes badly. Jock Stein, for example, would be thinking of an important Celtic game a few days after an international and of the possibility of a particular player getting injured and missing the game. It's a touchy subject and you can understand the manager's point of view in that situation.

It was disappointing to be omitted for several successive Scotland games and being left out in the circumstances I have outlined did feel like a bit of an insult. That was as nothing, though, in comparison with what was to follow when I would be subject to a snub that would prove to be one of the most wounding and irreparable blows ever delivered to a Scotland international footballer.

CHAPTER FIVE

THE STEIN SCENE

Jock Stein knew his players and knew what he wanted them to do and what he wanted from me was goals. It was clear from his arrival at the club in early 1965 that he wanted sharp, pacy forwards and I was to be one of those target men, a principal goalscorer for the team, a focal point of the attack. His approach was what made me and set me on the road to make history.

Jock thought I would score more goals as a centre-forward. He never spoke to me about it at great length – in fact, he never spoke to me at great length about anything. All he did, when he first got to the club, was to put me through the middle in wee training games to see if I would score goals in that position. I never at any time said to Jock or anyone else that I wanted to play in one particular position – I was simply happy to be in the team. If they put me in the centre, they had me there to do a job and I would try to do that job to the best of my ability.

It was soon clear to me that he was right; my best position in the team was to spearhead the attack. It was something that had never been fully obvious to me. I had always been quite happy to play on the wing or at inside-forward and although I had sometimes played at centre-forward for Celtic I had never settled there – the following week I was very likely to be switched to the wing or back to inside-forward. Jock found my best position and established me there and I suppose that's what makes the difference between a player and a manager.

As a winger you were up against one opponent, the full-back, and if you could exploit his weakness you could get past him and have some room in which to work. As a centre-forward you had the centre-half, the goalkeeper, the full-backs and the half-backs all on your case at one time or another. You would tend to get bumped about a lot more but you cannot just let people bump you about – you have to be able to give some of it back to them. I enjoyed playing centre-forward more and more – I grew into it and eventually felt it was more natural and better for me to be seeking goals than in a role where I would be doing more defending and knocking the ball about. I think Jock must have seen me in training swerving past someone and quickly getting in a shot on goal. I'd been doing that on the wing for years at Celtic but it took Jock to see that such talents ought to be used most regularly through the middle. At centre-forward, a big part of the role is about being cuter than the centre-half.

That is not to say that my progress under Jock Stein was serene and smooth. One of my most notable achievements with Jock at the helm arrived ten months after he had taken charge of Celtic, when we came up against Rangers in the derby match that would usher in the New Year of 1966 at Celtic Park. It was a very wintry day, typical of Glasgow at that time of year: grey, dank, freezing, misty; everything that early January stores up for our delight. I remember that the light was particularly poor that day and I believe there may have been some doubt beforehand as to whether the game would go ahead. Davie Wilson, the winger, scored for Rangers in the opening minutes and they went in 1-0 up at half-time, so we got a bit of a baiting from Jock to let us

THE STEIN SCENE

know he wanted more from us. We had struggled a bit in the first half and it looked as though we would have to try to grind out the second half to see if we might emerge with a draw or even a narrow victory. It has to be said that we did oblige Jock in terms of his demand for better things in the second half. Four minutes after half-time, I clipped the ball home from close range after a well-worked move had sliced open the Rangers defence. With little more than an hour on the clock, Charlie Gallagher sent over a corner-kick, I leaped into the air, got neatly in between two Rangers defenders and directed a header past Billy Ritchie, the Rangers goalkeeper, to put us 2-1 ahead. Charlie Gallagher added a third and Bobby Murdoch made it 4-1 before I slipped in for my final goal, a simple tap over the goalkeeper from just inside the six-yard box, in the final minute. We had simply clicked during that second 45 minutes and soon we had been whirring away like a wonderful machine.

I was delighted with my hat-trick. It makes me one of only three Celtic players to have scored a hat-trick in an Old Firm league match, numbering me alongside greats Jimmy Quinn, who got the first Celtic Ne'erday hat-trick in 1912, and Malky MacDonald, who also hit three against our closest rivals during the late 1930s. Mine was also a classic hat-trick: a left-footer, a right-footer and a header.

When I came into the dressing room after the match, I have to say that I was pretty pleased with myself – and it must have shown. I thought the manager would be absolutely delighted for me but instead I received a glower from Jock, who quickly attempted to puncture any self-satisfaction that I might be feeling. 'Just to let you know,' he said in his quietly forceful fashion, 'I wouldn't have picked you as the man of the match. I thought Yogi [John Hughes] had a great game, out on the wing.' Maybe he thought I had got my goals too easily. That was him trying to bring me down – from heaven. He'd have had his reasons for doing that but I still had the three goals – and I still have.

The thing about Jock was that although you might think you were doing all right, he might not think so. He might think that the club could get a wee bit more out of you. That, after all, was his job as a manager. He was a man who always had to be obeyed, without question, and we all knew, given that he was right much more than he was wrong, that that was the right thing to do. A manager, a good one like Jock, wants every ounce out of you. Having scored three goals against Rangers, I was selecting myself as man of the match – and I don't think that was unwarranted . . . although Yogi might have disagreed.

Scoring three goals is a wonderful achievement in any match and in any era, not least when it is achieved against your chief competitors. When you see how seriously the supporters take that game, you know that if you do a good job in one of them, it can only be beneficial for you. I realise now how much it means, especially given that we had been losing 1-0 and went on to win 5-1. It's a nice thing to be able to mention when I meet certain Rangers supporters.

In the modern era, some players have scored a couple of goals in an Old Firm match for Celtic and found themselves being given a lengthy contract extension on that basis. That did not happen for me, but mine is an achievement that people still discuss to this day. They were good goals to score. After my first two, Rangers collapsed. They had been teetering on the brink of disaster once we turned on the style in the second half but it took the hard reality of the goals themselves to breach their desperately constructed defensive dam and begin the flood.

When Jock Stein left Hibernian to become manager of Celtic in March 1965, you could do nothing else but welcome him because the arrival of someone like him was so badly needed. We also knew how good he was. Having been at Dunfermline and Hibs since leaving Celtic in 1960, he'd had a chance to look around at other players and other teams and deepen his knowledge of football and players and how individuals and teams played. I think everybody was delighted Jock was back at the club – whether they liked him personally or not. I think they were delighted that he had decided to take the job.

Jock wanted things to go his way, right from the start. He knew he would get cooperation from us because we were all desperate to get the team going again and saw him almost as our saviour. That helped him and there were few complaints about his methods – even though, during the first couple of months after his return, he would chop and change the team around almost incessantly. He was merely trying to learn more about the players he had, what they could do and where they could do it.

He would watch everything like a hawk, on and off the playing field and on the training pitch. It was a terrific thing getting him back at the club. He loved the club, knew what it was all about, knew that the directors had been putting their noses into team matters with Jimmy McGrory as manager and so before he took the job he told them, 'This is my job – no one else interferes.'

He would tell players what to do, explicitly, but if the player had something to say about it, Jock would listen. If he didn't agree, he wouldn't be long in telling them so. Big Tommy Gemmell used to have a bit of a go back at him and Bertie Auld would have a wee go. That was good, though. Jock would go through things and say, 'Has anybody got anything to say about this?' Bertie would always come in with a wee comment and the gaffer liked that. They weren't trying to tell the manager he was wrong; just providing some input. I didn't say much to him. I didn't feel as if I was big enough to say things to Jock. People's natures are different. Wee Bertie and Tommy are people you cannot keep quiet under any circumstances. Billy McNeill would also be good at discussing things with the manager. There were some players he would speak to roughly – but with me it would be more on the quiet. Other players would take abuse from him, but whatever way it was done it was always for the good of the team as a whole. At Seamill Hydro, in Ayrshire, where we would go to prepare for major matches, he would sit in the lounge there and talk away to the boys, asking people, 'What do you think of that?' There was always only one subject under discussion. It was football that he talked about all the time.

He would motor down to Liverpool and Manchester to watch evening matches but the following morning, almost without fail, he would be out on the training ground in his tracksuit. It was good having him there because he could see everything, good and bad, and would correct anything he thought could go better. He would join in training but he couldn't participate in practice matches because he couldn't really play – the ankle injury that had ended his career in the late 1950s plagued him perennially. He wasn't a formal coach – instead, he got to know the players as individuals and through being with them all the time. He would go to Seamill and have us as a large group and he would draw us

THE STEIN SCENE

together. He would also arrange, once or twice a year, a dinner for the players and their wives at one of the major hotels in Glasgow. Jock wanted to know the wives and he would threaten players, later on, that he would tell their wives if they had been up to something he didn't like. It also helped to get the support of the wives for those times when he would take us all away down to Seamill or for a pre-season trip for days or weeks at a time. He would talk away to the wives and get to know them. That was just one of his many cute moves.

If a cup final or a big European match was on the horizon, Jock would sometimes erect a tactics board and the whole squad would be gathered together to hear his analysis of the forthcoming fixture. He would set out on the board what he required from each of his players and what to expect from the opposition. I found that very helpful. You wanted to have something like that and he was the first person I had ever seen do it. He was very good at going to see games and coming back with ideas on how people played. He would try and see the strengths of different players. His knowledge, his strong powers of communication and his analysis all meant that when you left the room after one of his briefings, it was almost as if you had a mini-movie in your head outlining how the opposition would be likely to play. Jock was the first person I had met who would analyse the game and the opposition in that way – apart from my father.

There was also a degree of flexibility about Jock that had not been present on the managerial side prior to his arrival. He would announce a team and have you at outside-right but it wouldn't be long before he would switch you if he thought something else would work. I liked what Jock was doing – it was for the benefit of the team and for you as an individual. He was also a master of the psychology of the game. He knew what to say to motivate you to try harder, to do better for yourself and, consequently, for the team. If he had left you out of the side, and for the following match you were sitting in the dugout alongside him, he would lean across, nudge you and as the game was progressing say to you forcefully, 'You see that man playing out there, in your place. Look at him. You're better than him. That fellow can't play anything like you can. How can you be on the bench here when he is in the team? If you do what you're told, you'll be there instead of him. You build your game so that you're back in that position.' He'd then go on as if he was exasperated, annoyed, 'Look at him there – how can you not be in this team instead of him? You are better than him; you should be in this team.' He had knocked you down by omitting you from his team and this was him building you up again, giving you a lift. You knew, of course, that he would be reversing his sentiments neatly to the man whom he had named in the team in your place when he spoke to him, but you would always try to put that out of your mind and concentrate on trying to please Jock and get back into the team.

When you were on the field, you wouldn't always hear Jock from the dugout but if you weren't doing something, Jock would send Neilly Mochan, the trainer, out, round the park, with his sponge, to pretend he was having a look at your ankle or your shin in order to pass on some instructions from the bench.

When Jock spoke, you had to listen. He commanded your attention. Football players have a notoriously short attention span, but you could not betray any degree of inattention when Jock was in full flow. The only person who could get away with that was Jimmy Johnstone. We used to be standing with Jock for a wee talk and while Jock was speaking, Jimmy would be playing keepie-uppie at the back of the throng and chipping the ball up and down and moving around Jock with the ball. He wasn't being cheeky – it was just his desire to be on the ball all the time. Then he'd stop, pause, fold his arms and listen for a bit before he was off again with the ball. No one else would have been able to get away with that – in fact anyone who tried it stood a good chance of being drummed right out of the club. Jock, though, as with everyone else, knew that you couldn't really instruct wee Jimmy in how to play the game because Jimmy would always do what he wanted. In some ways, Jimmy's presence at team talks was just a token gesture. Sometimes Jock would collar Jimmy in the dressing room, eye to eye, and give him some specific instructions as to how to work back to deal with the opposition or to get more out of his own game. We would then trot into the tunnel to take the field and Jimmy would turn round and say, 'Who's he kidding?' Jock would occasionally drop Jimmy, which few managers would have done, but because the supporters couldn't believe it, it actually made Jock the bigger man in their eyes.

No one could feel utterly secure of their place in the team when Jock Stein was manager – maybe his idea was that a certain degree of pressure on your place in the team would be good for the club. There were times when Jock didn't play Jimmy at outside-right; maybe he would have had a wee battle with Jimmy. Jock would maybe have decided Jimmy needed a wee bit of a punishment and would tell him to watch the game from the stand. Those two had a lot of ding-dongs like that.

Jock had several means of punishing players. If someone was being paid well but not doing their job in the team, was dropped and started moaning that they were not playing, Jock would maybe tell the person running the second team to take the player up to Inverness for a friendly match but keep them on the sidelines. They would then have wasted the player's day, taking him up there and back without giving him a kick of the ball. That would reinforce the message to the player as to whom exactly the gaffer was and that when the gaffer gave instructions, they would have to be followed – to the letter. If that sort of thing didn't work, Jock would get rid of the player. Jock was good at building you up if you were one of his players – there was no one better at it – but he was also good at bringing you down. That ensured that there was always an edge to his relationship with his players; it kept everyone from becoming complacent, kept us all on our toes.

It was clear to Jock just how faithful his players were to Celtic, so if Jimmy was put in the stand he would be really hurt by it and he'd curse and swear about it – but he'd be aware that he'd been punished. I too was hugely loyal to Celtic – and I think the club knew it. I was one of the few players who never got an extended contract. I just took the year every time, delighted still to be playing for Celtic, determined to do my utmost to get another year once the contract in hand had expired. Perhaps the fact that I was never pushy or particularly assertive meant that they knew I would not demand an extension. I think a few clubs did come in for me but I wasn't told about it. People would let you know about it, on the quiet. There was a lot of that going on – Jock would only tell players that there was an offer in for them if it suited him. It would have been interesting to know which other clubs were keen on enlisting my services but I never wished to leave Celtic.

* * *

Jock chopped and changed his forward line much more than his defence. I didn't like that very much; it made me think that he wasn't happy with what he saw. It always made me feel as though my place in the side was under consideration. Sometimes it worked for him; sometimes it didn't. He tried a lot of things that just didn't work and if that had happened he'd come in at half-time and tell us to forget all about it. It is hard to pin down Jock's tactics to say that we were in a 4-2-4 formation or 4-3-3 or whatever. He changed things about an awful lot once a match was underway and he was, tactically, incredibly astute. He'd maybe tell Bobby Lennox in a particular game to come back a bit deep to pick up the ball and then go at somebody, depending on whom he was playing against. He'd maybe say, 'This fellow can't run. You've got to be able to get away from him.' He would show you on the board where he wanted you to play and what he was looking for from you. It wasn't as if a rigid system was enforced on everyone for every game. Everyone had roles that depended, often, on what the opposition might do.

It took only a month for Jock to achieve what had been unachievable for Celtic over the previous eight years: win a trophy. We faced Dunfermline Athletic in the Scottish Cup final in April 1965 and, although we were twice behind, we came through to triumph 3-2 thanks to a glorious header from Billy McNeill in the final minutes of the match. It was a great lift to all those of us who had taken stick from the crowd for all those previous difficult years. I felt we were reasonably well on top of them throughout the game but, overall, to me, it was just another hard cup tie. Its significance was huge, though. It established the idea that the players Jock had inherited had the potential to be winners and that the change required at the club was not so much one of personnel but of overall approach.

Part of the reason for our swift success was that Jock had started getting more out of the players right away. Everybody knew that if they didn't do it for him they would not be in his team. He was the boss and that was that. It helped enormously that what he was telling you was proven, time and again, to be utterly right. Jock would instruct you to do something and you would say to yourself, 'Why did I not think of that? Why did I not see that myself?' He was always a step in front of you and down the years he continued to innovate and improve.

Jock would maybe, for example, tell wee Jimmy Johnstone to drop back a bit in the outside-right position and leave a bit more of a space at the top of the right flank, in front of Jimmy and behind the full-back marking him. From the centre of the park, he would want Bobby Murdoch to send the ball over Jimmy's head and for me, from the centre-forward position, to dart diagonally out to the right, dragging the centre-half out of position. That would also give me a yard start because it would take time for the centre-half to catch on to what was happening – and a yard start means a lot in a game of football. Once I went out wide, my task was to get to the ball and whip it back quickly into the heart of the penalty area for someone such as Bobby Lennox to dart in from the opposite wing and slip the ball into the net. It could work equally well on the other side – I could veer out to the left and Bobby could come inside or Jimmy could dart in from the right wing to get on the end of my cross. Movement on the field of play is essential to success in football and under Jock it felt good to be asked to be on the move all the time, keeping the opposition on their toes constantly. You can have a good game simply through using open space to create room for other people to play. You might not see too much of the ball yourself sometimes but you would be carrying out a fine job for the team. If you take defenders into stupid positions, you're winning. Even if you don't get the ball, someone can move into your space.

I don't know if I would go so far as to say that I found it simple to score goals but I did a lot of it, let's put it that way, throughout my career, so I developed a knack for it. My play was always based on trying to get goals, without being too greedy. I was a forward after all. Being utterly selfish, though, the way some forwards, particularly strikers, are, was never my game – all through my career it was, to me, about playing for the team.

A year on from Jock's arrival at Celtic, we had become a team transformed. We were not only well on course to win the Scottish League title but also to reach the final of the European Cup-Winners' Cup. A momentous victory over Dynamo Kiev took us into a semi-final with Liverpool, who we defeated 1-0 in the first leg at Celtic Park in the spring of 1966. The second leg sticks in my memory for painful reasons. Before the game at Anfield, we were kicking in and loosening up and somebody crossed the ball for me. Ronnie Simpson, our goalkeeper, came out for it, without me realising he was doing so, and he came down right on top of me, scraping the studs of his boot down my leg as he did so. I didn't want to say anything so I played right through the game with the injury. It had been a really serious scrape right down the shin – maybe Ronnie was used to doing that to strikers. Blood was running freely from the wound. You had to expect these things in football – but not before the match. There was no way I was going to ask to have it strapped up or anything because Jock would call you for everything. So I just played away. It did us no good – we lost 2-0 and we were eliminated from the tournament.

We left Anfield with a grievance. Late on in the match, Bobby Lennox went streaking through on goal after having been played in by Joe McBride, who was in front of him when he made the pass, and put the ball in the Liverpool net. Joseph Hannet, the referee, from Belgium, disallowed the goal for offside but everyone knew the goal had been a valid one. Jock was furious, saying that the referee had beaten us, not Liverpool, and Mr Hannet would later admit, after scrutinising the goal on television, that he should have allowed it to stand. We had deserved to be level in the tie through that goal but I have to say that Liverpool were a difficult team to play against; they were a good, professional team that worked hard and played hard. They were not an easy team to beat or get a result against. They were one of the better teams we played during that era.

We were not too bad ourselves, though. Prior to Jock's arrival, we had trained with one or two balls so if, for example, you were training at Celtic Park and one ball was punted over the stand, you were struggling. Under Jock, everybody had a ball and that in itself made us feel that we were more professional and that we were expected to become more proficient in controlling and passing a football. To me, training is always much better when you've got a ball at your feet but before we started training, we would always do a bit of running; and running was always included in our training to a sizeable extent. I think that if you cannot run, and by that I mean run freely, quickly and well, you shouldn't be playing football. Allied to that, if you cannot control a ball and collect it and move away with it and use it, you should forget about playing the game as well. We needed a lot of the ball in training but that went hand in hand with fitness. It was never a case of one thing at the expense of the other. Under Jock, the training was no harder than that which we had been used to previously – it was just that it was that bit different. I thrived on training, loved it and could not get enough of it. I would never complain about getting extra training.

There were also greater demands on us in matches. Jock wanted his teams to play at a high tempo so you would feel afterwards that you had really been in a match and that great demands had been made on you. Your body soon adjusted to that and once Jock had been manager for a while we all went up a level in terms of the amount with which we could cope.

All of those elements in Jock Stein's alchemy were important, but the greatest effect he had on us was to transform us from perennial losers into winners. For every match, Jock sent us on to the field with a concrete-hard belief that we were going to win and it is hard to overestimate just how effective it can be for a football team to be winning. All my life, in whatever I have done, I have liked to be winning. I like to be doing things well and I always felt that deeply about football; that playing to win was essential. If I could score goals in the process of winning then that would be even better. It is a difficult bargain to strike sometimes for a forward. The most important thing is for the team to win but you are also aware that it is vital that you should score goals regularly. So, even if the team was winning, you could often get a bit anxious about scoring goals if you hadn't hit the net for a couple of weeks, especially with big Jock Stein grimacing and glowering away on the sidelines. I would always be trying to do better. As regards winning, I was hugely competitive in everything I did, in every sphere. When the children were young, I would take them to the local park and race against them, giving them a target of reaching a tree before me, with a suitable start – a start that would enable me to catch them and get past them, to win, just in time. It would only be once they had begun crying that I would allow them to win.

I remember the match on 7 May 1966, when we won the League Championship for the first time, as a team, at Motherwell, and the ground being so busy that day that several supporters stood on the top of the terracing roof. There was an official estimated crowd of 20,000 inside Fir Park that day, but the place was absolutely packed. Perhaps Motherwell had enlisted Desmond White to count the numbers for them. As with so many matches that season, it was another in which we got on top of the home side early on and never at any time looked like being beaten. It did take us until the closing minutes for Bobby Lennox to prod the ball over the Motherwell line for the only goal of the game, but we had won again and winning a game is just so much better than getting a draw or being beaten.

It's not a good idea in football to play for a draw – winning's the thing. There are times when you can play for a draw – when you don't need to have a victory – but it is always better to go all out to win. When we got in front in a match I would like to see people starting to try things on the park that they wouldn't have tried if the score was 1-0 to the other team. The thing about winning is that not only is it an end in itself but it brings with it extra benefits. If you are a winning team you become better as a team because you have the confidence to try things that you would never even contemplate if you were in a team that is habitually losing. Also, when you are winning, you never get tired during a match. If you are being beaten, you quickly begin to feel fatigued because you are running about daft, trying to get yourself right again. In short, if you are winning, football is an easy game.

The man who was responsible for that winning culture at Celtic Park, from the mid-1960s onwards, Jock Stein, had an infinite variety of means at his disposal for making sure that everyone inside the club was pepped up and prepared to perform to their maximum capacity for him. An important thing about Jock was his unpredictability. He could bite you about anything at any time. If, for example, we were on a trip and Jock knew that a player should have been at church on a particular occasion, he would be furious with them. 'Get yourself out of bed and get up to that church!' he would roar. That was something he didn't need to do but he would be aware of the players he was dealing with and would know from their background that on that particular day they ought to be at church. It was a question of Jock reinforcing with the player that he ought to carry out his duties properly. It also let people know who the boss was, although Jock would never leave a player out of any of his teams for something such as that.

Jock was always expert at taking a situation, weighing it up and working out exactly how he could squeeze every advantage from it for the benefit of himself, his players and Celtic Football Club. He could make players and people do exactly what he wanted them to do and he would make the press write what he wanted them to write. He would ring them up and tell them that a certain player was stronger than another – not always because he believed it but because it suited his purposes. That would duly be reported in the sports pages as if it were gospel and Jock's aim of building up one player at the expense of another would have been achieved. Or he would get in touch with the press and tell them all about this new system that we were playing and that he was confident that it was going to freshen up the team. We, his players, who were supposed to be at the heart of this new playing ploy, would read this in the papers and would all be looking at each other in puzzlement, given that Jock had not mentioned anything to us about a new system or style of play. He was absolutely masterful at using the press to his advantage.

I had a keen interest in photography and on European trips I would take a camera with me. It seemed a harmless enough means of combining a pleasant hobby with a journey abroad. I liked taking pictures of dramatic buildings, scenery and interesting, quirky things, such as the checkpoints on the borders between communist Eastern Europe and the West. Jock, though, objected to anyone introducing an outside interest or hobby into the business of professional football. He was a total professional and believed that we had to keep our minds on football alone. It wasn't that he had anything against me taking pictures – just that he wanted the very best from every one of us and anything that might have been considered a distraction was quickly vetoed. It did not upset me too much – I could see entirely his point – but it would be very good to have retained some personal souvenirs of those days through having photographs that I could look back upon.

But Jock's skills as a manager were not all about psychology and imagination – he was also extremely practical. Against Rangers, on 3 January 1966 when I scored my hat-trick, he sent us out wearing training shoes – Adidas Samba, with large suction holes on the soles – while the Rangers players were wearing boots. On a hard, frosty pitch it turned out to be a big advantage to us.

THE STEIN SCENE

Another clever thing that Jock did was to have around him people who had a light touch that complemented his sometimes more stern approach. Jimmy Steele, our masseur, was a great man to have on the bus when travelling to away matches. He was also in the dressing room for every game. He was a comedian, a raconteur, a mimic, a song and dance man; a lovely fellow who had been with the club before Jock but whom Jock encouraged greatly to be an integral part of the group. Jock would give Jimmy a hard time but it would all be laughed off. He'd stand at the front of the bus and put on a performance as if he was giving a running commentary on a boxing match or on the Derby, complete with the English-accented twang of Raymond Glendenning, the renowned, well-spoken commentator, and he'd have everyone in stitches. It was perfect for taking people's minds off a tedious journey or the tense match that was to follow. Later on, Steelie would frequently get asked to Manchester United by Alex Ferguson to perform the same function and he was often on duty, if you could call it that, with the Scotland international squad.

Even if we had not had Steelie with us on our travels, it would still have been clear to every one of us that the journey upon which we were embarking with Jock Stein was going to be a remarkable and hugely eventful one. Just how remarkable that journey would prove to be would have been beyond the creativity even of Steelie, our chirpy, cheerful, chatty masseur who was perennially inventive and imaginative in entertaining us grandly.

CHAPTER SIX

FORWARD MOTION

My sole encounter with one of the greatest goalscorers world football has ever seen proved to be a short and sharp and very painful one. Celtic were facing Bayern Munich in San Francisco in June 1966, in a match that was billed as a close-season friendly. Late in the match, we won a corner-kick. I was standing on the goal line, waiting for the ball to be delivered, when I decided to take a quick glance round to see where the opposition defenders and my various teammates were positioned. Next thing I knew, I was whacked, full in the face, by the fist of a stocky little fellow by the name of Gerd Müller, a forward back defending his goal, and the solidity of the blow stiffened me. The events that followed were rather funny; although only in retrospect, of course.

When I made to exact retribution on the little German, he took to his heels – so I followed. I pursued him across the penalty area, off the field of play and away round the back of the German team's goal. I eventually caught up with him in front of the stand – I don't know how because he was quick and he was ten years younger than me – but just as I got level with him, this massive Celtic supporter materialised in front of us. 'Just leave him with me!' he said. 'I'll get him.' I trotted back on to the park – I don't know what happened to Müller. I also have no idea why he punched me. His running away made the situation worse, as well as farcical. We were all a bit younger and more stupid back then but you lose your temper when you are punched like that. You can hardly do anything else. The inside of my mouth was cut badly afterwards.

After the match, Fred Reynders, the local referee who had officiated in the match, stated that he had intended to dismiss both me and Müller for scrapping on the track beside the pitch – or trying to anyway – but that as he made his way towards us an eight-man brawl involving other players from both sides began and he decided that he would either have to send off everyone involved or no one at all. So my teammates saved me because Mr Reynders took the sensible option of trying to cool everything down rather than dismissing half of the players on the pitch. We had thoroughly outplayed Bayern, the West German Cup holders, and following that incident Zlatko Cajkovski, the Bayern manager, had actually attempted to remove his team from the field of play. 'Celtic are good footballers but they are primitive,' Cajkovski imperiously told anyone prepared to listen to him after the match. In being outplayed, Bayern had resorted to foul tactics and hadn't liked it when we refused to be cowed. Jock Stein actually thought that we played our best football of the tour in that match, possibly because Bayern's unfriendliness stung us into treating the game as something more serious than a friendly. The following morning when we were leaving the hotel, which we shared with Bayern, and embarking on to our team bus, Müller was standing by the wall outside the hotel staring at us all, looking superior and smug. We were all on the bus shouting at him but he seemed to thrive on that.

Although I finished the 1966 tour of North America with that painful mouth injury from my meeting with Herr Müller, our visit to that vast continent had been a magnificent experience. If there was one thing more than any other that fused together all those Celtic players that Jock Stein took under his wing in the mid-1960s into a really tight-knit, near-inseparable bunch, it was criss-crossing North America in each other's company that early summer. That's not to say that it was fun and games all the way. We were away from our families for five weeks – and at the time, for many of us, those families would have been very young – and an absence from home for that length of time, even under the most pleasant of circumstances, is bound to incur certain stresses and strains. Some small things, such as making a transatlantic telephone call, required a gargantuan effort. The benefits though, far outweighed the inconveniences.

It was a terrific trip and one that I think really soldered us into a team, and Jock would have known all the time that things were progressing in the right direction. He enjoyed the tour as much as we did. There was good patter going on and people were being thrown into swimming pools all the time. On one occasion, Tommy Gemmell and big Billy McNeill tried to push Jock into a pool but, luckily for them, they couldn't move him. They probably wouldn't have played again for Celtic if they had managed to complete their prank. In Kansas, the boys threw one young newspaper reporter into a swimming pool only to discover, once he was spluttering and flailing around in the deep end, that he clearly could not swim. Sean Fallon, who had been a lifeguard in his native Sligo as a young man, dived in and hauled the struggling scribe safely out of the water.

As a means of defraying the overhanging debt of dullness, which results from living out of a suitcase in a series of hotels, Jock would switch room-mates around all the time. So when you went out on to the park, you were with your friends, not strangers or even mere teammates. Jock also ensured there were no cliques. Naturally, certain players would still have more time for some among their teammates than others, but that tour meant that even those who were not the best match temperamentally would get to know and understand each other much better. He made us friends for life, created a bond that would never be broken. It all meant that everybody in Jock's team worked for each other all the time.

The tour began on the beautiful island of Bermuda, with a 10-1 victory over a Bermuda national representative team, followed by a 7-0 victory over a team called Bermudan Young Men. From Bermuda, we flew to New York, and then took in places such as Toronto, St Louis, Vancouver and San Francisco. It was an 11-game, five-week-long tour, which began on 11 May 1966 when we flew out of Scotland, that would see us clocking up a total of 15,000 air miles. The match with Bayern took place on 9 June 1966, in San Francisco, and the 2-2 draw with the West Germans was the second-last match of the tour. Three days later we concluded our fixtures with a 1-0 victory over Atlas of Mexico. Overall, we had won eight matches and had drawn three, scoring 47 goals and conceding only six. We had defeated Tottenham Hotspur twice and had drawn with them once and, in contrast to the game with Bayern, the Tottenham games were really good – the boys from the London club appreciated that we were both involved in holiday-type matches, so they didn't go in too tough, didn't treat it too seriously and neither did we. Still, within the usual bounds of the conventions that surround friendlies, the matches with the club from White Hart Lane were good and competitive. They were a good, jolly crowd, who wanted fun off the park and a good but not too hard game on the day, which is just what you need. We also drew with Italian club Bologna, and won the rest of our matches against local representative teams.

Funnily enough, Jock, for reasons known best to himself, fielded me at right-back in one game, against one of the local teams. I'd love to be able to describe it as an outstanding success but the first time the ball came to me I went to smack it away and just about missed it altogether. The opposing winger robbed me of it, went flying in on goal and nearly scored. I looked over at the bench and all I could see was a blur of movement. Stein was signalling in my direction and yelling, 'Get out, get back up the park.' I was swiftly switched back to the forward line. That is how long the experiment of playing me as a defender lasted so I am in no position to comment with regard to the difficulties or otherwise of playing elsewhere in a football team. Jock would have known that I wasn't a full-back but he was always looking to have pace in his team and he may have thought it would be useful to have me as a possible emergency full-back in that, with my speed, I could whisk the ball upfield quickly once it had been distributed by the goalkeeper. He always looked to have his full-backs pushing up high, as illustrated by such great exponents of that art as Tommy Gemmell, Jim Craig and Danny McGrain. That experiment Stateside quickly showed him the stark reality of playing me at the back, and it was never repeated.

A squad of only 18 players were accompanied on that tour by manager Jock Stein, assistant manager Sean Fallon, club chairman Robert Kelly and trainer Neil Mochan. Jimmy Johnstone flew home during the tour to prepare for his wedding day, despite being asked by Jock Stein to remain and help out, given that we had suffered injuries to several players – by the end of the

11 matches, we had only 12 players still fit to play. It wasn't all football. We'd play golf and meet local dignitaries, go to watch horse racing, do a bit of sightseeing; it was nice to do things such as that. We also spent an awful lot of time together sitting around hotel pools, going for meals, taking it easy in hotel lounges. The camaraderie that was built up would sustain us for many years to come.

There were funny incidents galore. I remember that when we played Atlas, the Mexican club, in Los Angeles, the atmosphere was extremely humid. We were all preparing for the match and wondering how we were going to cope with this weather when Mr Kelly strode up and said, in his starchy voice, 'Not as hot as I thought it would be – quite cool here!' That became a bit of a standing joke among the players for a long time afterwards, especially as when we began playing that day the heat was steaming off of us. Things like that, shared 'in-jokes' and lots of other bits of fun, meant that by the end of the tour we had become, without being overly sentimental, almost like one big family rather than a squad of footballers.

For all that Jock Stein was very much a man who kept a degree of distance between him and his players, it was he who was responsible for creating close bonds between us, most especially over in North America that summer of 1966. Nothing happened by accident under Jock's managerial direction and he would have put a lot of thought and planning into everything that he and we did, on and off the field of play, on that tour. He also exercised strict control over the players even while inculcating an atmosphere of fun and togetherness among us. Although I knew Jock wasn't keen on it I took my camera on tour, took pictures of the boys and sent them back to the Scottish press for publication and they did use them. Eventually, big Jock got fed up with it and told me I was no longer allowed to use the camera. He said, 'You're no' here to play with photographs. You're here to win games.' He knew I was getting a few bob for it so maybe that was an extra annoyance for him.

The camaraderie built on that tour was to sustain us thoroughly when, as Scottish League champions, we entered the European Cup, the world's premier club competition, three months after our return home. As we launched ourselves into the club's first experience of that tournament, in September 1966, we had already enjoyed 18 months of Jock Stein's management and the positive feeling with which he had suffused the club. We had competed in the Fairs Cup and the European Cup-Winners' Cup and those had been good and interesting experiences, but the European Cup was always the big one.

Back in 1962, when we had faced Valencia, the then Fairs Cup holders and a supremely skilled Spanish side brightened even further by a couple of Brazilian talents, I had felt that we were not on the same level as them and had been involved in European football solely for experience. I must admit that four years later, as we prepared for the new competition, I still felt that it was too big a jump from the Scottish game to that level of competition. There were an awful lot of very good clubs to contend with, not least of which were the major Italian, Portuguese and Spanish clubs, who had monopolised the tournament ever since its inception. So we knew that any team from one of those nations would certainly be massively difficult opponents, let alone the top clubs from England, West Germany, France and Yugoslavia. We could not really afford to take anyone lightly.

For us, as a club from one of the smaller leagues in northern Europe in a tournament that had been dominated by the great football technicians and tacticians of southern Europe, the chances of lifting the European Cup looked infinitesimally small.

Our first step in the competition pitted us against FC Zurich, the champions of Switzerland. We treated them with respect, reckoning that they couldn't be a bad side if they were their nation's champions, but we felt that we would have a great chance against them because they were not one of the truly daunting names in European football. We thought they might be roughly on the same level as us. During that year's competition, our manager helped us to overcome any potential inferiority complex that might arise among us. He would tell us in the run-up to a match, 'You are as good a team as them.' Then, with a few minutes remaining before kick-off, with us preparing to go out on to the field, he might change that to, 'You're a better team than them . . .' He did it every time – and every time it worked in terms of making us believe him.

In the event, we won 5-0 against Zurich, over the two legs. I managed to notch my first European goal, scoring the second in our 3-0 second-leg victory over in Switzerland, knocking a loose ball over the line following a bit of a free-for-all at a corner-kick. That was an important goal as it put the tie out of sight for the Swiss. It may have looked like a simple, straightforward victory, but we had an awful will to win that permeated the entire squad. Without that, a tie against a club such as Zurich would have been a lot more difficult.

When we were drawn against Nantes, of France, in the next round, we felt that this was very much a step up. This was a club that had won the league in a major European footballing nation and several of the Nantes players had featured for France at the World Cup in England a few months earlier. We expected to face opponents who would be technically good on the ball and tactically aware, and we knew that it would be quite possible to lose to a team such as that. But we had people in our squad who had a fierce desire to win and, again, I cannot stress enough just how important that was. We went on to win both legs, each by 3-1, and I scored both home and away: a striker's classic tap-in in the first match in France, and a header in the return at Celtic Park.

One of the most pleasing things in making progress through those first two rounds was that we had scored 11 goals and not only that but they had been shared out among five players: myself, Tommy Gemmell, Joe McBride, Bobby Lennox and Jimmy Johnstone. Ninety-five per cent of eyes in the crowd inside a stadium are trained on the goalscorer, not on the man who makes the chance, so it's always quite a good thing if there are a number of different players scoring goals. It infuses the team with a spirit of togetherness in that the praise and the attention from press and public for putting the ball in the net is being shared more equally than in a team where there is a greater reliance on a single goalscorer. With that Celtic team, practically anybody could score goals – and everybody did. I was always happy to be making goals but you are always just that bit happier if you are scoring them, especially if you are a striker.

Following Christmas 1966 and as we entered 1967, we could feel satisfied with those two good wins against fairly accomplished opposition and a place in the quarter-finals of the Continent's premier competition, but further progress seemed less than likely.

We were always encouraged by the manager to win in Europe because of the all-round benefits that accrue to you, to the manager himself and to the club as a whole from each victory in that sphere of competition. But I never thought, as we progressed on that journey through the tournament, that we would win the trophy. It never even crossed my mind. We were simply pleased to be in the tournament and to have won a couple of ties, but, once we had won those meetings with Nantes and Zurich we started to enjoy the experience of playing against Continental clubs even more and we wished to have more and more of it.

When we were drawn against Vojvodina Novi Sad, of Yugoslavia, in the quarter-finals, the gradient on our uphill journey in that season's European Cup was increased considerably. Vojvodina were not one of the well-known names in European football but at that time European competitions would often see some really fine teams emerge from obscurity. It was more likely then, especially in the more secluded and far-flung parts of Europe, to come up against a team that had perhaps been constructed quietly over a number of years, a bit like ourselves, in fact.

Jock was never afraid to try new things and he deserves great credit for that. It kept things fresh in and around the club. As part of our preparations for facing Vojvodina, in early 1967, we played a friendly match against Dinamo Zagreb, another Yugoslavian club, in which he fielded some forwards in defensive positions and the defenders in attack. I remember the unusual sight of John Hughes, our dynamic, powerful forward, wearing a No. 5 on his shorts and being pulled away back deep. Again, Jock was quick to abandon the experiment once he had seen enough – at half-time he came in and said, simply, 'That's enough of that.'

For the second half everyone was restored to their more natural stations on the field of play. He never tried it again.

We were very hard-pressed during the first leg in Novi Sad and I think we were a wee bit surprised at them being such a good side. That meant we possibly did not play as well as we ought to have done. They were extremely accomplished opponents, a strong unit, almost flawless as a team, and we went down 1-0 over in Yugoslavia. On the strength of our performance, we returned home quite pleased to be only one goal behind.

We knew the return would be extremely difficult, and so it proved. They were just as hard to break down at Celtic Park but, finally, with almost an hour gone in the second leg, Ilija Pantelic, the Vojvodina goalkeeper, failed to cut out a cross ball from Tommy Gemmell and, after diving at full-stretch to intercept it, he was lying sprawled on the ground when the ball dropped in my vicinity. I controlled it quickly, eased away from a defender, let it fall and clipped it over the line to put us on level terms in the tie.

I loved those European games, with the pitch and the team colours lit up with a radiant sheen under the floodlights, and with the supporters masked by the darkness but still making their enormous presence felt through their powerful urging on of the team. They were so strong in their support that once a match appeared to have turned in our favour, the momentum from the Celtic crowd could push us on to get further goals and seal the game. The supporters were in full cry that night but even that couldn't quite break the resolve of our Yugoslavian opponents. Even after we had equalised, they remained resolute and they were holding us level in the tie as we entered its final minute.

With seconds to go we were awarded a corner, which Charlie Gallagher slung over. Charlie was great at crossing balls, especially when he was given plenty of time to do it. He put a beautiful ball into the penalty area that was directed unerringly in the direction of Billy McNeill's head and once Billy connected with a header his efforts were habitually powerful. Still, as with everyone, Billy could always do with a little help in getting the job done and as the ball came across I could see that the keeper clearly thought that he could intercept it if he was to race from his line and leap for it. I was sure that he was right too, because, for all that he was a nuisance and a big, arrogant, mouthy individual who had spent much of the evening moaning at the referee and indulging in delaying tactics, he was also an excellent goalkeeper. So I made a little run and accidentally got in his way as he moved towards the ball. That put Pantelic completely off his stride. Nobody told me to do it but I didn't want him coming out and getting the cross from Charlie, especially so late on in the game. I was keener to see how well Billy might head the ball than how well Pantelic could catch it.

Not a lot of people noticed my little cameo role, but it broke Pantelic's stride. It was not a dirty foul and I didn't trip him up or barge him, I just meandered across his tracks. I think his defenders expected him to come out and collect the ball, so when he was unable to do so they were caught unawares and it gave Billy an unhindered attempt at goal. He duly sent the perfect header into the net. The referee didn't notice my contribution and most people in the ground didn't see it but a few of my teammates saw what had happened. These things happen in football. Pantelic moaned about it to the referee but we were already on our way back to the halfway line for the restart and I am sure the referee would not have been too keen to disallow that goal when there were 75,000 Celtic supporters roaring their heads off in the belief that we had just sealed our entry into the European Cup semi-finals. You do a lot of things on the field of play and hope to get away with them and you've certainly got a better chance of that when you are close to the 90-minute mark. I jogged back to the centre of the park, in no hurry, because I was certain the referee would not disallow it. I was delighted to get through that tie because Vojvodina were such a good, all-round team. Interestingly, in late 1968, Celtic, and Rangers, apparently, showed some interest in signing Pantelic but it never happened. That would have been interesting.

Dukla Prague were to be our opponents in the semi-final and they were equally tough. This was a club with a real top-notch Champions' Cup pedigree. They were in the European Cup for the seventh time and in their six games prior to meeting us that season they had scored 15 goals and conceded only four. Josef Masopust, their midfield playmaker, had won more than 60 caps for Czechoslovakia, had scored the opener in the 1962 World Cup final against Brazil and had been named European Footballer of the Year the same year. As Dukla prepared to face us, he was regarded as having made a return to the form that had won him that accolade. Ivo Viktor, the goalkeeper, was widely regarded as one of the best in Europe.

Dukla, we felt, would have been confident of beating us. They were a team packed with Czechoslovakian internationals and had eliminated Ajax Amsterdam – the team that had scored seven goals in knocking Liverpool out of the tournament – in the quarter-finals. For our part, we thought we were going to beat them but you can often think that way and not get anything out of a game. It proved to be another vibrant evening at Celtic Park, with 75,000 supporters backing our efforts.

I made a sharp start to the match and after only a few minutes I put the ball in the net. Jimmy Johnstone cut in sharply from the right, got to the goal line and cut back an excellent ball that I headed past Ivo Viktor. I leapt for delight, feeling certain that I had begun the process of sending us into the final but the referee, inexplicably, disallowed it for an infringement that only he appeared to have spotted. Jimmy Johnstone actually opened the scoring, driving into the penalty box to lift the ball over Ivo Viktor. It was a brave effort on Jimmy's part, as the giant Viktor had come hurtling from his goal towards him in hugely intimidating fashion. It was good for Jimmy to get a goal – the opposition might have expected a lot of trickery from him but may not have expected him to score and perhaps they would have been marking other players more closely in and around the penalty area. So his scoring would have maybe forced them to reorganise although Dukla, who had started the match on fire, did continue to look impressive after going behind. Sure enough, they levelled the tie shortly before half-time when Stanislav Strunc scored after a neat, incisive move.

At the interval, Jock told us to press them much harder than in the first half. Dukla had looked very dangerous opponents and had had a lot of the ball but Jock must have seen that they might succumb to greater pressure from us and so it proved. On the hour, Willie Wallace reacted more quickly than anyone else to Tommy Gemmell's long, searching ball into the box to volley it past Viktor. With the score at 2-1 in our favour, I had a close-range effort beaten away by Viktor, on his line, and when, a few minutes later, Bertie Auld played a quick free-kick, Willie Wallace was again sharp to the ball to sweep it into the Dukla net. We continued to create numerous chances and by the end of the match, a Dukla side that had begun confidently were clearly grateful for the final whistle. Still, they had kept our margin of victory to only two goals, meaning they would have seen the return as manageable for them to obtain a victory and that, in turn, would make it a tense occasion for us.

Although we travelled to Czechoslovakia with a comfortable cushion in terms of the score, the trip held a good deal of anxiousness, and even a degree of fear, for me. There was always an increased level of tension on trips behind the Iron Curtain, the aphorism used by Sir Winston Churchill to describe the band of countries in the vicinity of Russia that stretched from the Baltic Sea to the Adriatic, which had been colonised by the Soviet Union following the Second World War and that were controlled ruthlessly from the heart of Moscow, making life grim and grey for their inhabitants. Westerners were not made to feel particularly welcome in those countries and Czechoslovakia was one of them.

You would be subject to low-level harassment in those communist states. On our way to Prague, they stopped the team bus at a checkpoint and opened up the luggage compartments to subject them to close scrutiny. I don't know whether they were actually looking for anything or just being awkward. Army operatives were swarming around the bus, some looking over the luggage and others staring up at the bus while some others, with rifles slung over their shoulders, were hanging back, in the background – and because I had been in the forces I knew what they were about. They were prepared to intervene if there should be any trouble. There were also guards in watchtowers surrounding the bus, glowering down, guns at the ready.

The communist countries all had clubs that represented the state security services and Dukla was the Czechoslovakian army club, so there was an extra element of threat surrounding them. From the moment we disembarked from our bus at the International Hotel in central Prague, there were people watching us all extremely closely: secret policemen. I was genuinely concerned that one wrong move could mean a long spell spent in custody in the Eastern bloc because once you went into the communist lands they were almost a law unto themselves. There was a nagging feeling in the back of my mind that I could end up in a Czech prison. Anything could happen and it was a big concern for me.

Dukla's home ground, the Juliska stadium, was unusual. It didn't look much like a traditional football stadium; it looked more like a place in which servicemen would exercise. The largest side was under reconstruction and closed to supporters and dotted with tree stumps. The other three sides were full but the crowd was no more than 25,000 and a number of those 'supporters' were actually servicemen drafted in to populate the ground. Because of that, they were less enthusiastic than if they had been there for love and not duty. Dukla were unpopular in Czechoslovakia because of their links with the hated security services and were never going to attract a huge voluntary following, so a number of the crowd may simply have been Czechs drawn to see a European Cup semi-final rather than being wildly supportive of the home club. The ground also didn't have floodlights and so the match was to be played in the afternoon, which added to the strangeness of the whole thing in terms of this being a semi-final of the most prestigious club competition on earth. It was vital on that day that we were not duped by our surroundings into thinking that this was anything less than a match of enormous magnitude and adjusting to those surroundings was a task in itself.

Before the match, given that we were looking after a two-goal lead from the first leg, Jock Stein told me that I would be up front on my own, keeping the Dukla defenders busy all the time. He felt that by deploying only one forward we would be more strongly equipped in midfield to preserve the team's lead. Such a role suited me – indeed any role in the team in that game would have suited me. I was so delighted that we were a fraction away from making the final that I would have run until I was dead wherever I was fielded.

On the field, the Dukla team were strong and well organised, resilient, as you would expect of army boys, and their approach to the game, which focused on them being particularly well drilled, set them slightly apart from the other teams that we had faced in Europe that season. On the day, I did not feel that I was particularly isolated although I clearly was. That was underlined when I got into a wee bit of bother at one point with their midfielder Jan Geleta, which ended with him on the ground. I found myself quickly surrounded by a vengeful pack of his team-mates ready to sort me out and there was not a Celtic player within 70 yards to offer me some backup. At the incident in question, I maybe went up for the ball with my elbow out and perhaps he connected with my elbow because when you go up for a ball you do have to stick your elbows out. They surrounded me to bring attention to me and see if they could frighten the referee into sending me off. They did not physically handle me at all but my fear at the time was that the referee might have been a fellow who thought he did not want to be badly treated by his communist hosts once the game was finished. My fears were not realised and I was allowed to proceed with my game as our lone wolf up front.

Any time I got the ball on that afternoon, I held on to it and took it away to the byline to waste a bit of time. From the dugout, Jock Stein kept yelling at me to push up the park and chase their defence down or to take the ball into the corners or away into an area from which they would find it difficult to build up play. Dukla wanted to win the match as much as we did so their players were kicking lumps out of me to try to win the ball and get it back in play. Maybe they knew they would be forced to do a lot more parade-ground exercises if they lost to us, I don't know, but they were desperate to win. I quite enjoyed the experience. I didn't mind it at all because I knew there was an end product and I must have done well enough because we got through the game, got our 0-0 draw and everybody thought I had done what I had done very well.

That was the one game in which Jock was really pleased with me. He was effusive in his praise of me after it and he really hugged me tight for the one and only time. He said that my performance had been great and that I had done everything he had wanted me to do. Jock possibly felt for me at Dukla because I was in scuffles a few times and got through them all right. I had certainly undergone a hard time throughout those 90 minutes but to think that we all now had a cup final to look forward to was wonderful and Jock clearly thought so too. I had run around up the park so many times it had been for me almost a test of stamina and athleticism as much as a football match – like running a long-distance race – but Jock was always a man who saw the bigger picture. He was delighted with what I had done for him and the team and it was after that performance, I think, that he decided he had to make sure I was playing in the final. The fact that I had also scored more goals than anybody else in the run to the final must have helped.

It was particularly special for me to feel that the final was within my sight because there had been a lot of extra pressure on my place in the team that season. A team always has room for improvement and, in December 1966, Jock had brought in Willie Wallace, an excellent forward, from Heart of Midlothian. With Joe McBride having scored regularly since signing for Celtic 18 months earlier, I felt a wee bit under pressure because we were competing for places. Joe was a good goalscorer, while Willie Wallace was not only a goalscorer but also a player who played off the front men. I was starting to worry a wee bit. I still scored goals once Joe McBride and Willie Wallace came to the club but Jock was always tinkering with his forward line. Maybe he was just adapting our side to play other teams but he never really changed the defence too much. I could never really fathom why he changed the forward line about so much – he did it incessantly, it was like a compulsion with him.

It wasn't only my own place in the team that was threatened. When Jock brought in Willie Wallace, maybe Joe McBride also felt it was going to make his place in the side less certain. More than one of my teammates at the time identified that in style Willie was very similar to Joe. Willie's position – playing just off the centre-forward – was something of a new one in football. It meant that he was expected to pick up the ball if it broke off the man who was spearheading the forward line. It reassured me to some extent that I provided something different to the other two. I reasoned to myself that if Jock decided he still required a sharp, direct forward, good at speeding away from opponents and at putting away chances – and half-chances – in and around the six-yard box, then I still had a serious role to play at the club. I turned 31 in the middle of that 1966–67 season but I felt as fit and sharp as ever. All that good living of mine was paying off in spades.

It was a funny thing, but Joe McBride had been a team-mate of mine at Rob Roy all those years ago. In fact, I had also played with Willie Wallace at Rob Roy, when he had been given a trial in a match against Blantyre Vics. We won 7-1. Another Celtic player, goalkeeper John Fallon, had also played in that match, for Blantyre.

Having reached the European Cup final, we liked the feeling that we were playing Internazionale of Milan, the richest and the most successful club in the world at the time. The Italians had won the great trophy in 1964 and 1965 and, simultaneous to us defeating Vojvodina over two legs, they had eliminated Real Madrid, the 1966 winners. All of that merely underlined just how hard it would be for us to make the European Cup our own.

Helenio Herrera, the Inter manager, was scheduled to watch us in action for the first time ten days before the final in Lisbon, when we were due to face Kilmarnock in our last league fixture of the season. Instead he flew in on a private jet to see us play Rangers at Ibrox in the title decider a week earlier, on 6 May.

It would be interesting to see Herrera's assessment of our performance that day – he sat in the main stand at Ibrox making copious notes. We played very well in a 2-2 draw and became Scottish champions for the second successive year but Herrera would have seen us running daft on the sodden Ibrox turf on a spring afternoon when it was pouring with rain. He would surely not have expected us to be able to replicate such a lung-bursting performance in the heat and humidity of Lisbon. Also, wee Jimmy Johnstone scored an excellent goal in the mud from quite a distance out, with his left foot, and Jimmy wasn't known to get that type of goal. He veered in from the right and sent the ball streaking into the top corner. I was right behind him and I was first to get a hold of Jimmy. I said, 'How on earth did you kick it that distance with your left foot?' Wee Jimmy failed to provide me with a considered reply – he just wanted to get away and run about in delight at his goal. So for all the trouble Herrera had taken to be in Glasgow that day, he must have been left with more questions than answers in his mind about our football team – and we were determined to pose a few more for him and his players when we came face to face with world football's most dominant team in the capital of Portugal.

CHAPTER SEVEN

OUT OF THE BLUE

My first stint in the dark blue of Scotland had come just as a team was being built to try to qualify for the 1966 World Cup finals so it was poignant that my recall to the side should come in the run-up to those finals. Scotland would not be there – after I had been dropped unceremoniously from the squad more than a year and a half previously, the team had narrowly failed to ease past Italy in their qualifying group and so it would be the Italians who would be billeted in the north-east of England when the tournament got underway.

When I did return to the Scotland team, in June 1966, my life was no less busy than when the selectors had last included me; indeed it was busier. Two days before we faced Portugal in a friendly at Hampden Park in June 1966, I flew into Prestwick Airport with my Celtic teammates after a 16-hour flight from Los Angeles that concluded Celtic's extended tour of North America. There were 200 fans present at Prestwick to welcome our VC-10 back and from there my next stop was Largs, just a few miles along the Ayrshire coast, where I joined up with the Scotland squad. My participation in the match with the Portuguese was not assured. John Prentice, the new Scotland manager, wished to assess whether I might be too fatigued after my journey to participate but I was keen to be in the team and I was feeling full of vim. Footballers had not yet heard about becoming 'mentally tired'.

It may seem strange but even though we were about to face two of the most accomplished teams to participate in the 1966 World Cup, in the shape of Portugal and Brazil, some Scottish players had opted to have a couple of extra weeks on the beach rather than perform for their country. I would never have taken that option and I never even considered whether other people would have been in the team ahead of me had they been available. Nor was I craving a holiday myself, even after a lengthy, demanding season and a long tour across the Pond that had followed on, immediately, from our winning the Scottish League Championship and also reaching both domestic cup finals and the semis of the European Cup-Winners' Cup. The desire to play as often as possible, which had been with me since boyhood, still burned brightly.

I liked John Prentice, as I had liked Ian McColl. I felt that he was a sympathetic manager, one who wanted to talk in depth to me and the other players, which was a good feeling to have. John Prentice accepted my assurances about being in good shape to play against the Portuguese and although he fielded Alex Young, the Everton player, at centre-forward in his team for the Portugal match, it had been agreed by the two managers that substitutes could be used after half-time, so when Alex suffered a knock I came on as his replacement and had a pretty lively game. We lost 1-0 but I had done enough to be considered for a start in the match with Brazil seven days later.

Otto Gloria, the Portugal manager, described Scotland as having 'no idea about tactics' after our loss to the Portuguese and the team had also displeased the Scottish crowd by playing a more cautious, defensively orientated game than usual – Billy Bremner, our normally tenacious, forward-driving, mid-field player, had been deployed as a sweeper behind the back four. So, with all this dissatisfaction flying around, there was a clamour for us to be more assertive against Brazil, even though this was a potential step up in class, given that the Brazilians were World Cup holders, having retained the trophy in Chile in 1962.

However, we knew that was easier said than done. The Brazilians had hit five – with Pele notching a hat-trick – against Atlético Madrid in Spain, watched by a crowd of 125,000, at the beginning of the week in which we were to play them. They saw the match with Scotland as assimilation for playing in British conditions and for meeting the type of northern European opposition – especially England themselves – that might be encountered in the World Cup finals. Vicente Feola, their manager, said that they were now 'full-out' in preparation for the tournament.

I was thrilled once I discovered that I had been selected by John Prentice to play in the Brazil game, and excited to be playing against such a team and finding out for myself whether they were just as good as they had looked on television. It was a great adventure.

Before the match, we went out on to the park for a warm-up and the Brazilians were kicking in at goal. I couldn't take my eyes off Pele. I said to Jim Baxter, 'Look at Pele. Isn't he brilliant?' Jim replied, in his lilting, broad Fife accent, totally cocksure, 'Never mind Pele . . . wait until you see me . . .' Baxter was as good as his word that day. He strolled through the game. He was super. He had no fears on days such as that.

After a week of training together – a rare luxury for a Scotland team in the 1960s albeit something the Brazilians took for granted – we were finely tuned for the challenge at hand and within a minute of the start I was in dreamland. Jim Baxter pinged a beautiful ball in my direction and, feeling fresh and eager, I got round Fidelis, the right-back, and, slightly off balance, got good contact on the ball with my right foot and clipped a shot past Gilmar, the Brazil goalkeeper, from just outside the six-yard box. He had no chance of saving it. My immediate sensation was one of almost uncontainable delight at scoring for my country in front of a wonderfully large Hampden Park crowd. Servilio equalised for Brazil after quarter of an hour's play, but during the second half I struck a sweet shot on target that looked sure to be a goal until Gilmar made a fine save to keep out my potential winner.

It's a great thing to have your name still recognised for playing and scoring against Brazil; after all, they haven't lost too many goals to Scottish teams. David Narey, with his wonderful goal against them at the World Cup in 1982, and John Collins, with a penalty in 1998, are the only other Scots who have put the ball behind a Brazilian goalkeeper.

It was a wonderful occasion, with a huge Saturday-evening Hampden Park crowd appreciative of our efforts against the world champions, who fielded players of the calibre of Jairzinho, Bellini, Gerson, Pele and Amarildo, but it was still clear to me, on a professional level, that the Brazilians were saving themselves to a certain extent. Pele had missed training the previous day and though the Brazilians had said this was normal practice, it turned out that he had been suffering from a stomach upset. Pele also claimed to be carrying a few extra pounds, which he intended to shed before they went into action in the World Cup.

Hampden Park that night was a stopping place for a Brazilian team gearing themselves up for the World Cup, so it was difficult to know just how much they put into the game. On the day it looked as though maybe they were not quite so keen to win as we were. Our players had really wanted to put on a show against the number one team in the world but the Brazilians had a bigger prize in sight. Their defence weren't playing at 100 per cent – they had the capability of knocking the ball about very well so they could cruise through a match and treat it like a training session. Even at their ease, they could make the ball just whoosh around all over the field. It was truly amazing to watch, especially from such a close vantage point as mine.

Pele had watched himself a wee bit. He was a strong fellow, stronger than you might realise given how gracefully and lithely he moved across a football pitch, but at Hampden he would try to keep out of tackles and the heftier challenges. He clearly didn't want to suffer any injuries as he looked forward to the World Cup. You could actually see that their entire team were watching themselves – something that was especially noticeable with the way our team was wiring into them! Billy Bremner did everything to try to stop Pele destroying us; Billy was right on top of him, trying to knock him out of his stride.

After the match Feola praised our 'good grasp of tactics', in contrast to Otto Gloria, and the Brazilian manager expressed his disappointment, given our performance, that Scotland were not participating in the finals. Not all of the Brazilians were happy, though. Their media and some officials, including Dr Hilton Gosling, their habitually urbane, charming general manager, complained about the 'rough handling' Pele had received from Bremner but I, for one, was quite happy that the Brazilians had been up in arms about Billy's treatment of the world's preeminent footballer. Had Billy been a bit gentler, played it more like a friendly, I might not have found myself with Pele's shirt.

During the match, Billy had clearly come to the conclusion that the only way to stop Pele was to injure him, which was not a very nice way to go about things. So when the final whistle blew and Billy made a beeline for Pele to exchange jerseys, Pele waved our fiery redhead away and instead turned around in my direction and offered to swap with me instead. It was certainly a snub for Billy, who had been certain he would get the jersey, but one that had worked fully in my favour. Pele's jersey is one of my favourite souvenirs of my time in football even though I was never one to go looking for jerseys from opponents at the end of a match. I wasn't ever a great collector of souvenirs from my career, whereas some players would ensure that they spent the final few minutes of a game making sure they were positioned closest to a certain opponent in order to have first claim on swapping shirts with them. It was just by chance that I happened to be in the right place at the right time.

Pele didn't speak very much English so he didn't say anything significant to me as we exchanged shirts. I was just so happy to wait for him to peel the jersey over his head and say thank you. When you think about it, it was quite a manly thing for him to do in turning away Bremner, to make a point of saying that he was not giving the jersey to an opponent who had, he felt, mistreated him during the match. I don't think Pele was a man that would kick people but he was a lot stronger than you would think. As John Clark, who was also in the Scotland team that day, says, if you tried to hit him with your shoulder, you would just bounce off of him because he was as powerfully built as could be.

He was like a rock. When Billy wasn't kicking away at Pele's ankles, the great Brazilian would be up against John. John was much more appreciative of playing against Pele because he was a serious connoisseur of world football; John would always be reading away at football magazines that dealt with the game on an international basis.

That evening there was a dinner given for both teams and officials and I could see Pele over in the corner of the room. I was desperate to go and thank him again for the jersey but he seemed to be a man who would rather sit happily there in the corner, out of the way, with a couple of the other players. He didn't dance about and say, 'I'm Pele.' I thought he was trying to be quite natural instead of being the star he was – and is – and I got the impression he was quite a modest fellow. Maybe he was fed up with all the attention he received wherever he went. I certainly felt a wee bit shy in terms of going over to him so I had to leave it. I have never regretted that at all because I saw that the man didn't want to be in the limelight all the time. I respected his privacy, even though he was in a public place.

The performance of the team had been excellent against Brazil – that full week of preparation in advance of the match to plan and prepare had been invaluable – and the same journalist who, back in late 1964, had described it as being simply 'tough', in his opinion, for me to be excluded from the Scotland team's future plans to make way for others, now described me as one of his 'heroes' from the Brazil game. What can you do but laugh? He also now described me and several others as being hard to displace from the team . . . but it was not as hard as I would have liked it to be.

* * *

Despite having done well against the Brazilians, even heroically, as my friend in the press had suggested, I was omitted from the next Scotland team, for a match with Wales in the autumn of 1966, and from the squad for the match with Northern Ireland in November. There was a lack of continuity in those days and the Scotland team would be chopped and changed on a whim. There were five changes to the team that had played Brazil when Scotland took the field against the Welsh, for example, and none of the forward line had survived the cull.

I was still as keen as ever to play for my country and so I dropped everything to join the Scotland squad when I received a distress call from the SFA to say that I was, after all, required for the match with the Irish. Forty-eight hours before the match, Denis Law had been declared unfit by Manchester United after having suffered a shin injury the previous weekend. I was asked to make my way quickly down to Largs, where the team was based for the match. My addition increased to seven the number of Celtic players in the squad of 13 for the match – two of the 13 being goalkeepers: Bobby Clark and Bobby Ferguson, of Aberdeen and Kilmarnock respectively. That squad selection may have owed something to the fact that Scotland now had a new acting manager in Malky MacDonald, then the manager of Kilmarnock but who, in the 1930s, had been a Celtic great. It was also nice, on the day of the match, to see my former Celtic teammate Bertie Peacock, who was now the Northern Ireland manager. On the night, six Celtic players lined up for Scotland – Billy McNeill was unlucky enough to be the sole outfield player in the squad who did not start.

Joe McBride and Bobby Lennox, making his debut, accompanied me in the forward line that day and I was happy to help set Bobby off on his international career. We went behind to an early goal but Bobby Murdoch equalised with a shot from the edge of the penalty area. Ten minutes before half-time, Bobby Lennox scored, swivelling superbly to hook the ball over his shoulder and shoot high into the net to put us ahead. Late in the second half, I was on the verge of adding a third when Terry Neill, the Northern Ireland centre-back, slid in with a fine tackle to relieve me of the ball. My other Celtic colleagues in that 2-1 victory were John Clark and Tommy Gemmell.

There was a gap of five months before Scotland's next match – lengthy periods between matches was another factor that mitigated against continued success for the national team during that era – and once again there was a heavy Celtic presence in the squad for the match with England at Wembley in April 1967. The SFA could not ignore Celtic's ongoing success in the European Cup and this match was to take place in between the two legs of Celtic's semi-final with Dukla Prague. I counted it to be my good fortune that I was part of the squad.

Friends of mine from Newmarket, Alan May and his wife Eve, whom I had got to know during my National Service days, came down to London for the game – they went to all the England matches – and I was very pleased to be able to give them a couple of tickets to say thanks in some small way for all their tremendous hospitality towards me during my time in Suffolk. They came to the Hendon House Hotel, our north London base, and I was able to introduce them to Denis Law and others. Rooming with Denis made me feel like I was in the big time and there was a good, confident atmosphere among all the boys before that game. Everyone was quite chirpy, even though we were going in against an England team that had become world champions at Wembley nine months previously and that had not lost in 19 matches and for 18 months. The confidence among the players was infectious and it was a wonderful feeling to be with that squad. What other motivation might a Scotland team require than to be facing our oldest rivals in their own den with the opportunity to dismantle that sort of proud record?

The team had been named in advance of the match and I was the first reserve in terms of the forward line. Frank McLintock, the versatile Arsenal player, was first reserve in defence. During that era, substitutions were only just becoming a part of the game and while in some matches substitutions were allowed, in others they were not and this match with England was one in which there would be no substitutions permitted. For such matches, what would happen would be that the manager would name a first reserve, a player who would then travel as part of the squad and who, it was accepted, would not be scheduled to play, but who would be ready to step into the team in the event of injury or illness to one of the named players. That was my role in the team and I was quite happy with it.

So when Jimmy Johnstone, who had been named in the forward line, did not travel with the Scotland party to London two days before the match, I got ready to step into his slot on the wing. I certainly wished Jimmy no ill and would have been very happy to see him wreak his habitual havoc on the England defence, but if he was going to have to withdraw I was more than prepared to replace him.

Following the European Cup semi-final first leg with Dukla Prague at Celtic Park on the Wednesday evening, it had been clear that Jimmy was struggling for fitness, as he had a strained thigh. Funnily enough, he had sustained the injury during the first half when, in cutting the ball back to me, he had suffered a kick on the back of the leg. So, as we flew south on the following day, Jimmy had remained behind at Celtic Park for treatment to see if he could be passed fit for the match with England on the Saturday. All through that Thursday, as Jimmy desperately tried everything in a bid to get fit, Bobby Brown, the new Scotland manager, and Jock Stein exchanged several telephone calls. The upshot of all those calls was that when, late that day, Jimmy finally had to admit defeat in his battle to prove himself fit and ready for the game, Jock had one last call to make. He telephoned Willie Wallace and told him he was to replace Jimmy in the squad and was likely to play in the match. Willie duly teamed up with us all at the Hendon House Hotel late on the Thursday evening.

I was pleased to see Willie and happy for him to be part of the squad but I wasn't very happy overall. I couldn't recall Willie playing on the wing for Celtic at any time whereas I had played there many times – and scored from there too. I felt as though the Scottish FA had not played fair with me. I am not the type of person to nurse a grudge or insist that I should have been in a certain team at a certain time, but the snub that was issued to me by the SFA that spring of 1967 rankled with me then and it still lingers today.

I wasn't bitter about it at the time but I have to say that my disappointment over that episode has never really dissipated. I wouldn't say it has grown but it has never really gone away. A disappointing aspect of it was that nobody came to me and told me why and how it had happened. I was very late in knowing they had sent for Wispy although I was still genuinely delighted to see that it was one of my Celtic teammates that was getting in because we were all a friendly team and I have nothing against Willie for taking the chance to play. Somebody said to me that Willie was coming down – I think it was Ronnie Simpson who told me. None of the officials said to me in any way that they were leaving me out and wanting Willie Wallace to come into the team. Bobby Brown, the manager, did not even discuss it with me. They should have had the gumption to come up to me and explain the whole thing.

I'm still as disappointed today as I was then. At the time I took it all right, I didn't take it too badly. If it had been someone from Rangers who had replaced me I'd have been sorely disappointed – not against the man himself but at the thought that the old, rumoured bias against Celtic had been at work again. Willie had been hit with a big present overnight and I did not grudge him that at all, but it would have been nice for someone to have explained it all to me, not least what the point had been of me travelling down to England in the first place.

It's impossible to know whether it was the Scotland manager or the SFA who made the decision. Or was someone else involved? Somebody did, ultimately make the decision. Someone decided Willie Wallace should be included and that bringing Willie into the team was a better option than playing me. I just didn't like the way that it had happened. The thing was, I had been picked as 12th man because I could play anywhere across the forward line – so if someone called off late or was injured I could slot into the team very easily. That was why they selected me – and then they never stood by that thinking. It was too easy for them to fly someone down from Glasgow to London – if we had been playing away abroad somewhere it would have been more difficult for them. I should have been automatically in the team but I wouldn't think Bobby Brown, who had been recently promoted to Scotland manager from his previous post with St Johnstone, would have been confident enough to tell the SFA or anyone else that he had a player in place and didn't need a replacement.

I was still determined to contribute to the cause so, on the Saturday morning, I slipped out of the hotel and took a trip into Golders Green to buy a bottle of whisky as a special treat for Ronnie Simpson, who always liked a whisky and lemonade prior to kick-off. It was not so much the alcoholic kick that players looked for when they took a wee swig of whisky pre-match – it was actually to help cope with a dry mouth, by providing them with a bit of moisture and a nice tingling sensation to calm the nerves.

It was such a big game, that one. It would have been a terrific game to play in, wonderful, Scotland taking on the world champions in front of 100,000 supporters. I still had a great thrill in terms of being with the party and being on the park before the game – in my suit – and seeing the Wembley terraces crammed with Scots making their usual din in support of the team. I loved the way the team played – so well – and while my disappointment at not playing in that match cannot be underestimated, on the other hand, and this may seem strange, I enjoyed very, very much being a part of the entire day. It was great to be in our dressing room before the match, and the enmity against the English team that was conjured up by our players was quite something. It was not coming from the players based in the Scottish League but from those who plied their trade down south and who were fatigued, let's say, by the constant reminders they had received from their teammates – some of them World Cup winners themselves – about England's great victory in the 1966 World Cup final. The English also had a tendency to rubbish the Scottish game and our England-based players were keen to set them right on that score too. They were determined that we would win this match to show that we were every bit as good as them and to shut their teammates up a bit for the coming year.

It would have been a great game to play in – as long as we had got the same result . . . a 3-2 victory . . . I'd have been right wing with Bobby Lennox on the left and Jim Baxter and Denis Law doing the fancy work through the middle. I enjoyed watching the match and I was sitting willing the team on like all the other good Scotland supporters, even though I wasn't playing. I felt fully a part of the team effort on the day and I was as pleased as any of the participating players that we had won. I thought we had the game completely under control that day at Wembley. It was so important for us to beat the world champions and be the first team to do so and I went out and celebrated the win long and hard in London's West End with the rest of the boys that night.

The disappointment of missing out at Wembley was still fresh in my mind when, in early May 1967, I was named in the Scotland squad for a match with the Soviet Union – a friendly that would take place just a fortnight before the European Cup final. It would have been harder for me not to be named in that Scotland squad: out of 16 players, no fewer than nine were from Celtic. Only Jim Craig and Bertie Auld, of the team that had defeated Aberdeen in the Scottish Cup final a few days before, failed to get the nod. We even trained at Seamill – Celtic's traditional base for pre-match preparation – so it was as if Scotland was becoming Celtic Mark Two. Bobby Brown made four changes from the team that had won at Wembley – Jimmy Johnstone was fit and available so Willie Wallace was relegated to the subs' bench and I was edged back into the stand. I remember very well Tommy Gemmell floating the ball, from quite a distance out, beautifully over the head of the goalkeeper early on in the match to open the scoring – and knocking it in very well. The only trouble was that the goalkeeper in question was our own Ronnie Simpson. Willie Wallace came on as a sub for Scotland at half-time and after the 2-0 defeat Bobby Brown explained that the reason his team had lost was that they had been too slow in attack. It was a charge that could never have been levelled against me. I couldn't be too bitter about missing that game, though; after Wembley nothing could top that.

I cannot say I was unlucky in my Scotland career. That's not really for me to say. If you look at it logically, I did not do a lot wrong for Scotland and I did quite a lot that was right. As for press intervention to guide the selectors in their moves, I always remember the time when Celtic were over in Nantes for our 1966 European Cup tie with the local side and Jock getting several of the football writers to take penalty-kicks. I think they had annoyed him with some stuff they had been writing about his players so he issued that challenge to them. They duly stepped up to the mark on our muddy training pitch at the end of our training session, in suits and shoes, and, with the lads crowding round and watching, amid much hilarity, it was quickly established that they could hardly kick the ball far enough to get it into the goal.

The thing is, and it applied not just to my Wembley disappointment but to my entire Scotland career, it was probably too easy for the SFA selectors to leave me out whenever they wished. People would know that I wouldn't cause any trouble so if they were going to leave me out of a squad or a team, they knew they could do it with few repercussions. I would be the last person to repeat the trick of the disgruntled footballer heading for the exit and taking a taxi away from the ground. If Scotland dropped me, I wouldn't make a fuss and the press would not make a fuss on my behalf either. The selectors would not have done that to a Denis Law or a Jim Baxter. I don't know whether it was the influence of my father but I would never cause trouble or draw attention to myself. If a photographer was around during my playing days, I would actually go out of my way to avoid them. I would never go in their direction as if I was keen to have my picture taken. I'd do the opposite. Maybe I should have sought more attention – players that do so seem to thrive on it and do well out of the publicity that it generates – but that is just not me.

I would say that it was always a great experience to play for Scotland. Coming from Scottish football and mixing with players from the Football League, in England, let you know whether they were better than you or if you had a lot to do to catch up with them. I found that a lot of those players also wanted to compare themselves with those from Celtic because we were winning everything, so it showed us how we were growing in respect from others. I know that at the time some Celtic players suffered a degree of abuse from the terraces – from our own supposed supporters – during Scotland matches because at that time the majority of the crowd were Rangers fans. I did not experience that too much – I never got a lot of abuse at those games – but I think Tommy Gemmell got a bit of abuse and Jim Kennedy really got abuse – Jim was an awfully strong Celtic man, a diehard Celtic supporter, and the fans knew that. For him, Celtic were never wrong.

There were always rumours of bias against Celtic and it is an old chestnut that Celtic players of that era did not win enough caps. Perhaps, though, that had less to do with bias and more to do with the Scotland team not being run particularly well at the time. After all, they selected all of those Celtic players for the match with the Soviet Union but the timing of that was awful – just a fortnight before the European Cup final – and the players who took part in that match would have been keen to avoid injury at all costs.

I loved playing for Scotland and you might think that, with me still to score some of my most important and well-remembered goals for Celtic, there might have been a place for me in the Scotland reckoning but no – after that match with the Soviet Union, and before Lisbon and all that, my Scotland career was over.

CHAPTER EIGHT

MATCHING THE MASTERS

There was something comical to be found in the way we prepared for the European Cup final on the eve of that momentous event in Lisbon in May 1967. It was not that we found it funny – far from it – but our opponents did. The footballers of the great Internazionale of Milan, European champions in two of the preceding three years and twice winners of the World Club Championship during the same period, had just finished their own training session and had remained to watch us as we went through a training stint supervised by Neilly Mochan, my former teammate and now the club's trainer. We could see the Italians, sitting like a cluster of pigeons on a wall of Portugal's Estadio Nacional, laughing away at us, as if they found our exercises something of a joke.

Well groomed and sleek, in the smartest of gear, they looked like matinee idols, which only emphasised their clearly felt sense of superiority to us, as, quite relaxed, they joked and joshed among themselves, pointing at this or that and chuckling away delightedly. They weren't hiding their laughter, either; it was loud enough for us to hear. It seemed as though they felt sure they would win the match the following day. But I think the idea that they were laughing at us added some bite to our attitude going into the game. Their apparent disdain provided us with a little bit of extra motivation, it made us all the more determined to beat them. They had trained before us and they should have been long gone by the time we began our session, but it worked well in our favour that they had stayed around.

The funny thing was that we were not deadly serious in our work, certainly not in the way they would be when they went through a stiff training session at the hands of Helenio Herrera. We were laughing and joking and you could see from the Italians' reactions that they thought that made us clowns. Inter were always deadly serious in the way they went about their preparations. They had their own training camp, close to Lake Como, nearly 30 miles north of Milan, a secluded area in woodland that comprised a hotel, tennis courts, seven football pitches, a swimming pool and top-notch medical and training facilities. Maybe they had heard about how we had to make do with Barrowfield, our training ground in the vicinity of the tenements that surrounded Celtic Park in Glasgow's East End, where we were used to muddy, rutted pitches through the worst of our weather. Maybe they'd even heard that we didn't get so much as a cup of tea after training.

Given Inter's experience at the top level of world football, it was perhaps no surprise that they might look down on us, treat us with a degree of ridicule. But I think their poor form in the run-up to the final had resulted in them getting a bit of stick in the Italian press and a number of their pressmen had started to say that they thought we could win. So a sense of insecurity may then have been transmitted to their players and their seemingly haughty laughter may have been laced with a degree of nervousness as much as anything else. Herrera had been saying for months that we were the one team he feared and that he knew Inter were facing a very powerful team. Perhaps, for all the offence we took at the Italians' laughter, there was a hollow, nervous edge to it. It ensured that we did not get carried away with having made it to the European Cup final and the Italians' attitude, for all that it appeared obnoxious, reminded us that they also had a degree of entitlement in terms of thinking they were the masters and we were the whipping boys in waiting. They had the medals to prove it and it reminded us that we would have to work awfully hard the following day if we were to destroy that sense of entitlement and dislodge them from the pinnacle of European football.

In the run-up to the match, Jock Stein was as cute as usual. He was quite happy for the Italians to watch us training, and he was no doubt pleased that they had shown us a degree of disrespect. If Jock hadn't wanted the Italians to see our training he would have made sure they didn't, and it wasn't as if we revealed anything surprising or innovative that would help them deal with us the following afternoon. Indeed, while Jock was quite happy for the Italians to watch us, he had kept us away from the stadium when they were training in advance of us. Big Jock didn't want us to see anything they were doing. Quite what he had in mind by this, I don't know. The manager sometimes had ideas that were, while not exactly strange, certainly distinctive. He would maybe think that by telling his team that we were not to watch the Italians train, that that would show Herrera and Inter that we were a confident team, one that was not interested in observing them. All through that year, Jock did unusual things, things you would not expect. He constantly changed things to keep everyone on their toes. Inter were top of the tree but Jock wasn't interested in seeing them – an act that would have shown Inter that we were not their admirers, rather that we were a professional outfit there to do a job on them and not gaze upon them in admiration, like tourists, admirers or fans. Jock was always good at doing the unexpected – it was one of his greatest strengths.

Jock Stein was also keen to point out to the Italian press that the European Cup final would be no more demanding for us than a match with Rangers and it helped us that he kept a degree of perspective on the whole thing. The preparations were much the same as for any other game. On the morning of Thursday 25 May, the day of the final, we had nothing more than a wee, quick, loosening-up session – albeit after a restless night's sleep. I always found loosening up quite easy – I have never carried very much weight and have remained at slightly over 10 stone all my life. Jock would have known that the players would be feeling enough self-induced tension without him adding to it by overstressing the importance of the occasion. So all we did that morning was to have a light session on the immaculately manicured lawn beside the swimming pool in the grounds of the Hotel Palacio in Estoril, which was our base for the match.

During the Second World War, the Palacio had been a base for all sorts of spies and they might have appreciated the ability of Jock Stein to divert and distract his opponents. Long before he arrived in Portugal, he had concocted a plan that would leave the arrogantly confident Italians dazzled and confused. Jock was a winner and everything he did was calculated to eke out every advantage in terms of securing victory. I wasn't too nervous before the game but you do have to have a degree of nervousness about you to become tuned up for a match. Jock was just as excited as us on the day but he hid it better. He gave us the impression that he was ready for anything.

* * *

We would not have been there in that final had it not been for Jock Stein. He was so cute it was incredible. He was always one step in front. I think that as we went through each stage of the tournament and were making progress and seeing how strong we were, strong enough to go further and further, we increasingly saw the Italians as the one barrier that might just be insurmountable – they were the top people – but we had worked hard to get there and we were going to have a good go at it.

Despite the misgivings of some Italian journalists who were dismayed at Inter's poor domestic form – Herrera's team had, during the weeks before the European Cup final, begun to falter in the race to win the Scudetto, the Italian championship the Italians' confidence remained very high. Herrera was not known as 'The Magician' in Italy for nothing. There was some evidence though that that magic might owe itself occasionally to base means, not least when Inter drew on aggregate with CSKA Sofia of Bulgaria in the semi-final and had the play-off switched from neutral Austria to Bologna in Italy by offering the Bulgarian club a greater share of the gate money from the play-off. With 'home' advantage theirs, Inter duly seized their place in the final with a 1-0 victory. That episode betrayed the fact that there was a degree of anxiety around Internazionale.

On the day of the final, I got the distinct feeling that things were not right between the Inter players and their manager. I could not quite put my finger on it but, as a professional football player, you often get an idea as to how the other team is feeling and I sensed some discontentment among our Italian opponents. Still, in a one-off match, whatever the circumstances inside the club, Inter's experience at club and international level was always going to make them formidable opponents and football 'experts' in magazines and newspapers across Europe had been, in advance of the big day, utterly sure that the great Internazionale of Milan would lift their third European Cup in Lisbon. 'Soccer is said to be unpredictable,' wrote Roger MacDonald in the April 1967 edition of *World Soccer* magazine, 'but Inter, with their ruthless, relentless tactical system, have reduced uncertainty to complete insignificance. When Inter win the final at Lisbon in May . . .' Herrera himself was, he said, certain that Inter would win the European Cup, although after beating Real Madrid in the quarter-finals he also said that the only team remaining in the competition that gave him concern was Celtic. 'They are very fast, very robust and quite ruthless when their opponents make a mistake. But I doubt whether they would beat us in the final at Lisbon. After all, we would need only one goal to win.'

On arrival at the National Stadium, an unusual venue in that it was situated in woodland six miles from Lisbon itself, we had a long walk up to the stadium and realised just how many of those good Celtic supporters had come to see us. We had been warned beforehand that there were going to be piles of people supporting us at the stadium but actually seeing it was wonderful. A lot of them couldn't really afford to be at that game but they had made it there and that says a lot for them.

One thing that maintained my focus and concentration all day in Lisbon was having it in my mind that I would never have that chance again. I felt that I would run until I dropped to try and get this victory – no British club had won the trophy, indeed none had previously made it to the final, so that emphasised how hard it was to get there and it reinforced the idea in my mind that it was essential to seize the day. It helped that ours was a bunch of people who lived in close proximity to one another – we were almost a street team – we had no big-money signings or big earners. That helped the sense of camaraderie and fellow feeling that imbued everything we did.

I had not been sure at any point that I would be in the team for the final. You never knew what Jock was going to do and very often he would do things you didn't expect. If Jimmy Johnstone could be dropped, none of us were safe; none of us could feel sure that we would figure in any given game. It kept us on our toes; it kept complacency at bay. Still, I always had a feeling, coming up to the final, that I knew the eleven that Jock would name. I kept it to myself but for all that Jock liked to switch his personnel around, he fielded an identical team in all of the really vital matches in which we participated in the month prior to meeting Inter. The team that got the crucial draw in Prague against Dukla in the European Cup semi-final, the team that defeated Aberdeen in the Scottish Cup final in late April and the team that drew 2-2 with Rangers to clinch the 1966–67 league title in early May, consisted, in each instance, of the eleven players that took the field at the National Stadium in Lisbon on 25 May 1967.

Anyone watching that final closely would see right from the start of the match that the Celtic players were taking up unexpected positions. It was Jock Stein's intention to outmanoeuvre the Italians by coming up with the unexpected. That was his starting point, although once we were on the field of play we had to adjust to the development of the game and work out for ourselves the best way to continue to bedazzle the Inter players. We moved about a lot because every time you move you take someone with you. The Italians went one-for-one in terms of marking, which meant that, as our players constantly moved around, they would be dragging opposition players around with them, pulling them into unfamiliar areas.

From the opening minutes, it was clear that that was going to be one of our major traits in the match. Jim Craig, our right-back, went screaming up the wing, acting as an outside-right, to cross the ball into the penalty area from a pass that was hit from very deep by Bertie Auld, the midfield player. We wanted to play an attacking game and the manager had told us beforehand that he expected us to run Internazionale off the park. Jock had a knack of saying things, predicting the way in which matters would transpire, that we would quickly find to be true. We could see, from early on in the match, that the Italians did not want a quick, hard game, just as Jock had anticipated. Now, the temperature was very high, it was baking, so from the very start of the match you were soaked in sweat and the Italians, naturally, wanted to play a very slow game. It was true that they were more used to playing in the heat than we were, but they were not used to playing a game at this speed in the heat, they tended to conserve energy and play the game at a steady pace. We had turned convention on its head and unsettled them by opting to play a ferociously fast game that went in the face of what they might have expected, given that we ought to have found the humid conditions more draining than them. We had decided we were going to take the game to them from the first minute to the last. That neutralised the advantage they had of playing in the heat and, in fact, it turned it our way.

We were all tuned into the idea. I felt strongly that this was our big chance and that we might never get this chance again. That added fire, determination and a real edge to our play.

MATCHING THE MASTERS

For us it was the match of our lives; a match we simply had to win. We felt that there was no option. Would the Italians, having enjoyed so much more international success than us, have felt quite the same way, been quite as determined to put every last ounce of effort into that game? It seemed unlikely. This game meant an awful lot more to us than it did to the Italians. I think the Italians weren't in quite the same determined frame of mind as we were.

It was a sporting game, on the whole. The Italians have a reputation for gamesmanship but I thought they were not too bad on the day. I do think that they knew we were a good side and all the newspapers and sports papers prior to the match had said that we were going to go at them and really take the game to them. I don't think they had been looking forward to that at all, but they were probably bemused at just how far we went in terms of giving them no respite, no rest, at all.

One thing that was not in our plans was for Inter to take the lead, but in the seventh minute of the match we took a corner-kick, which was cleared and moved forward swiftly to Sandro Mazzola, the Inter striker. He saw an opening and made an incision in our defence with a clever diagonal ball for Renato Cappellini to chase. Just as Cappellini moved on to the ball, Jim Craig, who had followed the Italian's run, appeared to make the slightest contact with him, which was followed by Cappellini tumbling to the ground, rolling over four times and Kurt Tschenscher, the West German referee, pointing to the penalty spot.

It was a soft penalty and Cappellini had played for it – Jim didn't hit him hard, if he hit him at all. He may have just stumbled into him but Jim shouldn't have been making contact with him in there because it was well inside the penalty box and the slightest contact was sure to see the Italian making the most of it. Jim should have manoeuvred him out of the box and then tried to tackle him – easier said than done, perhaps.

We tried our best to get the referee to go over to speak to his linesman. You couldn't just give in and accept the award against your team. Things happen so quickly during a match that you can rarely be entirely sure either way whether the referee has made a correct decision, but you have to protest just in case the referee might change his mind. Funnily enough, I was the Celtic player who was most agitated, very angrily so, in directly confronting the referee. I raced back to our penalty box, going face to face with Kurt Tschenscher in my protests about the penalty. That's not usually my style so it showed how revved up I was that day, in terms of wanting to win. We had fought all the way through to the European Cup final, had found a way past all those difficult opponents in the earlier rounds of the competition, and had done so well to get there that I didn't want us to throw it away at the final stage.

For all the vehemence of my protests, Herr Tschenscher refused to change his decision. It actually took Billy McNeill, our captain, to come up and shove me away, quite roughly, from in front of the referee before I would cease my protests. These things happen in the midst of a highly charged football match and Billy was probably doing that for my own protection as much as anything. We didn't need a player cautioned to add to the loss of the penalty-kick. There was not much chance of the referee changing his mind. Few referees do so. Mazzola stroked the ball expertly past Ronnie Simpson to put Inter 1-0 ahead. He took the penalty well, tucking it away neatly, low into the left-hand corner of the net – Ronnie did not have much chance.

Once they had the goal, Inter tried to hold on to their lead by playing things cagily. That suited us. Undeterred by the goal, we continued pressing them hard. That did not suit Inter at all. Jock had said beforehand, 'We will attack and keep on attacking until we win this game.' We did just that but it was not blind attacking, it was done in a very sophisticated fashion. Prior to every match that season, Jock had told us that it could turn out to be an extraordinary season for us. His words gathered weight as the season rolled on and we had won everything else in sight – Scottish League, Scottish Cup and League Cup – so by the time we got to Lisbon we really believed that anything was possible for us. Going a goal behind was never going to affect that deeply held belief. We were one step away from the European Cup – we could not back off now.

The Inter players may have been laughing at us during our training session the night before but we were the fitter team when it came to the action on the park. They were soon struggling. The Italians are good at slowing the game down and then moving the ball forward on the break and Inter's game was based on them sitting back, sucking up the efforts of an attacking team such as us and then hitting back, slyly and speedily, principally through the wiles of Giacinto Facchetti, their pacy left-back, who constructed breakaway moves as an extra man moving forward. It should have suited them to be facing a team like us, geared up to go forward, but it was soon clear that they were failing to cope with the extraordinary pace and relentlessness with which we took the game to them.

The referee was so-so – not great but not bad – but it was possibly a good thing that we had a northern European referee in that he allowed quite a few hard, but fair, tackles to be put in by players on our side early on in the match. Our men were going in hard and fast on our opponents – people think that the Italians can be rough but our boys were going in to win the ball without giving any quarter. The Italians' tackling was perhaps not quite as fierce as it was from our side. Even though we had lost that penalty so early in the match, and even though that gave the Italians a bit of a lift, they still knew that we were gaining the upper hand. Every one of the tackles that had gone in, powerfully, during the opening stages, had been from our team so they knew they were in a game with determined opponents. They weren't bad tackles – our players were going in after the ball and there were no appeals from the Italians to say that they were being kicked. That transmitted to them the message that we would not be cowed and that, despite the loss of the goal, we were going to impose ourselves on this game.

During the first half, I didn't get the ball as much as I expected, especially in a match in which we had so much possession and were continually going forward. It's not, though, as if I was doing nothing. I may not have been at the centre of the action but I was continually moving into space. If someone is marking you – and in Lisbon I was being marked by Gianfranco Bedin – by moving around you will be taking him into stupid places and leaving a gap in their defence into which one of your players might take the ball. That was happening all the time. Bedin was one of the younger players in their team – he was 21 years old – and he was all right in the way he played me, there was no bother from him or anything. He was simply doing his job in a system set up for them to play man-for-man. It might have appeared to those supporters watching the match that I would disappear for ten minutes at a time, and that I was hardly in the game, but I was working hard all the time, making space for other people. Even the shortest of runs can be enough to create a glimmer of space that someone else can use. Or, if I came close to Bobby Murdoch in midfield and he noticed there was space behind me, he could ping the ball in behind, knowing that I would turn sharply to pursue his pass.

All of that goes some way towards explaining why, for me, the 1967 European Cup final was something of an odd experience. Given that I was centre-forward and given that Celtic created chance after chance from the beginning to the end of the match, very few of them fell to me. When the first of my few chances arrived, well into the first half, it proved a tricky one to take: a ball that came in from the left wing, one of those where you are unsure whether to go for it with your boot or your head. I tried to head it but misdirected it, back in the direction whence it came. It was not a good header at all. I could only hope that I might be able to do better in front of goal later on in the match. The only other chance to fall to me during the first half came after I had dropped back to the inside-right position in another effort to confuse Bedin. The ball fell to me outside the penalty area and I took a swipe at it but it went flying well wide of the left-hand post. If I was going to score, I thought to myself, maybe I would have to find a way of doing so from a bit closer to goal.

For all the work I was doing off the ball and for all that I knew it was valuable, I didn't feel that I was in the game enough, but the manager was happy with me because we were playing to a pattern. Celtic correctly received enormous praise for the way we attacked incessantly that day, and quite rightly so, but that has tended to mask the fine tactical sophistication with which we approached that match. The Italians did not like being moved around the park by us at all.

Another reason why people might not have noticed me a great deal during the first half is that when I did get on to the ball I was often in the most unusual positions and, given how fast the play was proceeding and how quickly we were switching the ball around, they may have presumed I was someone else entirely. Those watching on television and, indeed, those inside the stadium, must have wondered if I was even playing at all so rarely did I figure at the heart of the action. During the first half, I was even to be seen, by the more eagle-eyed among the onlookers, collecting the ball in the right-back position and then racing all the way up the wing with it. Going away back into defence was one way of losing my marker.

With me manoeuvring my way all over the field, no less a person than Jimmy Johnstone could be found occasionally filling my position at centre-forward. At other times, Jimmy would be out on the left wing, while I might be found in a playmaking role inside the centre circle. With the match swirling around us, spectators could easily have missed these details of positioning, but they were key to the whirl of confusion with which we obscured the vision of the Italian players.

If Jimmy was playing in the centre of the attack, it meant that the Italian left-back was in the middle of their defence while Bedin, the player assigned to mark me – the centre-forward – was all over the place following me, that is, whenever he could keep up with me. With Willie Wallace and Bobby Lennox making similar runs and with our full-backs overlapping frequently, it is easy to see how the Italians' finely tailored marking system was rapidly coming apart at the seams after years and years in which they had made it the most fashionable style in which to clothe a team.

It was not always entirely clear that things were going our way. Certainly we were attacking a lot during that first half but the Italians were happy as long as the score remained 1-0. It was also slightly frustrating to me, as a centre-forward, that other people were getting into key scoring positions, even though I appreciated the way Jock Stein had set out to confuse the Italians and the necessity of us playing, tactically, to his instructions. More than anything, we were still, as the first half wore on, 1-0 down and in that situation you want to see something happen in terms of getting a goal back. As long as we didn't score, the Italians could feel they were on top, regardless of how the game was going.

Bobby Lennox and I, the two principal goalscorers in the team, along with Willie Wallace, were continually moving out of the way to allow the full-backs Jim Craig and Tommy Gemmell, and the playmakers Bertie Auld and Bobby Murdoch, to have a pop at goal. I found it an odd feeling on the day to be displaced in such a fashion but I was not unhappy about it. I was happy; happy simply to be in the team on the great day. Also, I appreciated that if we were to beat Il Grande Inter, the most illustrious name in European football during the mid-1960s, we would have to do it as a team and that meant playing for each other. And if it was puzzling me, how much must it have been bamboozling Helenio Herrera and his players that, for the entirety of the first half, none of the goalscorers in the Celtic team ever really looked as if they wanted to be where they could best put the ball in the net?

When the match reached half-time, we were not downhearted in any way. We knew it was there to be won. We were certainly a wee bit annoyed about the penalty-kick but that was over and done with. Nor was there any sense of frustration that we were still behind. Jock was still confident in terms of how the match was going and he made sure that we too were confident as the minutes ticked down towards the all-or-nothing second half.

Throughout our run to the final, Jock had given us confidence that we would get through. He was always positive. During the break, Jock did not begin speaking right away. He allowed us time to towel ourselves down because of the heat – the game kicked off in the late afternoon and it was 85°F – because we did not have enough time to have a quick shower. We then changed into a fresh strip. Jock bided his time and then, just before we were due to go back out, he told us that he felt we could win. The players felt that too, so as we took the field for the second half we were bursting with confidence.

JUNIOR INTERNATIONAL MATCH SCOTLAND v. IRELAND.
PLAYED AT CELTIC PARK, GLASGOW, 12TH MARCH, 1921. RESULT: IRELAND, 1 GOAL; SCOTLAND, NIL.

Above One of the biggest influences on my life was my father, David (front row, third from right). A goalscoring midfielder, his proudest moment in the game was winning this Junior international cap for Scotland, against Ireland, at Celtic Park on 12 March 1921.

Left At school I could think of nothing else but football. I played for the Glasgow Roman Catholic Select a number of times, including in this match against our Dundee contemporaries in May 1948 (that's me aged 12, middle row, third from right), building an appetite for the game that has never left me.

Things really took off for me when ed Ashfield in 1957. The premier club in the Glasgow area, they a side that wanted to win. Here I ongside the talented Neil Duffy, g advice from manager Louis Boyle.

Left I did my National Service in th[e] RAF, despite a lifelong fear of flyin[g]. It was pretty tough and even cruel times. But, stationed at RAF Stradi[shall] in Suffolk, I made some good frien[ds] – here I am (front row, far left) – w[ith] some of them. What got me throu[gh] was playing for the RAF team as w[ell] as for local club Newmarket Town

Below On our wedding day, 18 June 1960: the ceremony, held in [St] Aloysius Church in Springburn, wa[s a] delight with both families and frie[nds] in attendance. This picture shows: (left to right) David Chalmers, my father, best man Benny Friel, Mar[y] Chalmers, my mother, the groom, the bride, Sadie's mother Maggie, bridesmaid Ann Mitchell and Sadi[e's] father Willie Brackenridge.

Below By the mid-1960s we were a growing family: having been joined by (left to right) Paul, Stephen, Carol and Ann, who were all ferried around in our light blue Beetle. The family grew further in 1970 when Martin (inset: left) was born and completed in 1976 when Clare (inset: right) arrived.

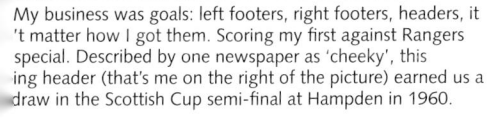

My business was goals: left footers, right footers, headers, it 't matter how I got them. Scoring my first against Rangers special. Described by one newspaper as 'cheeky', this ing header (that's me on the right of the picture) earned us a draw in the Scottish Cup semi-final at Hampden in 1960.

e One of my best days came in the 1964 League Cup ter-final against East Fife. We lost 2-0 in the first leg in il; it was a shocking defeat for Celtic. But in the second leg von 6-0, of which I scored five, including this left-footer to e it 5-0.

Above Although I enjoyed scoring myself, I was also happy to celebrate goals by my teammates; as long as Celtic were winning, I was happy. Here I am in the net after 'Yogi' Hughes' goal in a 3-1 win against Rangers at Parkhead in September 1964.

Below As well as scoring goals, I loved training. In the early days at Celtic Park we didn't do much ball-work but we ran, and ran, and ran. This sprinting session featured: (from left to right) Charlie Gallagher, Willie Fernie, John Hughes, me and Alec Byrne.

Left Although I didn't always see eye to-eye with Jock Stein (pictured left) I owe a great deal to someone who believe was one of the finest manag in the world. I will never forget him leading me on my greatest footballi adventure, which began here, outsi Celtic Park, when we boarded the b for our tour of North America in the summer of 1966.

Below I loved the European matche with the pitch bright green under th lights and the huge support we alw had. One of the best was the 1967 European Cup quarter-final against Vojvodina. We were 1-0 down from the first leg, but I scored this equalis before Billy McNeill's header put us though.

Below Another memorable game was the semi-final against Dukla Prague. We won the first leg 3-1 in Glasgow but travelled to Czechoslovakia knowing we were in for a tough game. We were right. I played up front on my own and took a lot of kicks and bumps for my troubles. Mind you, I gave as good as I got as you can see from the Dukla players in this picture. Jock was so pleased with me that he hugged me after the game, the only time he ever did such a thing.

Left Skipper Billy McNeill leads the team out at the National Stadium in Lisbon on 25 May 1967. It was to be the greatest day in the history of Celtic Football Club.

Below It may have looked like a lucky touch, but it wasn't. We'd practiced this time and time again; I knew the ball was coming, I knew where I should position myself and it was in the net before the keeper could even move. As soon as the goal went in we all knew it had been the winning touch.

Inset left I'm not a great keeper of memorabilia from my career as a footballer, but my European Cup winner's medal is one of the most precious items in my small collection.

We didn't really celebrate our victory until ... ot home to Glasgow. Scenes in the streets ... e way from the airport were astonishing, ... ve had a marvellous reception at Celtic ... too. A day or two later, Sadie's aunt and ... , Mitchie and Sally (front centre) gave a ... in my honour, at which the whole family ... share in the success, complete with replica ... ean Cup.

Left My first Scotland cap came in the Home International against Wales at Ninian Park, Cardiff in October 1964. The line up that day was: (back row left to right) Alex Hamilton, Jim Kennedy, John Greig, Ron Yeats, Jim Baxter, Campbell Forsyth; (front row, left to right) Jimmy Johnstone, me, Denis Law, Davie Gibson, Jimmy Robertson.

Above and right Two years later, in June 1966, having been out of the side for much of the time, I was selected to play against Brazil at Hampden Park in a friendly that was part of the world champions' preparations for the forthcoming World Cup in England. Within a minute of the start I scored with this right-footer. It was a brilliant moment, matched only by an incident at the end of the game when Pele refused to swap shirts with Billy Bremner, preferring to exchange with me instead.

Left I left Celtic and moved to Morton as player-coach in September 1971. Although I felt it was a step down, it was good to be able to work again with my former teammate John Clark.

Below left Two chips off the old block: me and my sons Paul (left), who joined Celtic in 1980, and Stephen, who played for Queen's Park between 1982 and 1984.

Below Aside from football, my greatest sporting love has always been golf. One of the most memorable rounds of my life came at the Sean Connery golf tournament in 1970 over Troon's Old Course where among others I accompanied the famous wartime RAF pilot Douglas Bader.

Perhaps the best memory of Celtic's ill-fated trip to Argentina to play the second leg of World Club Championship was the chance to play some golf in an exotic location. Here I am teeing off with Ronnie Simpson and Willie Wallace while some local boys act as our caddies.

Above I still love football a[nd] still love Celtic. At the mom[ent] I stand as the fourth highes[t] goalscorer in the club's histo[ry.] It is an achievement of whi[ch] I am very proud. One abov[e] me on the list is Henrik Lars[son] (second left), a player I adm[ire] very much and with whom [it] is an honour to be compare[d.] The other players in this pic[ture] are Lubomir Moravcik (far right) who developed such [a] good relationship up front [with] Henrik and Mark Burchill, a[young striker who showed [a] lot of promise.

Above I can't say enough about my family and how much they have supported me during my life. Here are Sadie and I surrounded by our grown-up grandchildren: (from left to right) Vicki, Paul, Chris, Natalie, Martin, Michael and Stephen.

Right And here am I with the very latest in the line: Scott, aged three, and baby Jack, who was born in 2011.

CHAPTER NINE

THE WINNING TOUCH

The goal that Tommy Gemmell scored for Celtic in the 63rd minute of the European Cup final in Lisbon in 1967 was the perfect equaliser. Everything about it was just wonderful, not least our left-back being in position on our right flank just outside the Inter penalty area to meet the ball and, from 22 yards, latch on to the perfect pass from Jim Craig, cleanly and at full pelt, and despatch a shot past Giuliano Sarti in the Internazionale goal. The style in which that goal was scored was symbolic of our forward-rushing momentum in the match and from then on the Italians were finished as a force in the game. As long as they had held on to their single-goal advantage, they could feel that it might turn out to be their day and Tommy himself felt that it might just be one of those games in which we would have all the play but fail to score. Once their goal had been breached, it seemed only a matter of time until it happened again.

That goal was also putting on a formal basis what everyone on the field knew: that we had proven ourselves to be more than the equals of Inter. The momentum was also with us to an enormous degree; we were tilting forward like a high-speed train and nothing could get in the way of the force that we had created. The one thing I could not believe was that the Italians did not put anything extra into their game to try to retrieve the day. I could not believe how lackadaisical they were. Whereas we were fighting to win, they were taking it too easy. You hardly ever saw them in and around the Celtic goal – apart from at the penalty-kick. I think Ronnie Simpson only had to make one really good save.

Once Tommy had scored, we continued to go at them with the same intensity as before and I continued to hurl myself around all parts of the pitch like a demented dervish. Early in the second half, I dropped into the right-half position and once or twice I even gathered the ball inside my own half and dashed furiously at the Inter defence from deep, weaving past several challenges before I was stopped. No one was more amazed at the way I was playing than I was myself.

As the match went on and the final whistle neared, we were maybe becoming a bit desperate to score. Everyone was at it to get the game finished before the 90 minutes were over. I realised that their team was tiring, we all realised that, and we wanted to seize the chance to capitalise on having taken them by surprise. We didn't want them to get the chance to regroup; and we didn't want a replay. You could see, when the score was 1-1, by the number of our boys that were having potshots at goal, how desperate everyone had become not only to win the match but also to be the individual who got the winner.

It helped us enormously at Celtic, particularly in that game, that Jock Stein was a lucky manager. I don't mean that to be derogatory or denigrating in any way with regard to his talents. He had all the other qualities that a manager requires: he was brilliantly inspirational as a motivator, immensely clever tactically, he knew how to knit a team together and he was exceptional at reading people, in terms of their moods, intentions, strengths and weaknesses. Like every manager, though, having done all his preparation for a match, he needed a certain amount of luck in the one thing he could not control entirely – the sway of the game itself – and in Lisbon his clever tactics helped produce that little bit of necessary good fortune. But not even Jock could have possibly foreseen a situation whereby his nominal centre-forward would become so frustrated with playing to instructions and moving off the ball that, with minutes to go, he would have had enough of it and decide to return to the centre of the penalty box action, in which position he would score a goal. Although you never know . . . maybe Jock Stein had anticipated that very thing happening.

Jock's instructions as to how I should play against the Italians had worked very well for us in terms of knocking them out of kilter, but as the match wound towards its end, I had had enough of veering here and there away from my position and not really getting on the ball very much. I decided that the time was right for me to get back where I belonged and this was maybe where Jock's luck was in. Having unsettled and confused the Italians by straying from my position for so long, at Jock's insistence, perhaps the last place they now expected me to pop up was in the heart of their penalty area. They were so flustered by that stage that they had no longer come to expect the expected.

All afternoon I had been making runs to free up space for other people and in the 85th minute – as Tommy Gemmell played in Bobby Murdoch for a shot at goal – I had the favour returned, beautifully. Willie Wallace made a run to his left, drawing his marker, and Jimmy Johnstone made a run that freed up a lot of space in the middle of the penalty area, allowing Bobby a clear sight of goal. Bobby duly shot and that put me on high alert to get into position in front of goal to take advantage of the space that opened up. As the ball left Bobby's foot, I had an inkling that it was not going to be on target. That sort of thing is down to instantaneous judgement and instinct. I was on the blind side of Armando Picchi, the Inter captain and sweeper, as the ball came across, and he never twigged that I was moving around him. Their players were watching Bobby and not really paying attention to what I was going to do, coming from deep into the centre of the penalty box, where I knew the ball was heading.

Maybe Picchi believed that the goalkeeper had everything covered and was leaving it for him. Maybe the sweeper was thinking that if he went for it and got some contact on the ball, it could go anywhere and so he ought to leave it to the goalkeeper to come out and shut it down. I wouldn't think he was counting at all on someone nipping in to nick it into the net. Maybe he had lowered his levels of concentration through tiredness or through counting on his team hanging on for a wee while longer, given that they had done so for 85 minutes despite our incessant attacking. Maybe it was all just too quick for him even to think about what he was going to do at all.

I knew what was going to happen – I had my mind made up – and if a forward knows what he is going to do it gives him a huge advantage over a defender. In such a situation, the forward acts and the defender reacts. Picchi had barely moved from the moment Bobby had struck the ball until I had nipped in front of him. My timing must have been just right to prevent him making a move. I had been only slightly behind him to begin with but as soon as I saw the ball coming into the box I was off – and Picchi was rooted to the spot. I made sure I was a wee bit away from him so that I could get a start on him and I got myself right on to the six-yard line – just far enough away from Picchi to prevent him getting in a block. I think Picchi was ball watching. I'm not sure that he knew where I was. I think he thought he was covering the near post but one of the themes of the match was that our team was much fitter than them and, in saying that, I am not taking anything away from them in terms of them being fit. They would have been fit for the type of football they played – they wanted to slow the game down and play short passes – but we countermanded that by forcing the pace of the game up to a level with which they were clearly never comfortable.

I nipped in and hit the ball, first time, with the instep of my right boot and it went to the left of Giuliano Sarti, leaving him standing, frozen – maybe he expected me to shoot to his other side or maybe he too just didn't see me coming.

The ball was in the net before I knew it. The whole thing was too quick for Sarti; for once he could not set himself up properly. Picchi and he may have been caught out because in the period of the match prior to that, Celtic had had a lot of efforts on goal that Sarti had saved directly or that had narrowly missed the target. Many of those shots at goal were also from long range and so that was maybe what they had expected from Bobby Murdoch's shot – the ball whistling wide of target. The goal was down to sheer instinct on my part, because the ball had come across goal too quickly for me to think much about what to do. I have to say, all things considered, that I'm glad it went in . . .

A lot of people said that I was lucky to score a goal like that. It wasn't lucky at all. Bobby Murdoch was a beautiful striker of the ball but he didn't hit it very well that day in Lisbon. He was actually trying to have a shot at goal, but Jock was so thorough that we had even prepared for one of our players miscuing a shot. In training, he would have two groups of players running, in parallel, up each wing and sending the ball into the heart of the penalty area, often hitting the ball hard across the front of goal. If that happens and you are the centre-forward and you allow it to hit off your boot, it's going into the net. We practised that just about every day in training and we scored a lot of goals that way.

It is interesting how many shots at goal Tommy Gemmell and Bertie Auld had that day and yet it was me who put the ball in the net. By the 85th minute I had become fed up watching others shooting for goal and I had wanted to have a go myself. You didn't associate lax defending with the Italians and certainly not with the great Picchi, cornerstone of their successes, but we had pulled them around so much on the day that by that time they were all pretty frazzled.

It didn't immediately hit me just how important that goal was when I scored it. You don't want to think about it too much until the game's finished. I was very conscious that the team should keep the ball away from our goal, which was fairly straightforward, given that Inter barely mounted a semblance of an attack in the remaining five minutes. They looked as though they were out of puff... done. When my goal went in it was almost as though the Inter players were relieved that it would soon be all over, that the inevitable had happened. I think they had been run off their feet. I don't think they came forward at all after I had scored. If we had been 2-1 down we would have thrown everything at the opposition.

I think it upset Inter on the day that they could not slow us down and prevent us going at them at full tilt for the full

90 minutes. I was also a wee bit surprised that they didn't put on a better performance on the day because I feel they were a much better side than they showed. Herrera, their manager, was already being credited as one of the greatest footballing tacticians ever, but clearly even he did not have a clue how to stop Celtic flooding forward incessantly in the direction of their goal. When Inter scored their penalty, they weren't keen to try and get more goals – they were quite happy to knock the ball about, rather sedately. Our team were hungry and fired up; you could see the difference in the way the two sides went into tackles. I was very surprised when the first goal went in that they didn't look to try and get more. I feel that if we had scored the first goal we would have sought more. Even after I scored my goal they hardly crossed the halfway line to try and get an equaliser.

It was understood that Herrera was expert at setting up his team to take the sting out of more adventurous opponents, but if that was his plan in Lisbon, he made a bad job of it, especially as they had first-class players: four of that Inter team would go on to play for Italy in the 1970 World Cup final, against Brazil, in Mexico City. I don't know the set-up with Inter – but to me they played as if they weren't getting on with the manager just as well as they should have been. They had had four draws in a row before that game, which was unusual for them, so their players were perhaps tired of Herrera. Or maybe he built them up the wrong way for the match.

Some of the boys told me that I looked as if I was in a daze during the minutes after my goal, which had its origins in Jock's half-time team talk. He had told us to vary our tactics a bit and one of his points was that we should try angling the ball low and hard across the goal. That's what Bobby did. He was at the left edge of the penalty area when he let fly. The ball was going like a rocket, going fast but wide of the goal.

I've been asked many times how I felt after I'd scored that goal in Lisbon. The answer is exhausted. I could feel cramp coming on after an afternoon pounding the pitch at the National Stadium in that sapping heat but the goal pepped me up somewhat and enabled me to see through the final five minutes.

After my goal, we knew we had won the European Cup. It was left only to Bertie Auld to take the ball into the corner and wind down the time; something that he used to love doing.

It had been the complete team performance. The full-backs had overlapped magnificently, but when it was time for them to tackle they had done that more traditional part of their job to perfection. Well, apart from Jim Craig's slip in giving away the penalty but we'll say no more about that . . . Bertie Auld and Bobby Murdoch, the two midfield players, had been strong and perceptive in their passing throughout the game. Everyone had played their part but I have to say this: that I am utterly sure that every one of them would have loved to score the winning goal. I bet to this day that if you asked them, they would admit that they had wanted to score the goal that I got! Tommy's goal was magnificent but I'm sure he'd admit he would have loved to strike the winner. It was, though, the type of goal that had my signature mark all over it; few of my teammates were in the habit of scoring goals such as that. It relied on the art of hovering alertly in and around the penalty area before darting into the six-yard box and pouncing sharply to administer the finest of finishing touches.

Although Jock's tactics worked brilliantly on the day I have to say that I'm still a wee bit disappointed that I wasn't more directly involved in the game in terms of being in and around the penalty area. I was allocated a job on the day and I fulfilled it to the best of my ability. It was how the gaffer wanted the game played but it's hard to say whether I could have done that job and also been more in the box. That's a moot point. Jock Stein knew that Bobby Lennox and I had the speed to draw people away quickly so that's what it fell upon us to do.

Minutes after the end of the match, the supporters flooded on to the park. I made a run for it because they were tearing everything off of you, they would even grab players' tops and pull them over their heads. As I made a run for it, I could see big Jock on the park tearing into someone who had gone too far – an extraordinary sight. There was no question of all of us returning to the pitch afterwards because there were so many people wanting a piece of us out there, literally. It was great that people were able to go on to the park and not be thrown off or get themselves into trouble. It would have been a joy for them to get on the field after spending all that money in getting there from Glasgow. They were getting a hold of the players and players were losing boots, strips and everything, but I must say that at the time, I had never been so frightened as I was by being engulfed suddenly by that crowd. I did not think I was ever going to get off that field. I made for the dressing room as quickly as I could after I had swapped shirts with Bedin, my marker for the day, the Inter No. 4, and there was no way anyone else was getting that strip. That was mine. It was a beautiful jersey – beautiful quality, as you would expect.

Shortly after the match I was asked by a reporter from *Mundo Desportivo*, the Lisbon sports daily, for my thoughts on the match. My immediate analysis of that momentous day was to say, 'We were the better side. It was very warm in the first half and we felt it. Inter were very defensive. We appreciate the way the Portuguese public got behind us for we are admirers of Portuguese football, particularly Eusebio and Benfica.' A nifty summing-up of the game I would say. The writer on *Mundo Desportivo* was kind enough, in assessing the match, to single me out as one of the three 'motors' of Celtic's victory, alongside Bobby Murdoch and Bertie Auld. That was good because while it was obvious that Bobby and Bertie had played magnificently on the day, my contribution was less to the fore – apart from the goal, of course. He went on to describe me as 'an agile centre-forward who was constantly on the move', one who impressed with his 'highly intelligent and effective movement off the ball.' The latter qualities were especially highlighted, he said, by the way I stole in on the blind side of Aristide Guarneri and Armando Picchi to score the winning goal. That reporter must really have known his stuff, mustn't he?

World Soccer asserted that Jimmy Johnstone and Tommy Gemmell had made the difference in our victory. They had both been fantastic and were perhaps particularly noticeable because of their heads of burnished red hair. Tommy played a vital role in both goals and put in a powerhouse performance streaking up and down the left all afternoon. Wee Jimmy was immense too, with his dribbling, and he even sent in an early header that would have been a goal but for a world-class save from Sarti, when he arched backwards to tip the ball up and over from underneath his crossbar. Jimmy did tire a wee bit towards the end – you knew that he was getting tired when he made it clear that he didn't want the ball.

There were some terrific individual performances from our players on the day in Lisbon, but we won the European Cup as a team. We had known that this was our chance to win and that we could not reach a higher stage or win anything more significant than we could do that day by seizing the European Cup. Every one of us had a great feeling of commitment that day. The work that our players put into the game collectively only highlighted just how disunited the Italians were. For me a measure of our teamwork can be shown in that John Clark, our largely unheralded sweeper, was maybe the best man on the park. The work he got through in that match was quite incredible – and most of it was work that people didn't notice. He was continually breaking up play in the centre of the field and sustaining our momentum by moving the ball out to the players who were situated wide and to the playmakers in the middle. Additional to that, John would be filling in for Tommy Gemmell, Jim Craig and Billy McNeill, his fellow defenders, when they eased forward or moved sideways out of position, as happened when Tommy was supplied with the ball by Jim Craig to score his goal. John's use of the ball, when he was on it, was superb. He typified how we were not a team of stars but one of good players who played to the full extent of their own capabilities and as a team. 'No manager has ever been given so much by his players,' Jock said afterwards and, as with most of Jock's pronouncements, that was unerringly true.

We had a very good squad and the strength of that squad did an enormous amount to push us on to the final. Several players who did not feature in the final had contributed a great deal to our victories in the early rounds of the European Cup, but the players who made the starting eleven for the final felt, I believe, that they had just that wee extra edge on the others.

Joe McBride had been unfortunate in that, having accumulated a stack of goals in the first half of the season, he had suffered a cartilage injury at Aberdeen at Christmas time that sidelined him for the remainder of the season. Might he have been in the team for Lisbon if he had remained injury-free? Joe was a great goalscorer but maybe I had the extra asset that I could play in several different positions. He couldn't play as an outside-right as I often did in the final. Joe would hold the ball up and lay it off for other people, but that wasn't really the way we played in Lisbon.

It is slightly irritating to me when people raise the question of whether someone else, in different circumstances, might have taken my place for the European Cup final. I must say, in all modesty, that whoever it might have been could hardly have improved on my contribution to the game. Not only did I follow Jock's instructions to the letter but I also managed to score the winning goal just as it appeared as though we might be running out of time. At the age of 31 I was the oldest outfield player, but that meant I had lots more experience than most of my teammates and, as anyone watching the game was able to see, I was as quick as ever.

The Scottish press noted that I had scored the goal, of course, but they largely overlooked the amount of work that I had put into the match. Such is life. The Portuguese sporting press were different. Apart from *Mundo Desportivo*, one publication that did make a point of giving me credit for all the grafting that I had done on the day was *O Globo*, the Portuguese sports newspaper, which was very nice and perceptive of them.

Our celebrations were not as riotous as might have been expected from a team that had just lifted the greatest prize in club football. There was so much excitement after the game that we almost forgot to celebrate properly. The 90 minutes had been over for quite a while by the time we had fought through the crowd and into the dressing room, and in there we found Jock Stein with Bill Shankly and a few pressmen around them. There wasn't space for too many people, especially as the dressing room was split into two parts in a kind of L-shape. Everyone was just holding one another and enjoying the feeling of so much shared joy that it made it difficult for us all to have a moment together with Stein. There was so much glorious confusion and chaos, so much singing and shouting in the dressing room, that we didn't even know that Billy was away up to get the cup. Funnily enough, nobody was looking for the cup so nobody noticed that it was not there until Billy returned, clutching it. It is only in retrospect that our team is a wee bit disappointed not to have seen Billy going up to lift the trophy in the traditional way.

Once Billy McNeill had returned to the dressing room with the European Cup, it was filled with alcoholic beverages and we all had a refreshing sip. Jock Stein, who was teetotal, refrained. He needed no elixir other than victory in the match itself. It was very noble, I thought, of Bill Shankly, the Liverpool manager, to be inside that dressing room to congratulate Jock. Bill had been desperately pursuing the European Cup with Liverpool in the preceding years but he clearly did not begrudge us our success at all. One thing I cannot understand is why Jock Stein was not given a knighthood in the wake of Lisbon. Alf Ramsey was knighted that year, 1967, for his achievements in leading England to win the World Cup and Matt Busby became Sir Matt after winning the European Cup with Manchester United in 1968, and yet Jock's achievement with us did not obtain for him the same recognition. Those other great footballing figures certainly deserved their honours but why was Jock Stein not also a recipient of a knighthood?

Once we were all dressed and ready, we headed into a post-match reception in central Lisbon, which we shared with the Inter players, who now showed true sportsmanship by applauding us. It hadn't yet sunk in even at that point, as far as I was concerned, that my winner was going to be a very famous goal. Our team coach collected us after that dinner to take us back to the hotel in Estoril and the only person who opted out of that was Tommy Gemmell, as he had a wild night planned with some pals of his in downtown Lisbon.

I was rooming with Bobby Murdoch and when we got back to the Hotel Palacio, Bobby was desperate for a pint but we were so late in returning to the hotel that all of its bars and restaurants were closed and although some people were talking about going back into the city, most of us felt too tired to do so. Jock Stein celebrated with tea from room service. The heat and our exertions meant we were actually ready for nothing more than drifting off to sleep and we were just doing so when we heard that the aeroplane that had been scheduled to take the girlfriends and wives back to Glasgow had been delayed until the morning and that they were now on their way to Estoril. We all had to rouse ourselves from our beds to look after our partners.

The whole thing was a lot to take in and that dizzying sensation lasted into the following day, when we returned to Glasgow and disembarked to discover the Rangers chairman John Lawrence awaiting us, and offering Bob Kelly, in particular, his congratulations. That was good to see. Once we boarded our coach and began motoring through Glasgow, we could not believe how many people were waiting on the corners of the streets to greet us. On every corner from the airport to Celtic Park they were there to cheer you on – and you have never seen as many people crying as there were on that bus. I had a wee cry as well. We knew there would be a reception for us at Celtic Park, although Jock tried to pretend that there was nothing arranged. When we turned into London Road, we were greeted with the colourful sight of hundreds of people hanging out of their tenement windows and there were flags everywhere.

Inside Celtic Park, the stadium was crammed with supporters. It was such a grand occasion and it was completely hectic by the time we got on to the rear platform of a truck to take us round the park. It was shoogling about quite a lot – it wasn't a smooth ride on that truck, which was supplied by Mr Stewart, a fellow who undertook all the maintenance work at the club. It was hard work keeping your balance on the back of that truck, which had been decorated with bunting. There was a band marching in front of us – a flute band – and big Jock, I think, didn't like that. They were allowed to go on so long then were stopped and told to take their leave. Maybe he thought it did not quite fit in with the mood of celebration of a great footballing achievement.

Once we came off the lorry we got back home as quickly as we could. I had a friend awaiting me at the faraway gate at the back of the ground and he whisked Sadie and I and the kids back to our home in Bishopbriggs, just to ease the pressure. It was an absolutely terrific day.

Celtic never again played the way we had done in Lisbon. I don't think Jock would ever have played a game again where he sacrificed, for so much of the game, the two players in his team with the most regular record of hitting goals: myself and Bobby

Lennox. In the wake of the European Cup final, Jock never, ever took me aside and expressed gratitude or special appreciation for the goal that I had scored. Not that I was looking for it and not that I felt particularly upset that it never happened. That was just Jock. As centre-forward my job in the team was to score goals and that was what I had done on the day. From Jock's point of view there was probably no need to draw any special attention to the fact that I had been the one who had scored the goal. I had been, as he probably saw it, simply doing my work.

That goal has brought me nothing but happiness; it has had nothing other than good effects for me. It meant a lot to my family too in the immediate aftermath; my brothers and sisters would go into work and people would congratulate them on my action. My only tinge of regret is that my father never got to see it; he had passed away shortly before we got to the final in Lisbon. It would have been lovely for him to see that.

We had stunned Inter, not only through our utter commitment to attacking them incessantly throughout the 90 minutes but also because they had clearly not expected a team from the Scottish Football League to be so replete with talented footballers as our team proved on that day. Or else they thought they were simply so good that if they played their normal game, they would sweep us aside. Helenio Herrera had believed that a 1-0 lead would have given his team the trophy. He was wrong and afterwards he was big enough to say that we had deserved our victory, that it had been a victory for sport. Yet he had known all about us. After the match with Rangers on 6 May he had assessed us as a team and his summing up of our talents was near exemplary. 'Celtic are a very strong team,' he had said, 'perhaps the strongest we might yet meet in the European

Cup. They're an accomplished side, well coached, full of energy and capable of competing for 90 minutes. It will be difficult to contain Celtic's attacking power, given their dizzying interchanging of positions. Celtic's greatest strength, however, is in their teamwork. Inter have the classier players on a man-to-man comparison, but Celtic's dynamic style and approach makes up for their deficiencies.' Apart from that final mention of supposed deficiencies and apart from his suggestion that his players were classier, I couldn't have put it better myself. For Herrera on that day in May 1967 though, forewarned had not been forearmed.

CHAPTER TEN

DESCENDING FROM THE SUMMIT

The fact that I had scored the winning goal in the European Cup final would have been of no consideration at all to Jock Stein once the following season got underway. Nor would my having been his leading goalscorer during the exceptional 1966–67 season. Both of those statistics would have been immaterial to him as he looked forward. I knew I would have to work hard to remain in his Celtic team but I was ready for that. The one thing for which I was not ready was for him to be prepared to jettison me entirely from the club that I loved.

During the 1967–68 season, following Lisbon, Jock chopped and changed the forward line endlessly, fielding me as a winger or an inside-forward, sometimes naming me as a substitute and sometimes leaving me out altogether. I had been his regular centre-forward, settled and successful in that position, during the previous season but it was not Jock's way to leave things as they were and to wait and see if they would continue to go well. I had made 54 appearances in all competitions during the 1966–67 season and that was whittled away to a mere 25 in 1967–68. Jock never explained to me why he was not playing me quite so much but I quickly arrived at what I considered to be the only sensible conclusion: Jock wanted me to leave the club. That may seem a strange idea given that this was only shortly after I had scored the most important goal in Celtic's history but it was an inescapable one for me.

There was only one solution and that was to follow the method that had served me well all through my time at Celtic: to work as hard as possible at my game and do all I could to remain at the club. That was how I had dealt with all the testing times prior to Jock's arrival and that was how I had ensured that my contract would be renewed every year. There was no alternative; I was never going to confront the manager. That wasn't me; it wasn't in my personality. Those that did knock on his door, to demand an explanation for this and that, usually received short shrift and often exited his office in a worse situation than the one they had been in on entering. I don't think it was ever a particularly good idea to question Jock Stein. If he had not been successful as a manager, then, yes, you might question him, but clearly Jock did not fall into that category. Jimmy Johnstone would be dropped and question Jock in no uncertain terms – and then receive a nice fine for it. I couldn't afford that, for one thing...

It did not pay to meddle with the boss. If you challenged him, in any way, it could lead to you being out of the team for six weeks and if he was having doubts about your worth to the club as a player, for whatever reason, then confronting him could be the thing that made him decide it was time for you to leave. Within days, if not hours, you could be on your way out of Celtic Park.

It is worth remembering that Jock had an awful lot of goal-scorers available to him: forwards such as Bobby Lennox,

Willie Wallace, John Hughes and Joe McBride, while others, such as Lou Macari and Kenny Dalglish were bubbling under in the reserves. Bertie Auld and Bobby Murdoch, our principal midfield players, also scored an amazing number of goals. That must have been a great delight for the manager. He had a fair sprinkling of world-class talent upon which he could draw and I was just one of several options available to him. It was amazing how many of our players got hat-tricks down the years. Not only that, but several of those players were versatile enough to be able to play in a variety of positions. You might be sent out with a particular number on your shorts but that did not mean much – Jock would shift you around during a match. If the centre-half was a big monster, for example, he'd maybe play John 'Yogi' Hughes against him and hope for him to outmuscle him even though Yogi might have a No. 11 on his shorts.

As a professional, I had to get on with things and forget the winning goal in Lisbon, as far as that was possible. You don't want to be selected or think you should be selected on the basis of scoring such a goal, important as it was. Jock would have had it in his mind that he could soon be bringing a stronger team through. When we had returned to training in the summer of 1967, for example, a certain Kenny Dalglish, a precocious 16-year-old who was not afraid to assert himself, had been among us. With Jock Stein around, complacency was never allowed.

As Jock experimented with his team, I would maybe be one of the easiest players for the boss to leave out because I wouldn't make any fuss about it. I wouldn't be pleased about it but I knew it wasn't worth the bother of creating a kerfuffle about it all. He would know he would get it easier from me because I wouldn't kick up a row. Any time I did get back into the team, I would be trying so hard to make an impression.

Another factor, one that I could do little about, was that I was getting on a wee bit – I had been 31 years of age when I had scored the winner in Lisbon and even scoring such a life-enhancing goal had not provided me with the elixir of youth. Jock would have been aware that at some point I would start falling away and would have to be replaced. Looking at the matter from his point of view, I could see why he might choose to shuffle the pack. If I had been the manager I would probably have done the same thing, but as far as I was concerned, being a part of a great panoply of talent at the only club close to my heart was a more appealing scenario than moving to another club.

I was completely happy to be fielded in a position other than centre-forward. I would never get precious about not being played in my favourite position. There was only one thing that mattered to me, especially at a club where there was such huge competition for places, and that was to be in the team. If I was left out I would be awfully disappointed; being fielded, on the wing, at inside-forward, anywhere at all, was great. If you were up against a certain team, Jock might have seen something in them that meant that he felt that was where you would be most effective. He would maybe field Bobby Lennox and I on the wings to see whether we could run the backside off of the opposition. Also, with all these very good players at his disposal, Jock would want to move everyone around the forward line to see who could do what and where.

It was not as if Jock would drop you without there being a good reason for it. He was not a manager who would explain things to his players, but on those occasions when he did speak to me, it would be to say that he thought I needed a bit of a rest. As a professional man I would dislike that because I wanted to play in every single game, but it was not possible to complain about that because he knew I was getting on and that I would benefit from a break. Additionally, Jock knew better than anyone else what was good for me and whereas my judgement as to how fit and ready I was to play was clouded by my deep desire to be so, Jock could see matters more objectively and therefore more clearly. It was essential for Jock to have new players continually infusing the team with their enthusiasm and verve or to have longer-serving players regain their zest by missing a game or two. It is also worth noting that Jock secured 25 trophies in ten years, including the European Cup, the trophy of trophies, so any reasonable person would have to come to the conclusion that he got his team selections and his decisions right an awful lot more often than he got them wrong.

I think the thing that was driving all this constant change on Jock's part was that he had looked at the young players coming through and had decided that he could replace the older guys with them and build another team to win the European Cup. He would discover that it wasn't that easy.

Early in that 1967–68 season, we faced Dundee in the League Cup final and this was one match for which I was chosen, even though I had not always been in the team during the weeks beforehand. I always found it quite a good game against them. They were a fine footballing team, they'd allow you to play, but you had to be pretty alert against them because if you weren't too careful, they could punish you. I scored with a good header early on in the match but Dundee seemed to come back into the game. I scored again, late on, to make it 3-1 and ease the match further away from our opponents. We scored through Willie Wallace with a couple of minutes remaining, just to crown it, completing victory with a 5-3 scoreline. Dundee had made it a good match and it was great for me – notching two goals in a final would have shown Jock that I could still do it.

Immediately after the match, we flew out to South America for the second leg of the World Club Championship against Racing Club of Argentina on 1 November. Jock was extremely keen for Celtic to be named world champions but it wasn't a good game to play in – the Argentinians had lots of ability but they instead just wanted to destroy us. Funnily enough, I didn't get too much trouble from them in terms of being kicked. We expected them to dole out the rough stuff so I took heed of the warning and kept out of their way as much as possible. Perhaps a side-effect of that was that I didn't do anything particularly great in the match at the Avellaneda Stadium, which Racing won 2-1 in front of a 120,000 crowd. Added to our 1-0 victory in the first leg in Glasgow, that meant a 2-2 aggregate draw in the tie and the prospect of a play-off four days later at the Centenario Stadium in Montevideo, Uruguay, the venue for the first World Cup final, just across the river from Argentina.

It had been a long trip to get there – via a lengthy stopover in Spain – and once we arrived in Argentina we were given a police escort from the airport. When you see that, you immediately wonder just how bad the situation is. The security people were very anxious around us, very careful in terms of keeping us safe, so when you are in a situation such as that, you begin to feel concerned about just what they might be expecting the public to do to you if they were to get the chance. It plays on your mind.

If we wanted to go out for a walk at all, no matter where we went, we would have a police escort, albeit on foot this time. Even when we went to visit a church, we had policemen with us, all the way inside. They never allowed any of us to stray off on our own. All that enforced protection instils a degree of fear in you.

Those matches with Racing Club were hard for anyone to referee but the quality of refereeing was poor. For the third game, I was sitting in the crowd and I don't know which was the worst place to be – in the stand or on the park – because we received enormous abuse from their supporters from beginning to end. On the park, it became a bit silly. At times our players were doing things that they shouldn't have been doing but they were being treated terribly, the refereeing was dreadful and it had got to the point, I think, where our boys were determined not to take any more from the Argentinians. I remember Yogi went in and collided with Agustín Cejas, the goalkeeper, gave him a real old dunt, and was dismissed. Afterwards, someone asked him, 'What did you do that for?' He said, 'I didn't think anybody would notice.' He seemed to have forgotten that the match was being beamed around the world on television. All the boys had a great laugh about that. Racing won the match 1-0 while Celtic had four players dismissed and Racing two.

Once we had been back in Glasgow for a couple of weeks, following the Racing matches, Robert Kelly, the chairman, convened a meeting of the players in the table-tennis room at Celtic Park. This was on a Saturday morning, late that November, and we had all gathered at the ground early in the day in advance of travelling up to Kirkcaldy for a league match with Raith Rovers. Mr Kelly announced that he was going to fine everyone in the Celtic squad, and no small amount either.

Instead of paying us our win bonuses for defeating Dundee in the League Cup final, he was going to withhold them. Everyone was due £250 each for triumphing in that game and that was a considerable amount for us – equivalent to approximately six weeks' wages.

Although it was a difficult situation for Mr Kelly, I don't think he should have fined the players. Racing had subjected everyone to extreme provocation during the first two legs and our players had behaved with real restraint in both games, but it was too much to expect the Celtic players to stand back and suffer in silence for a third game in which they were subjected to serious brutality. Also, Bobby Lennox, a player of great character, was dismissed for nothing at all in the third match and Jimmy Johnstone, who was also sent off, had been subjected to the most appalling behaviour. Our players were spat upon incessantly and were subjected to sly hair pulling in all three matches, with Racing Club players nipping and fouling and dunting players with the shoulder when the ball was nowhere near. Ronnie Simpson was hit by an iron bar, thrown from somewhere close to the pitch, while warming-up minutes before the second leg and suffered such a serious head-wound that he had to be replaced in goal by John Fallon. Players who were sitting in the stand in Buenos Aires were urinated upon from above, the water supply to our dressing room was cut off at half-time and the crowd, baying for blood, were kept at bay, only just, by 1,000 police officers, several on horseback, some with the fiercest of dogs, armed with whips and swords.

On the field of play, in the second leg, key decisions went against us: two players were clearly offside for Racing's first goal and Jimmy Johnstone scored a goal that was disallowed for no reason. Even before the third match, the Celtic players still had the aim of defeating Racing by getting the ball down and playing, but once that match began it was clear that that was never going to be allowed to happen and that they were going to be knocked around for the entirety of the match. In such circumstances, perhaps Mr Kelly, who had actually complained after the second match about Racing's 'controlled ruthlessness', might have reflected that it was a miracle that our players acted without retaliation for quite as long as they did.

If Mr Kelly thought that a point had to be made by Celtic FC, he should have made it after the second match and withdrawn the club from the play-off. That would have sent out a message to the world. There had been a great deal of discussion among the Celtic directors after the match at the Avellaneda, as to whether to proceed with the third game or to withdraw honourably: that way Racing would have been unable to claim even a hollow victory. Once the Celtic directors had agreed to go ahead with the third match, they had to expect our players to react in some way. Jock Stein said, before the game at the Centenario Stadium, that the time for politeness was over and that Celtic would be hard, if necessary, and would not stand the shocking conduct of Racing Club any further. Anyone with an understanding of football would know what that meant. If you're a player and you're being kicked and bashed about, you have to let the opposition know that you are not going to lie down. There was also nothing coming our way from Rodolfo Osorio, the Paraguayan referee in Montevideo, nothing at all, and he was making mistakes all the time.

At the time we won the European Cup, we were on a weekly wage of £45. That was not bad but none of us was going to play forever and that level of pay was unlikely to set any of us up for life. Given what we had done for the club, in winning the European Cup, perhaps Celtic ought to have considered a means of providing a long-term financial benefit fund for us. Just under a fortnight after we had won the trophy, we played Real Madrid at their Bernabeu stadium in the testimonial match for Alfredo Di Stefano, the Argentinian who was one of the all-time great international footballers. It was, of course, a great honour to be invited to Spain for that match but I think what Celtic should have done was to have insisted on a return match at Hampden Park and used the proceeds to set up a pension fund for everyone, players and backroom staff, who had been involved in the victory in Lisbon. They'd have had 120,000 at Hampden Park and Real would surely have agreed to such a clause.

Ronnie Simpson, Tommy Gemmell and I didn't play in Madrid and Jock Stein put it nicely by saying that we were having a rest. In reality, he did not want Real to be facing the team that had won the European Cup because he would not have been happy if that team had been beaten in its first outing after becoming champions of Europe. Real, who we had deposed as the top team in European football, had been making all sorts of noises beforehand about how they were going to show that they remained the true champions but, instead, our team merely highlighted that we were rightfully the elite among the elite. In a match that was far from being friendly, Jimmy Johnstone was on fire, holding on to the ball and making the Real defenders spin madly around in his orbit. They could rarely get near him and it was Celtic's due reward that we should win the match, 1-0, through a superb goal by Bobby Lennox.

* * *

Such highlights seemed far away, though, as I found myself, in the succeeding season, deprived of my regular place in Stein's side. I was like anyone else when Jock omitted me from the team. I could not quite understand why I was not in the starting eleven and my only desire would be to get my place back. I never, though, thought about any omission from the team as being a disaster. I always believed that if I could continue to prove my worth, there would be a place for me at Celtic. As it turned out, I was correct. At the end of that 1967–68 season, Jock renewed my annual contract. He must have seen enough determination and fire, not to mention residual ability, in me to convince him that I could continue to make a contribution to the Celtic cause, even though I had now reached the grand old age of 32.

Strangely enough, after reducing my number of appearances drastically in the season after Lisbon, Jock began playing me much more frequently the following year, which actually seems a bit odd. I found myself fielded in major European Cup ties too – testing matches against Basel, St Etienne, Red Star Belgrade and Milan, really tough, tight, tense affairs. The thing was, I had never let him down and had shown that, whatever his opinion of my age, I could still do it for him, still score goals and contribute to the team. Jock never said too much about things or his reasons for doing this or that. He was a big man in every sense and you just didn't get in his way. Everyone knew that.

I remember a couple of the boys went in to see Jock in his office one day. They had been offered the chance to do a wee bit of modelling, with the opportunity to get a little bit of money for themselves from the assignment. This was in the late 1960s, when that sort of thing was beginning to happen as footballers were becoming more famous. Jock's response was, 'If you go along with that and do that, you'll be looking for a new team on Saturday.'

A feature article on which I cooperated with John Rafferty of *The Scotsman* newspaper during this era focused on my professionalism, something in which I always took enormous pride. 'Although he was, on the field, the man who was always in a hurry,' Rafferty wrote, 'off it he was a quiet, sensible professional, a model player, one whom, later, managers elsewhere were to seek, for he was a good man to have in the dressing room.' I said of myself in Rafferty's feature, 'I'm always looking after myself. I'll eat anything that is good for me even if I don't like it, like honey for instance. I eat for my health's sake. I train conscientiously and rest sensibly and play golf for relaxation.'

One aspect of looking after myself carefully was that I always wanted a rest in the afternoon. Before an evening match, Jock would often offer you the choice of either coming in to Celtic Park to loosen up or to spend the afternoon resting in bed. I'd almost always choose the option of resting – and poor Sadie would have to go out with the kids to let me have peace. She'd be out and about with the pram and have two or three kids hanging off it, causing mayhem, while I would be blissfully tucked up in bed. Before a match I would have a steak with lots of vegetables – the steak was cut down a bit, really, just to make it a light meal. It would quite often be just a plain steak on its own. There were no dieticians involved. You knew what you were supposed to eat.

One record that I'm not happy about is that I was Celtic's first substitute and the first player to be substituted in a European match. Those were records that I didn't want. I was never happy being a sub or being substituted. I would rather start a match and remain on the field of play throughout the 90 minutes.

All that professionalism paid off when I helped Celtic to the Treble in the 1968–69 season. It was a terrific feat and one of its great highlights was the autumn evening on which we faced Hamilton Academical in the quarter-finals of the League Cup. It was a match that had looked likely to be something of a routine affair, with us pitted against Second Division opponents. Instead, it proved to be one of the most extraordinary evenings in the Jock Stein era. As might have been expected we had a lot of the ball from the start, but for the opening 25 minutes could not get the ball in the net, thanks largely to Bill Lamont, the Hamilton goalkeeper, performing very well. At that point he must have thought it was going to be his night. Then Jim Craig crossed and I nicked a header into the net to put us ahead. Three minutes later I almost got another, but when my shot was blocked by a defender, Bobby Lennox slipped home the second. Bobby got a third and I scored a fourth before half-time to put the tie beyond our opponents. I notched my hat-trick shortly after the break, weaving through the Hamilton defence, sidestepping Bill Lamont and tapping the ball into an empty net. That made it 5-0.

Jimmy Johnstone set me up to score my fourth and Celtic's sixth goal, then Jinky did the same for Bobby Lennox, who made it seven, before Bobby got his own fourth to make it 8-0 with five minutes to go. With only one minute remaining I headed home from the heart of the penalty area to make it 9-0 but Bobby, with a few seconds remaining, eased us into double figures to make it 10-0 – just one goal short of Celtic's record victory.

Once we got to the point at which we realised we were getting goals easily, it built into a mini-competition between Bobby and me to see how many goals each of us could get. It was an easy game for us – Hamilton simply weren't up to it, at all.

That's perhaps something of an understatement – after a 10-0 defeat, they certainly could not have claimed to be in the game . . . It developed into something of a fun evening, through Bobby and I, after a certain stage, betting each other that we would score more than the other.

Even more memorably, I topped off the 1968–69 Treble – only the second in the club's history with the other being completed during the glorious 1966–67 season – by scoring in our victory over Rangers in the Scottish Cup final. That was the last part of the Treble and my goal proved to be the final flourish in a magnificent season for us.

We were 3-0 up and the match was entering its closing stages as I collected the ball from very deep to get a counter-attack moving swiftly, following the breakdown of a Rangers' move. They had thrown everyone forward in an attempt to salvage at least something from the game; so that meant that their half of the field was almost empty, apart from the figure of Norrie Martin, the goalkeeper. It is perhaps that vast, dramatic, empty canvas of half of Hampden's expansive turf, so unusual for the habitually closely contested Old Firm game in which time and space is usually at a premium, that provided the goal with its timeless appeal and that makes it stick in the minds of so many people. That, together with the fact that it was the last rapier thrust of a memorably emphatic victory over Rangers, a win that gave us the Treble and that emphasised our ongoing superiority just at a time when our great rivals had thought they were in a position to challenge us seriously again.

I ran three-quarters of the length of the park to score that goal and even though I make the suggestion myself, it was an extremely good one. I ran from inside our own half, up the left wing, received the ball from Bertie Auld's fine cross-field pass, before cutting into the Rangers' penalty area and spearing a neat shot into the net. I actually owe Bobby Lennox an apology because I think he was in a better position to score than me. He had run up the right-hand side of the park as I was going up the left, and he was free, but we were so much in charge and so far in front that I thought, 'I'm going to have a pop myself.' There were only 15 minutes remaining and the prospect of Rangers getting back into the game was so remote that I could take that chance.

Bobby still says to this day that I should have passed it to him and he would have finished it off properly. My father always told me that I should act as a team player but it's the man that scores the goal that gets all the praise and attention. Players that score goals command the biggest transfer fees. A funny thing about that goal is that even though I had to run almost the length of the park, I felt as though I had no one from Rangers chasing me. That, again, was a very unusual sensation in an Old Firm game. Rangers hadn't played very well and it was odd for them to leave two fast men, Bobby and I, unmarked and free to do our work. Of all the times I played against Rangers, I think that was the worst performance that they put on against us.

When that goal went in, in front of the west terracing at Hampden, which is often referred to as the 'Rangers end', I was quickly enveloped in hugs from happy teammates and as we were congratulating each other I could see the Rangers supporters making hastily for the exits, slipping away from the terracing like water down a drain. It was a memorable goal. People speak to me about that goal nearly as much as they do about the golden goal, the one that won us the European Cup.

My next cup final at Hampden Park was equally memorable but for much less pleasant reasons. We had made a bright start to the League Cup final with St Johnstone in October 1969, scoring early on through Bertie Auld. But St Johnstone had begun to play well and were committed to getting something from the game. With the first half proving taut and competitive, I went into a challenge with their right-back John Lambie. It was a fair challenge; I could see no malevolence at all on John's part. The outcome was immediately painful for me but I just thought I had suffered a heavy knock. A few other players, though, who were in the vicinity when it happened, said that they heard a crack. It wasn't John's fault and it wasn't mine. It was just the two of us going for the ball and I came off worst. I was carried right round the park by the stretcher-bearers, taken into the dressing room and set down on the treatment table.

In such a situation, the trainer and the doctor don't want to say to you right away that you have got a broken leg but Dr Fitzsimmons, Celtic's club doctor, said to me, 'We'll need to get you to the hospital.' That sounded like the right idea to me as I was suffering enormous pain but the doctor told me that he could not take me there right away because he had to stay and watch the team in case any other players went down with injury. I was left sitting in that dressing room on my own and even at half-time no one made any arrangements to whisk me off to the hospital. When the teams returned to the field of play for the second half, I was again left in the dressing room, laid up in absolute agony, on my own. It was only after the game, and only after the doctor had looked at everyone else to attend to any minor knocks, that I was finally taken away, a couple of hours after sustaining the injury. He helped me into his car and drove me up to the Victoria

Infirmary where a specialist diagnosed that I had a fracture. I had a plaster put on it that night all the way up to the knee of my right leg.

Several weeks later I went back to the hospital so that the specialist could see how I was progressing and how the injury was healing. He said, 'Get yourself up on that big table and let's have a look at you.' He removed the plaster and had a glance at my leg and then he said, 'Let's see you walk round that table.' I said, 'Doctor, I cannot walk around that table.' He said, 'Don't be stupid. You must be able to walk. Just take a walk around the table.' I said, 'I can't. I can't do it.'

So he stood and thought for a moment and then he said, 'We'll need to go up and X-ray it again.' Having had that done, he told me to wait for him. I did so patiently, wondering where all this was going to end, before he eventually returned. I watched him making his way into the room where he had left me and he was the very picture of jollity. He was holding the X-rays in his hand, high above his head, as if they were inscribed with some excellent news, as he came bustling happily into the room, with a big smile on his face, to say, 'You wouldn't guess this at all. You really wouldn't guess it! You've got another fracture that we didn't detect the first time we worked on your leg. We never picked it up.' He said this as if it was a fantastic surprise; wonderful news that I should be happy to share with him. 'Imagine that,' he said. 'We've got another fracture!' This time I had another stookie put on my leg, up to the top of my thigh, and it was another month before I would even get back on my feet again. That specialist would have been getting paid by Celtic to be on stand-by for any emergency, he was their specialist for dealing with broken bones.

I thought that was terrible. After that, I decided I would take matters into my own hands and enlisted the help of Des Lamb, a physiotherapist, to get me through my rehabilitation. He lived close to my home in Bishopbriggs and came round one day to install a pulley system with a heavy weight on one end that I could use to strengthen my leg muscles. He was very good – and his advice helped me greatly. If Jock had known about this he would have given me a serious dressing down. I could just see him asking me, 'Think you're special, eh? What's wrong with what we've got here at the Park? Not good enough for you, is it?' In truth, that was correct. I wasn't certain that the treatment that I would get from the club would be exactly what I required. After all, they had in their employment a specialist who had let me down badly but, as far as I know, no fuss was made of that. I would have thought the manager should have taken it upon himself to tighten up things on the medical side after that. Maybe if it had happened to wee Jimmy Johnstone they might have made more of a fuss.

Jock did come out to the house in Bishopbriggs to see me after he heard of the doctor's pratfall, to show some sympathy for my plight, and he was fine. It was good of him to visit and he had a cup of tea and a chat and thankfully he didn't see the pulley. I don't know whether Jock went and visited other players when they were recovering from injury, but if he came to see me he must have gone to see everyone. He told me to rest, to get myself fit and not to rush back. I do remember one Sunday morning going into Celtic Park, as I was recovering, to run round the track and when Jock turned up – he often spent a Sunday morning at the ground – he took me off the track immediately and said to me to get inside and not to be in such a hurry. I didn't know whether that was him showing genuine concern for me or whether it was another instance of him showing he was boss and that if I was to have a recovery schedule, he was going to oversee it.

Fortunately, I got through having the double fracture all right and got back to fitness, but following that injury I didn't play a lot in the Celtic team. Things went steadily downhill for me. I was sidelined for the remainder of the 1969–70 season and made only a handful of appearances in the year after that. I'd been in decent form up until that break – I was still a fixture in the first team for cup finals, European ties and Old Firm games – but it was maybe a good excuse for the manager to move me on and get in someone else. You have to consider the manager's way of thinking. He had several boys in the reserve team that he was hoping to introduce and he would have had it in mind that I was now in my early thirties and that if he could get someone else in he would be happy to get rid of me. I could see his point of view – at that time Celtic had the best reserve team that you could ever see, featuring players such as Davie Hay, Danny McGrain, George Connelly, Kenny Dalglish, Lou Macari, Vic Davidson and Paul Wilson – fantastic players. Jock had every right to move people like me aside. I was getting older and maybe wasn't just as fit as I thought.

One problem for Stein, though, in introducing all those young, hungry players to the Celtic first team, was that those young guys all knew that the Lisbon Lions had been poorly rewarded for winning the European Cup. They knew that the club had not improved our pay following that triumph as well as it might have done, considering what that had done for Celtic Football Club and its reputation worldwide. It is an effect that still lingers to this day. All of those boys would eventually prove different to us in that respect. We were all happy to stay with the club but those young guys were aware of the chasm that had developed between those playing down south and us. They knew what was being paid in England. I would say that Jock had it in his mind almost immediately after we won the European Cup that he would build a new team to win the great trophy again – but Jock seemed at times a little too hasty in disposing of the players that had made the triumph in Lisbon possible so that he could get on with the business of bringing in the youngsters. If he had held on to some of us a bit longer, and had a stronger squad, he might have been a bit less vulnerable when those newer players made high wage demands and started being unsettled by interest in them from major clubs in England.

I was pleased to see Celtic continue to perform with excellence while I recovered from my injury. They won the league title again in the spring of 1970, for the fifth successive time under Stein, and had held on to secure the League Cup by defeating St Johnstone 1-0, the scoreline that had been in place prior to my injury. But even more impressively, the club had reached a second European Cup final. In the semi-final against Leeds United in April 1970, I thought the team did really well. After Celtic won the first leg 1-0 at Elland Road, wee Billy Bremner, the Leeds midfield player, said, 'That was a fluke. We'll beat you easily in Glasgow. You've no chance.' At Hampden Park we hammered them, playing them off the park for the second time in a fortnight and both Billy and Jack Charlton, the big centre-half, who tended to hurl words at other people as if they were cannonballs, admitted that they had changed their minds about Celtic and acknowledged that they had been beaten by a truly great team.

DESCENDING FROM THE SUMMIT

I went out to Milan with the club for the final at the San Siro on 6 May 1970 but I wasn't in the playing squad for the match against Dutch champions Feyenoord. It was nice to be with the lads and I can always remember being in the dressing room prior to kick-off of the final and doing what I could to provide support for them. I also remember them running out on to the field and me being left with the manager in the dressing room and then saying, conversationally, to Stein, 'What do you think, boss? Do you think we can get a result?' He turned to me and he said, 'If we play at all, we'll take six off of them.' What about that? That's a confident man, saying that. As it transpired, Feyenoord proved an excellent side and Celtic were outplayed on the night and beaten 2-1.

I would say that the players in 1967 were determined to win the European Cup, come what may. The players that faced Feyenoord in 1970 were maybe just not quite so strong in terms of their desire to win the trophy. I was disappointed with the way we played that night. We did not play very well. There could have been a feeling among the players that Jock thought we would win the game easily and had consequently ignored the threat from the players in Feyenoord's team, which contained footballers such as Wim Jansen, Wim van Hanegem and Ove Kindvall, who were emergent world-class stars and who were to the fore in doing the damage to us on the night. But I was awfully disappointed with the way we performed. You do get that – you get off-nights.

My leg had healed and I had started playing again by the start of the 1970–71 season but I found myself being used only very sparingly indeed by the manager. The break was never going to stop me carrying on and my leg was actually in a better condition than it had been after suffering the chipped bone against Barcelona in 1964. However, I only made half a dozen appearances for Celtic that season, the first of which was in the second leg of a European Cup tie against Kokkola of Finland after Celtic had put the tie beyond any reasonable doubt by defeating them 9-0 at Celtic Park in the first leg. For the second leg, in Lapland, the temperature was well below freezing even though it was September. A roaring fire kept us warm in the dressing room before the game but that only brought home to me how cold it was out on the field. We warmed up well enough to win 5-0 and at the end of the match the Finns, despite being on the end of a 14-0 aggregate defeat, sportingly announced two men of the match: Bobby Lennox and me. The two of us had been inside the dressing room with the rest of the team when it was announced, relieved at getting a chance to get a good heat from that big fire, and we had to return to the pitch, shivering away, to be presented with our awards, which in my case was, very appropriately, a fur hat.

It was obvious that with all those good young players coming through, Jock would have to get rid of a few people – that was his business – but I was not keen to be one of them. Things tended to happen quickly under Jock Stein, though, and I got an indication of what might be in store for me when he hauled me into his office one day and told me I had to go and see someone at Hearts the following day to be transferred. I came in the next day and Jock said, 'Just forget that.' I was not keen on the idea of leaving Celtic and I don't know what happened to kill the move so swiftly. It was on and then off just like that. They presumably had been unable to complete a deal even though the two managers had possibly agreed that I would make the move. Maybe there was a disagreement between the two boards of directors over the transfer fee. Maybe Jock was asking for too much for me and told them to forget it when they were unwilling to come up with the cash. I didn't want to go to Hearts but it could have become a case of being forced to go by Jock and I was relieved when it failed to happen.

That meant, among other things, that the Lisbon Lions could all be together for one final time as a team in the spring of 1971. Celtic had been closing in on a sixth successive title all season even though Aberdeen, our closest challengers, had pushed us so hard that we still had points to gather to secure the championship as we entered the final week of the season. A final week that would see Celtic play their final three fixtures in five days – playing on Tuesday, Thursday and Saturday.

I was a substitute at Paisley on the Tuesday evening when, in the first of those concluding fixtures, we drew 2-2 with St Mirren to edge closer to the championship. I then played for the reserves on the Wednesday, against Falkirk reserves, a match we won 4-0. On the Thursday evening a victory over Ayr all but clinched the title for Celtic. The only possibility of us losing it to Aberdeen would be if, in our final league match, Clyde were to win by 12 goals and hand the title to Aberdeen on goal difference. So, with a record-equalling sixth successive title as good as ours, Stein announced that, for the last time, the Lisbon Lions would take the field at Celtic Park for the final league fixture of the season. Ronnie Simpson, our goalkeeper, was by then no longer a registered player with the Scottish League – having retired – but he got stripped and walked out with the team. Bertie Auld had been awarded a free transfer the day before so the outfield side was definitely about to break up – although it had been three years since all eleven of us had played in the same team.

Celtic Park was packed that day – Jock's announcement of our final collective appearance had doubled the crowd for what had otherwise been something of a dead rubber. A quirky aspect of the occasion was that the 40-year-old main stand was in the process of being demolished, so we didn't come out of the tunnel that day and instead walked on to the field through a door at the end of the stand.

We were 5-1 ahead and the game was coursing towards its conclusion when Tommy McCulloch, the Clyde goalkeeper, saved my shot from inside the six-yard box but failed to gather the ball. I followed up to put the rebound into the net. It was surely fitting that the scorer of the winner in Lisbon should also net the final goal for the Lions. In the background, the old main stand, which had been the place from which so many of our exploits had been overviewed, was making its own last stand. Canvas wraps covered the seats where fans had roared with delight on all those great European nights and the old press box, where our adventures had been written up, and which had sat slanting down on the roof, was already being pulled apart piece by piece, ready to be replaced. It seemed appropriate that the stand was being dismantled just as time was finally being called upon us as a collection of players.

I had scored in my final Scottish Cup match for Celtic, been prevented from scoring for the team in my final League Cup match by breaking my leg against St Johnstone and had been named joint man of the match in my final European Cup match. Now, I had scored in what proved to be my final league match for Celtic, even if I did not know it at the time.

Early the following season, after I had signed my habitual one-year extension to my contract at Celtic, Jock Stein got rid of me so quickly, moved me on to Morton so swiftly, that I hardly recognised what had happened. He simply told me one day that the club was going to sell me to the Cappielow club and that becoming player-coach there, which was the proposed arrangement, would be a great experience for me. He was cute enough to get in touch quickly with Sadie and tell her that he was helping out the Chalmers family by providing me with an opportunity at the Greenock club. A number of my contemporaries at Celtic were despatched equally quickly. Lisbon Lions would be summoned to the manager's office and within hours would be departing Celtic Park with their belongings entirely without ceremony, goodbye, thanks, all the best.

I was certainly not happy to be told I was on my way to Morton. It was always a decent little club and I had nothing against it but I didn't want to leave Celtic. If I hadn't gone to Morton though, Jock would have sent me somewhere else. Managers have to get rid of people all the time – you should not take it personally – you must think of it in footballing terms, but although I could see Jock Stein's point of view, I hated him the moment he told me that he was letting me go and that he had arranged a transfer for me.

I had been at training that fateful day when Jock came to the mouth of the tunnel at Celtic Park, called me into his office and said, 'I want a wee word with you. Morton have been on and you have a chance to go there.' When he told me I was going to be allowed to move on, my first thought was, 'That cannot be right. How can this be happening to me?'

John Clark had gone to Cappielow three months earlier so I

should have got hold of him and said to him, 'What kind of a club is it?' Instead I went home, in a bit of a daze, and spoke to Sadie and she, being practical about it, suggested that it was maybe for the best and that I had maybe had my time at Celtic Park. I was taken on as player-coach, with John Clark named as assistant player-coach. Hal Stewart was the manager – a position he had held since 1960.

To me, it wasn't clear that my time at Celtic had come to a natural end. Fitness-wise, I could have played on very handily. I feel I could have performed a similar role to Bobby Lennox, who, in common with me, was always an extremely fit professional. Bobby remained at Celtic throughout the 1970s and only retired from Celtic – after a brief spell in Texas with the Houston Hurricane – on the doctor's advice after sustaining a serious injury in the late 1980s. During the latter part of his Celtic career, as Bobby eased into his thirties, he would spend a lot of time on the bench and would be brought on late in matches to inject some speed and urgency into the team. He would run some younger opponents right off their feet immediately because he had such terrific fitness. I felt I could have been deployed similarly and would have been quite happy to have a similar future at Celtic. It wasn't that I didn't want to go to Morton, as such, more that I felt I could still do a job for Celtic. I was very surprised to be asked to move.

There seemed no option when Jock told me to go but I still cannot believe how easily I agreed to do so. I decided that if he wanted rid of me, out of the door, that there was not much good in me doing anything about it, but I could have done more. Morton were struggling to hold their own in the top flight at the time so I should have said to Jock that I knew he wanted me to go but would it be possible for me to wait and see whether I might get a club that was better positioned in the league or maybe even be given a free transfer so that I could see who might come in for me. I don't know why I didn't query it or do anything about it at all, maybe because Jock Stein was the type of manager who would decide something and that would be that, no use arguing with him.

Jock said that if I wished to come back to Celtic Park there would always be a place for me. I took that as meaning there would be a job at the Park for me. It was so easy for him to move me on that it was daft. Someone like Tommy Gemmell would be a wee bit cheeky to Jock but he knew I would not do that. Tommy would bite back at him. Jock wouldn't have wanted to give me a free transfer because then I would have been able to find a club that was anxious to get me and maybe I would then return to Celtic and do Jock's team some damage. I didn't complain at all because I didn't want to make any trouble. So, my mind in turmoil, I lost something that had sustained me throughout my life until that point: the idea of being a Celtic footballer.

CHAPTER ELEVEN

REACHING THE RIGHT CONCLUSION

There was quite a difference between being involved in European Cup finals and going down to Cappielow to work as player-coach at Morton. As if to emphasise the distinct change, the road to Greenock, at that time, was a winding, difficult one that veered inland in various directions until you finally got down to the port itself. Morton was, and is, a good community club that has produced some very good teams down the years, but going there at that time from Celtic and the level to which Jock Stein had taken us, made for quite a drop. It would have been a real wrench to be going to any other club but it felt more pronounced to be going to one with modest support, a tight little ground and which was doing all it could simply to try to remain in the top flight of Scottish football.

I soon began to feel it to be a hard task to go up and down to Greenock every day from my home in Bishopbriggs, on the other side of Glasgow. That old, not very good, back road down there took you away from the banks of the River Clyde and seemed to mirror the haphazard, footballing journey on which I had now embarked. Matchdays could be equally dispiriting. You would be driving down to Greenock for your game and passing you in the other direction, en route to Glasgow and other parts, would be coaches full of Celtic and Rangers supporters. Then you'd arrive at Cappielow and wonder how many – or how few – would be turning up to see the local team. The whole thing soon began to get me down.

It had all started brightly, though, when I took up my position of player-coach in early September 1971. On appointing John Clark and me, Hal Stewart, who was both the owner of Morton and the team manager, described us as the 'future of Morton' and our first match in our new roles was at Cappielow, against Falkirk, just two days after we had been appointed. John and I had discussed the match in depth beforehand and had decided that Billy 'Sugar' Osborne, the Morton centre-forward, should put pressure on George Miller, the Falkirk centre-half, while I played in a more withdrawn role. It worked very well and we got off to a fine start in our coaching careers, with both John and I playing well, especially in the first half, in a 3-1 victory. Falkirk had been going well – only a few days before the match Willie Cunningham, their manager, had turned down the opportunity to become Scotland manager and they also had in their team a forward who had once been at Rangers – one Alex Ferguson. For us to defeat a team managed by Mr Cunningham in our first match looked promising.

I trotted out in the Hoops again at Celtic Park one week after that win over Falkirk – but this time I was in the blue and white hoops of Morton, with Celtic switching to a change strip that featured all-green shirts. Bobby Lennox opened the scoring for Celtic early in the match and John Clark, sadly, put through his own goal before Borge Thorup, our Danish midfield player, got one back for us late in the match. A minute later Harry Hood scored again to make it 3-1 to Celtic. Afterwards Jock Stein was encouraging, saying that he could already see signs that we were reshaping the Morton team and that we would improve.

We won again the following week, beating Partick Thistle, another club doing well, and late in September 1971, I scored my first goal for Morton in a Texaco Cup tie with Huddersfield Town at Cappielow. It was a good one too. I latched on to the ball 25 yards from goal and at an angle and fairly lashed it into the net. Unfortunately, by the time I scored that goal we were out of the two-legged tie. There were only four minutes remaining of the second leg and two Frank Worthington goals for Huddersfield made them 2-1 winners on the night and 3-1 victors overall. We might have run out of gas in the Texaco competition – a tournament contested by English and Scottish clubs in the early 1970s – but it had been a test during those first few weeks for John Clark and me to experiment and try things as coaches. For all that I disliked Jock Stein picking me up and packaging me out of Celtic Park, maybe he thought that I was being given a good chance at Cappielow in terms of getting a foothold in coaching and management. After all, more than a decade earlier he himself had taken the chance of going to Dunfermline Athletic, in his first position as manager, when they had been struggling desperately against relegation, and his subsequent managerial career had worked out incredibly well. So, after my initial misgivings, I thought that maybe I should try to make the most of the opportunity that I had been given at Morton.

Hal Stewart was one of those individuals in football who are never out of the press if they can help it, and often he would be making enormous boasts about what his team were going to do in the next match, how great they were going to be; it was almost like a fan's angle rather than that of a professional from inside the game. He'd tell the press that Morton were going to 'set about this team' and 'march on by winning this match with the fans behind us'. Behind the scenes, matters rarely matched the rhetoric.

Hal was a pleasant enough person on a one-to-one basis – you could talk to him easily enough, although you couldn't be sure how much was going in and I'm not sure how much he knew about the game. He was trying to keep Morton in the top flight so he was always looking for transfer money. That was the best way he saw of gathering income for the club to keep it going. He was working to a tight budget – Morton was clearly a club short of cash. The difference in the level at which I was now working was regularly brought home to me. You would go into the boot room and say, 'Let's throw away that old pair of boots – they're burst.' Hal would reply, 'No, no, no, we'll patch them up and give them to some youngster coming into the club.' There was a league rule at the time that a brand new ball had to be used for every match. Hal, aware of the need to make the most of his resources, would tell a player that, at a certain point in the match he was to belt the ball away up and over the stand, which was fairly easy to do as Cappielow is a nice, tight, compact, little ground; atmospheric but with a low stand over which a ball can be easily punted. A ball boy would be waiting to pick up the ball and scurry off with it and it would then be recycled as the 'new ball' for the next home fixture. The players were well aware that they were representing a club with cash-flow problems. Any time they received cheques as payment from the club, there would be a mad dash for the bank to get it cashed before the money ran out.

REACHING THE RIGHT CONCLUSION

Hal was never about when we were doing training, something we did at some playing fields near Port Glasgow, where we would do our running, our games, ball-work and where we would provide practice for the goalkeepers. Even though he never took any interest in training and never gave the impression that he really understood the game, Hal would still select the team. He might ask me what I thought the team should be but I never knew whether he was really taking any notice of what I was saying at all. We did not have that many players so they had to be shuffled about quite a bit and you had to get them to do a job for you.

Morton was a club that was happy just to float along; that quickly became pretty clear to me. Prior to matches, Hal would maybe say a few words as a team talk to try and encourage the team. I would have worked hard in training all week with the players and then, on a Saturday, he would come down to see us all just as the lads were getting ready to run out for the game. 'Now, look, lads, here's a good reason for you to play well, today,' he'd say to them, giving them a wee pat on the back, 'there's a scout from Newcastle United up there in the stand today so if you do well there could be a move in it for you.' That was not exactly what you would call an exercise in team building. If the players came in and had done well, he would say, 'Good game, boys. You could soon be on your way to one of the bigger clubs.'

My relationship with the players was pretty good – I always felt that they tried to do their best for us, within limits, but it was hard to try and build up a team and instil in the players some team spirit when Hal was trying to sell every player on the books. The playing squad consisted of experienced men who had been at a number of other clubs, along with some enthusiastic local youngsters, such as 'Sugar' Osborne, who was a big, stocky fellow, a nice, big lad, who received his nickname from working in the Tate & Lyle sugar factory on one of the many streets that go up the hillside in Greenock. He was a boy who could use his bulk to muscle players out of the way and a useful player for Morton at the time. John Murphy was another I liked particularly; a good, solid, hard-working midfield player who could use the ball well.

Following our encouraging start to coaching in September 1971, we began October by defeating East Fife 6-0 in Methil but we then went on a lengthy run of defeats, in a number of which we were a bit unlucky. At Cappielow, against Aberdeen, we lost the only goal of the game after 30 seconds and we lost 6-1 to Heart of Midlothian at Tynecastle on a day when our keeper Erik Sorensen only saw one of the goals go past him – he was concussed early on in the match and only fully conscious of seeing the final goal go into his net. This was long before substitute goalkeepers were allowed. By mid-November only three points covered the bottom ten teams in the top division and, although we were seventh-bottom amid that anxious pack, we were only one point better off than the four clubs at the foot of the table.

Matters barely improved, if at all, after that point and as we entered the final month of the season we had drifted down into third-bottom position, only three points ahead of bottom placed Dunfermline Athletic, and one ahead of Clyde in second bottom. The slightest slip could see us drop into those relegation positions and just as we prepared for the crucial month of April, in which the season's fixtures would be concluded, George Anderson, our centre-half, and Billy Osborne, our centre-forward, were both suspended. We had signed some useful players that season, among them Chris Shevlane, a full-back and former club-mate of mine at Celtic, who joined from Hibernian in October, and Don Gillies, a useful 19-year-old centre-forward from Inverness Clachnacuddin, who would score frequently for the club. But neither had been able to do enough to prevent us sliding seriously into danger.

It always seemed to be raining down in Greenock and it was raining again on the April night in 1972 on which we faced Motherwell at Cappielow, battling for our lives in the top flight. John Fallon, my former Celtic teammate, was in goal for Motherwell that evening and early in the match Don Gillies headed powerfully past him to put us ahead, while I scored with a strong free-kick from the edge of the penalty area after half an hour. Matters looked a lot brighter for us than the Greenock weather but then after half-time Kirkie Lawson and Brian Heron got goals for Motherwell that drew the teams level. Near the end, Denis Laughton burst forward for us and hit a shot from just outside the penalty area to beat John Fallon for a third time and secure the points. When we defeated Clyde 4-0 a week later, with two goals from Billy Armstrong, a striker signed from Stirling Albion, and two from Don Gillies, we were as good as safe. I was pleased to cross nicely for Gillies to hit home the first of his double and the team played very well on the night, belying our poor position in the league.

All in all though, as the season ended, I was not convinced that I ought to persevere as player-coach at Cappielow. When I first went to Morton, I had thought that being the team's player-coach would be a job I could do with little bother but it had proved much harder than that. I didn't seek advice from Jock Stein, although I certainly tried some of his coaching exercises, and I put in as much effort as I could to try to help

Morton, most especially the young players. It was when the results showed that it wasn't going well, with Morton struggling to escape relegation, that it was outlined to me that I maybe was not cut out for that business of managing and coaching. I found it very hard.

It took both John and I quite a while to work out what we should be doing in our new roles, especially as we both came from an environment at Celtic Park where we were told exactly what we had to do and what was expected of us as players. It is hard to make the transition from that to being in charge yourself and I was someone who had, at the time I left Celtic, still been thinking very much in terms of remaining a player. I had not begun planning for or even thinking about management or coaching. Nor had I been on any coaching courses prior to going to Greenock, so I was really struggling at the start. I was very disappointed to have been involved in a relegation struggle near the end of that 1971–72 season and I came to the conclusion that it was time for me to leave.

I found that the double demands of coaching as well as playing were draining my fitness and that left me struggling badly to fulfil the demands of the post. If you have to supervise training and get other people to train and are watching them do so, you are not doing quite as much yourself. If you've got players under your supervision, you've got to keep it interesting for them, through devising wee games and suchlike, and you cannot do that properly and do your own training properly. Your own fitness starts to suffer and once you are in your mid-thirties, as I was, you are losing it considerably more quickly than you were a decade previously. Of course, I would still do as much work on the park on a Saturday as I could.

REACHING THE RIGHT CONCLUSION

There were some very difficult moments. Big Erik Sorensen, the goalkeeper, went to Hal Stewart to say that he wasn't happy with me making him do running work in training. He said he should be carrying out his training between the goalposts. So I agreed to give him some exercises in which he would be saving shots and getting up and down, on and off his knees between the goalposts. I would have six balls and I would hit them across the goal from one side to the other and he was expected to try to save each shot and get up on his feet quickly for the next shot, but he would not do the exercises properly. He would demand a rest and wouldn't get up to save the shots. He would go into the back of the net, at his own pace, to pick balls up so he could get a break. I was trying to help him – he had complained about having to do the running and this seemed a good alternative – but he didn't take to this either.

I didn't care which position a player had on the field – I felt that they all had to run to maintain a high level of fitness. A fitter goalkeeper would be a better goalkeeper as far as I was concerned because he would be able to be more agile and flexible and better able to clear danger in and around his goalmouth. Sorensen had a pub in Greenock – I think he had married a Greenock girl – and you could see some of the effects of his new job in that it was changing his body shape, so he needed some good training. He was a Denmark international and he had played for Rangers before returning to Morton and was one of a number of Scandinavian players that Hal Stewart had brought over to this country at a time when foreign players were few and far between in British football. The policy had been a bit of a success for the club. I didn't like Sorensen's attitude in going to Hal to say he wasn't a runner but I got on all right with him after that. Maybe a different coach would have made a stand about all that and demanded that the player do as he was told, regardless of interference from Hal, and maybe my feeling unwilling to do so was another reason why being player-coach was a role for which I was not cut out.

Lack of success in that job at Morton hurt me badly. It was hard to know how much of that lack of success was actually down to me and how much to other people. I was not the type of coach that would run around the training park shouting at people to move themselves and that sort of thing and it is hard to know whether things would have gone better if I had been. It was also hard for me to understand the attitude of some of those in my charge. The more experienced players did not want to take instructions on board if it didn't suit them – they just wanted to play the way they had always played. Several of them had been at good clubs prior to Morton and had certainly worked harder at those clubs than they did at Cappielow. Some of them were good players but they had been in the game for a long while, and they were maybe not that keen to extend themselves as fully as they had been when they were younger. Some were maybe just seeing out their careers rather than being entirely committed to turning Morton into a team that could compete strongly in the top flight.

While the older fellows weren't killing themselves in training, it was still gratifying to be able to help the youngsters. We had one very good young player called Neil McNab, a slight, lightweight boy, and I tried to help him with his attacking game by teaching him how to shield the ball and move away from opponents. He worked hard at his game and I'm pleased he went on to have an extremely good career down in England, most notably at Tottenham Hotspur and Manchester City.

An added difficulty for me at that time was that shortly after joining Morton I had taken over an off-sales in Maryhill, in an edgy section of Glasgow called The Botany – although known to the locals as 'The Butney'. A flavour of the area can be provided in that it had got its name because many of those who had lived there had been sentenced to exile in Botany Bay, Australia, the well-known destination of British convicts. They were good drinkers in that part of the city of Glasgow so we had some very regular regulars. I took over as proprietor in December 1971, named it the Steve Chalmers Off-Sales, and Tommy Gemmell, my fellow European Cup final goalscorer, who was on the verge of leaving Celtic for Nottingham Forest, and Tommy Callaghan, a teammate from Celtic, were guests of honour at the launch of my new venture.

In trying to play for Morton, keep fit, coach the team and look after the shop, I had maybe taken on too much. I would be there most nights of the week although on a Friday, the busiest night of the week, my sister and brother would run the shop so that I could get my sleep for the football. The other people who staffed the shop were also very good but for me it was a very demanding job. I would finish a match on a Saturday at Cappielow, or wherever we were playing, drive to a cash and carry, collect stock for the off-sales, take it there, get it sorted out and only then get home to have my evening meal. It was not ideal.

I could have finished with football after my experiences in Greenock because I was not too happy with the job I had done at Morton. Then Davie McParland, the manager of Partick Thistle, came down to see me at the off-licence one day. I always had a high liking for Davie because he was such a nice fellow who came over well – I had come up against him often when he had been a player at Partick. Davie said he wanted to sign me but I said to him that I didn't think I could do much for him as a player at my age and stage. He said, 'Don't talk rubbish. You'll do what I want you to do.' He persuaded me how much he thought I could help him with his young team and I was delighted to get the chance. I had thought that my time as a player was just about over.

Partick were a notch or two up the Scottish football pecking order from Morton – during the preceding season they had finished seventh in the top flight and, much more notably, had defeated Celtic 4-1 in the League Cup final; a result that had resonated across Britain because things such as that just did not happen to Jock Stein's Celtic. Partick had a lot of young players who were very good prospects and Davie had done well to assemble such a squad. He had a good scouting system and found players in places that Glasgow's big two might not look, such as Stirlingshire and Clackmannanshire. He had Alan Rough, a goalkeeper who was great with the patter and who would go on to play in two World Cups for Scotland; John Hansen, a Scotland international full-back; Ronnie Glavin, always a very smartly-turned-out individual and a midfield player who, along with striker Joe Craig, would go on to play for Celtic; Alex Forsyth, who would play for Manchester United; and Alan Hansen, a teenager who would later win European Cups with Liverpool. These were all young players with top-class potential and Davie wanted me to mix with them and encourage them and the other younger players at the club.

I think Davie respected me as much as I respected him and mutual respect is not a bad thing to have if you are trying your best to achieve something. Davie would take the training and I would help him out occasionally, maybe by keeping the boys busy if he was working inside or if he was away scouting or trying to get someone to sign for the club. I was not a regular coach – more an assistant to the manager, as and when required. Scot Symon, a former Rangers manager, was the general manager at Partick, and I found him to be an absolute gentleman, someone with whom I could very easily get along.

At Partick I got back to a level of fitness that I had lost at Morton. I could concentrate on my own training and getting fit and was given the time and space in which to do so because Davie realised that I needed a degree of leeway if I was to get fit again.

The young players at Partick were great with the pranks. After training, Roughie and a couple of the others would go into Glasgow city centre and rake through the bin at a bus stop, pretending to look for cigarette ends. They would do it so that the people standing in the queue would say, 'Look at those football players! Why are they doing that?' It was Roughie's idea of a laugh.

John Hansen was fairly quiet – a kind of low-key, intelligent guy – but Alan was anything but quiet. Alan was a good player and he could talk a good game, even back then, but I honestly did not think he would reach the heights in the game that he did. He did very well to get the move to Anfield and, for me, did well at Liverpool because he was in a team with a lot of good players who brought the best out of him. Joe Craig was a true prospect – I thought he would do really well. He was young and fit and, as a fellow striker, I was certain that he would make it at a big club. A more traditional Partick player was Denis McQuade, who I believe was a student of classics at Glasgow

University and then a schoolteacher. Denis would get on the ball and show some lovely touches, do a lot of wee tricks, and then lose it. Denis wanted to do things on the park that suited him and looked good to supporters but he would lose possession for the rest of the team.

Alongside all those talented and entertaining players and with a supportive and sympathetic manager, I could hardly fail to enjoy thoroughly my time at Partick. I was still a winner and would always do my utmost to try to help the team to win matches and even though we knew we were not often going to be close to the top of the league, everyone still tried as much as they could to deliver good results for the club. I still wanted to win – so badly. It was in my system that I wanted to do as well as I could. That was a large part of the reason Davie had been determined to persuade me to go to Firhill. He wanted me to show the other lads how anxious I was to do well and to let them try and build up to the same type of thing.

My Indian summer in Glasgow's West End lasted for two very good years and then, in the summer of 1974, Davie McParland left Partick to become manager of Queen's Park. His replacement was none other than Bertie Auld, my former teammate and Lisbon Lion. I had always thought Bertie could become a good manager and his coming to Thistle was a great thing for him because he had been brought up in Maryhill and in his early days would have been familiar with Firhill.

It was a slightly awkward situation, because Bertie was reluctant to give me stick in the same way as he did all the other players even though I would have been quite happy for him to do that. The Lions, though, were still such a family that you could not do that to one another, really. However, Bertie had loved the managerial style of Eddie Turnbull of Hibs – Bertie had gone to Easter Road after leaving Celtic – and he would do the type of things that Turnbull would do. He had a great delight in telling you how hard Turnbull was and how he really made the players graft. He had been a good role model for Bertie and the Partick players were really made to knuckle down.

It became progressively harder for Bertie to keep me in the team – I had just turned 38 when he arrived and I sensed that I was close to finishing as a player. I almost felt that by hanging on I wasn't doing Bertie any good in terms of his management of Partick. You know when you're not doing it any more as a player – you cannot do what you want to do or what you could do a couple of years previously. You think you can but you get caught out. Bertie was a tough wee fellow and he always wanted the players to give him everything they could. His training sessions were hugely demanding and you had to do as much as you could and not drop below the standard he required. In tandem with feeling my playing standards drop, it was hard for me to keep up with his training and that too let me know that my time as a player was finally at an end.

CHAPTER TWELVE

UP UNTIL NOW

The dilemma I faced in the summer of 1975 was the same as that which confronted all footballers of my generation. I was too old to play the game I loved but too young – and not rich enough – to retire. I had dedicated my life to professional football and knew the game inside out, but that knowledge would now be of little use to me in entirely practical terms. I knew I had to seek some sort of employment to provide for my family but, having tried the coaching side of football, I was not sure where life would next lead me.

I was still running the Steve Chalmers Off-Sales but, even though I was putting an awful lot of time into it, it was not proving to be quite the success that I had envisaged. It had been John Dunn, a friend and a Glasgow city councillor, who had started me off in that business and I was grateful to him for the opportunity it gave me, not least because he had meant well in doing so. He had persuaded me to take one of the shops in his off-sales chain but it wasn't a business from which you could make a lot of money because the competition was so fierce. The bigger shops always had discounts on their products but, counterbalancing that, I was lucky in that even though I might be slightly more expensive than larger outlets, I had an awful lot of people coming into the shop that were doing so through admiration for what I had done for them as a footballer. They would pass other off-licences to come into mine and they would tell me that and I appreciated them doing so. I also felt well protected in that off-sales is something that you need in a part of town such as The Butney. The type of people who hang about street corners were among my customers and they made sure that I did not get any trouble in running the business. I had built up a good client base, as you might call it, of people who liked to come in and have a chat and who were streetwise and made sure I could go on with my work with no bother.

I worked at the off-sales business all through my days with Partick Thistle, but soon after retiring as a player my time as an off-sales proprietor drew to its natural conclusion. The building that housed my premises became subject to a compulsory purchase order because the council was looking to demolish it. If I had wished to continue, I would have been able to begin again in a new district but that was something on which I was not keen.

It was then that, by good fortune, I was given the chance to return to Celtic Park, when I was asked to join Celtic Pools as sales manager. The role of Celtic Pools is to raise money for the club's youth development arm – and my name and the reputation that I had earned as a player helped me to get business from people. I was almost as determined to make something of my new post as I had been as a player.

Just as I had done a good deal of hard running for the club as a footballer, so I covered an awful lot of ground for Celtic in that new role. If someone had ceased to be a Pools agent, I would go to their home and chap their door and they would get a big surprise when they saw me standing there. I would try to persuade them to continue as a sales agent and that shock tactic, as you might call it, would often succeed and they would agree to re-commence their work with Celtic Pools. If they were not willing, I would ask them if they knew someone else in the area that could take over their role. They usually would do and I was then able to maintain the Pools' foothold and strength in the area.

It was not that easy for people to do the Pools. They had to make weekly payments and they might not see the collector for a few weeks so what they owed would mount up – and it is always harder to get money back from people once it has accumulated. It required all of my skills of persuasion when attempting to get people to remain involved with the scheme.

Nobody pushed me too hard in that job – it was up to me to use my initiative to make a success of it. I was based at Celtic Park, in the small building that sits between the stadium and the primary school on London Road. There was a lot of travelling to be done and it was up to me to make sure I worked out how and when to put in the miles. It was important to travel the length and breadth of Scotland – there were people involved in Celtic Pools on the islands and in the Highlands and as far south as Dumfries. Greenock, funnily enough, of all places, proved a fertile area for Celtic Pools agents; so I was down there particularly often, which was something that I had not expected after my disappointing time at Cappielow. I think I did well in the job – I enjoyed it, especially as I was my own boss in terms of organising my working days. There were approximately 1,500 agents when I was sales manager and my job was to ensure that that level was maintained.

One good thing about the job was that the hours were extremely flexible. I would attend functions for the supporters and try, through a mixture of good humour and friendly chat, to get people to do the Pools. I would often not get home until midnight and so I would be able to take a bit of time to myself the following day. That enabled me to indulge in one of the other great, enduring passions of my life – golf.

One of my golfing colleagues at Cawder Golf Club in Bishopbriggs once said that he couldn't believe the change in my personality when playing sport and with golf, as with football, I was interested mainly in winning. The scenery when playing a course like that of Cawder, with the Campsie Hills as a wonderful backdrop, is superb, and it is good to get out into the fresh air, but it was winning, more than anything else, that motivated me when playing the game.

As a footballer, I spent a lot of time playing golf. There was a rule at Celtic that you were not supposed to play golf during the two days prior to a match but they were prepared to turn a blind eye to that as they knew you could be doing an awful lot worse than walking about on a golf course, getting some gentle exercise. I would adhere to that rule for the really important matches. A lot of the time I would go to the course and just practise, hitting a dozen balls, then picking them up, bringing them back and hitting them again with another club. I was extremely keen on the golf. I would not be out every day – that could possibly tire you too much – but at least every other day.

I would say the football helped the golf because it made me a lot fitter than many of the people with whom I played. I was a member at Cawder, which is a fairly hilly course, and

I would get up and down the slopes without any bother but I would be standing on a hilly tee, waiting to hit the ball, while my playing partners would be struggling upwards, and having to stand for a bit to get their breath back before teeing off. I'd sometimes go round with smokers, get to the tee and they would all be coughing and wheezing away whenever they had to exert themselves to climb a hill, they would be hardly able to get a breath.

I liked the idea that I had to work hard at golf if I was to improve. I could practise for as much as an hour before I started my round. I was stupid enough, as a younger man, to go out in all weathers. Rain, sleet and all sorts, I'd put on my waterproofs and have my umbrella up and do my best to keep dry. But nowadays I just don't like those conditions at all. At my stage of life I would rather stay dry. Nowadays, if it is raining or the ground is frosty, I simply will not play.

I do not mind bunkers, driving, fairway iron shots or pitching but I have always found putting a bit tricky, even though I used to practise like crazy to get it to as good a level as possible. My strength as a golfer is consistency. Every time I hit a shot it tends to be a good one, all the way round the course, even though I possibly do not hit the ball as far as other people. Nowadays I play only just enough medals to keep my handicap, which is at eight. My lowest handicap was one and I maintained that for three or four years. That was when I was at Celtic. At Cawder there were quite a lot of medals and so plenty of opportunities to move your handicap upwards. There was also a team competition, a league, in which you would play the better players from neighbouring courses, in Kirkintilloch, Bearsden, Milngavie and Bishopbriggs itself. It was good to play against first-class golfers, in the amateur sense, and that sharpened even further my competitive instincts.

I would also get a chance, now and then, to play with professionals, through my fame as a Celtic footballer, and you could always learn something from a pro and get a tip or two from them about your own game. I also, memorably, played in the Sean Connery Golf Tournament in 1970 over Troon's Old Course, with Max Faulkner, who had won the Open Championship, and Douglas Bader, the RAF pilot who had lost his legs in the war. Sean was a fine host on the day and Ronnie Simpson, another dedicated golfer, also played, with Gary Player, the South African who has won everything in the game. Despite playing in such exalted company, we could not find any accommodation for that weekend so we stayed, not in the Marine Hotel beside the course, but in a caravan.

All that stimulating company helped me to do well at Cawder, where I played in the final of the club championship four times, winning it on three occasions, which made me captain for the year. My name is on the board and inscribed on the trophy. That was the highlight of my golfing career. Cawder was not a stuffy golf club; it was a friendly club where I was a member from around 1963 until 2009. I loved the course and I think I have walked every inch of it. It is such a friendly game. It is great to play courses other than your own and to meet other people. If it had not been for football, my golf would never have become so good. I had plenty of free afternoons in which to improve my game and I also had the money to pay membership and course fees and to fork out for the best of equipment.

In turn golf did a lot for my football – it kept me moving and fit all year round. In the summer, especially, it would maintain my level of fitness so that when I started pre-season training, which was usually in mid-July at the time of the Glasgow Fair Holiday, I would be feeling fairly fit – although nothing could completely prepare you for the ferocity of the assault on the senses that was Jock Stein's pre-season work. You could always see who had done a bit of training on their own before facing Jock and the hard stuff. It was hard on your feet, you'd be getting blisters through doing so much running in a concentrated period. You'd be getting timed and they would be checking your weight and seeing how you lost it but, through golf, I would not have let my fitness drop too much over the close season. I did appreciate getting a break from football every summer – I felt a serious degree of relief at getting away from the game for a while. I think it helped me, as a footballer, to get a lot of rest. At that time, the season would conclude in late April or early May so you would get a decent, refreshing period away from it before returning to training in the summer. I feel now that the footballers do not get a long enough break, away from it all, during the summer. I think they play too many friendly matches. You see a lot of injuries early in the season and I'd be concerned that it's because they are not getting enough rest.

One morning, during the late 1980s, I was going to golf early on a Sunday morning and began feeling rather unwell. Sadie quickly fetched Dr Kennedy, a neighbour, who had been in his bath. It was about eight o'clock in the morning. The doctor came right away, attended to me and I began to feel a bit better so I said to him that I had to get to the golf for nine o'clock or I wouldn't get into the sweep. He told me, quite strictly, not to move an inch because he had an ambulance coming for me. It took me straight into Stobhill Hospital and intensive care, where I remained for three days. I had suffered a heart attack.

That proved to be something of a watershed for me. It made me a bit more careful – for six months I was not allowed to do any driving and we went to Kelly's Hotel and Spa in Rosslare for a week's convalescence, where I was given swimming lessons for the first time in my life and where the emphasis is on total relaxation and enjoying their wonderful food. It is a special place.

I didn't go back to work at Celtic Pools after that. The heart attack had been brought on by stress through worrying about work. I had also just started playing badminton shortly before I suffered the heart attack. I would go to Bishopbriggs Sports Centre with some golfing pals to play badminton when the weather was too poor to play golf, and, as with everything I did, I became extremely competitive in playing the game. I would return home after those matches utterly exhausted and drained. That participation in badminton had begun for me about six months before I suffered the heart attack.

The first person to phone Sadie to ask after me was Alex Ferguson. That meant a lot to me. I was also a guest at the Celtic supporters' rally in Glasgow's Royal Concert Hall shortly after my release from hospital – maybe they thought they should get me there while they could.

We had moved to Bishopbriggs during the late 1960s as part of a general progression that saw us move home on a regular basis, for practical reasons, as our family grew in number. Having begun married life in Dennistoun and then moved to Easterhouse, we then moved to Springburn in the mid-1960s, where our neighbours were two very refined ladies and their brother who had been most apprehensive about this family with four children moving in, but they ruined our children, spoiled them rotten, plying them with sweets and presents. We were three floors up in a brand new flat and close to Sadie's mum and dad, so it was perfect in terms of babysitting. We then moved to Bishopbriggs and to a house, where, next door, we had a Mr Radoman, a Yugoslavian baker, who brought us a full board of buns and cakes every Saturday night. Martin was born while we were living there, on 28 March 1970 and Clare, our surprise package, arrived on 9 December 1976. We then moved to a five-bedroomed house, still in Bishopbriggs, where all the children grew into teenagers, then adults and, eventually, got married.

I have to admit that I found it a bit hard to watch Paul, my second-oldest son, play for Celtic. I was very happy when he signed for the club in 1980, as a 16-year-old, but he took a lot of knocks and he wasn't a particularly heavy boy so he did not look to me too well designed for all the punishment that was dealt out to him. Another reason I found it difficult to watch him was because I would see him making mistakes and I had decided to follow the same tack as my father had taken with me and make sure that I was not going to interfere with him or contradict what he might be getting told by people at the club. If he was being told one thing by the club, it would not be good if he turned round and said, 'But my dad said . . .'

Paul was a good goalscorer and would muck in even though he got knocks. Bobby Lennox, who was the reserve team coach, always said that Paul was an absolute glutton for training and that he just wanted to be running and doing all his exercises. He would work very, very hard. He did not play many first-team games, though, and I have to accept that that was probably fair.

Celtic obviously sized him up and decided he did not have exactly what they were seeking. I thought they might have given him a bit more time to prove himself but they had a lot of good players on the books at that time. He moved on to have a good career representing St Mirren, Swansea City, Dunfermline Athletic and Hamilton Academical.

There may have been a bit of extra pressure on him, especially at Celtic, with me being his father – it couldn't have been too easy. I never helped him much with his football, in terms of him learning the game, but he may have been motivated through trying to catch up with his father and trying to get as much out of the game as his father did. He is a sensible fellow and he knew that, after he had been at Celtic for several years without making a serious breakthrough to the first team, it was best to move on to another club. He knew that by finding another club and getting first-team football, he would maybe make a wee bit more money out of the game than I had – and he probably did. He still had to get a job to keep himself going once he finished football and he now works for an Edinburgh letting agency. At one stage he helped out in finding houses for Celtic's foreign players.

Stephen, my oldest son, works in the American Golf shop in Stirling; Carol is married to Gerard; Anne works at the Marine Hotel in Troon, where her husband is the chef, and she organises weddings and functions; Clare, the youngest, has two young babies; and Martin, my youngest son, was working in York recently when he found that he was feeling fatigued an awful lot of the time and discovered he had a heart condition called cardiomyopathy. He was dangerously ill with that for quite a while but he is now back in Scotland, living close to us, and getting on not too badly. We are also lucky to have nine grandchildren:

Stephen, Christopher, Martin, Paul, Natalie, Michael, Victoria, Scott and Jack.

I still love my football and, unlike some former players, I think that, as with most things in life, the game has improved. It is awfully hard, though, to judge whether players today are more skilled than in my time – how could anyone be more skilled than Jimmy Johnstone or Jim Baxter? Perhaps the biggest difference, overall, is the amount of televised football on our screens, and television is not merely reflecting the game, as it did in my time as a player, but is affecting the way players see themselves. You see players in the modern game who seek out a TV camera after they have scored a goal and they go and hug it with all their teammates on their back. I would never have done that – I would never have drawn attention to myself in that way. The thing is that all those players have got on; they have made big names for themselves. Television is in danger of ruining football and leaving the fans jaded by it. In the past, you would really anticipate a match being on television. Nowadays, there are so many games on TV – and sometimes one after another – that you often cannot be bothered with them.

Celtic remain one of my principal considerations in life and I have maintained a close interest in the club and how it is progressing. It is nice to be acknowledged as Celtic's fourth-highest goalscorer but I must say that, in 1973, when Bobby Lennox surpassed my record to take over from me as the second-highest scorer in the club's history, I was entirely unaware of the fact. At that time, people didn't worry much about statistics. Maybe I'm wrong, maybe other people were concerned with statistics, such as being top scorer in this or that, but I was not and I do not remember too many teammates or opponents or fellow Scotland players being particularly concerned with things like that. If I were starting again as a footballer, in the present day, I would keep records of what I had done because it means so much to score goals now in terms of transfer value and all the benefits of being regarded as an effective goalscorer. I simply felt good through scoring goals and looked forward to scoring the next one. That was enough for me. It was no disgrace to lose my record to Bobby – even if I did not realise it – because he was a fantastic footballer, exceptionally fit and a magnificent all-round player. He had a great shot in either foot, both in terms of power and accuracy and he was unselfish in assisting teammates and providing chances for others. He also played in a lot more games than I did so that gives him an unfair advantage over me in the scoring stakes . . .

There was a lot more made of the situation in 2004 when Henrik Larsson became the next Celtic man to score more than me. I thought Henrik was terrific, not only for himself but for those who played beside him. Henrik had everything that you could ask for in a footballer. He was not such a big fellow yet he scored a lot of goals with his head, while his fitness was fantastic. His all-round play was very good. They had it in the papers that Henrik had pushed me back down to fourth place and while I would have liked to have remained second to the incomparable Jimmy McGrory, the people who passed me – Bobby and Henrik – are worthy of their standing. It is great to be even near Larsson's record and to be regarded as worthy of any kind of comparison with him is something I regard as an honour.

John Hartson was another very good goalscorer of recent times at Celtic, and one whom I would select as a personal favourite. I attended a function in his honour at the Hilton Hotel in Glasgow at which they showed a film of all the goals he had scored for the club. I could have watched that film on a loop all night; as a centre-forward I could really appreciate it. Those were such good goals.

Mixed in with so many great memories of Celtic and football are one or two that are rather less pleasant. Back in the spring of 1980 Tommy Callaghan and I attended the Scottish Cup final and waited behind after the game, which, infamously, was followed by a riot on the pitch, when young supporters of both Celtic and Rangers confronted each other and indulged in some serious violence after Celtic had won the trophy. That was the day on which mounted police had to be brought on to the turf at Hampden to disperse battling supporters. Tommy and I waited and waited until we thought the crowds would be away and then left the ground to head for Mount Florida. As we were walking away from the stadium, we encountered a large group of Rangers supporters who began calling us all the vilest names of which they could think; and they had an extensive repertoire. They were keen for a fight so the two of us dashed for a gate at Lesser Hampden, told an official what was happening and he admitted us into the ground, where we remained until the storm blew over. It's a terrible thing, all the trouble that surrounds the Glasgow derby. It makes you despair, not least because I have always had very good relations with people from Rangers, not only opponents from my time as a player but with those who have played and coached and managed there since I left Celtic, such as Ally McCoist.

Life, for me, is now lived at a more relaxed pace than it used to be. During the late 1990s, with the family having flown the nest,

Sadie and I opted to leave Bishopbriggs and move to the seaside, to a two-bedroomed flat in Troon. We always used to come to Troon on holiday and hire a house if we had decided not to go abroad that year. Once it had become clear that I would be unable to go back to work following my heart attack, we decided to move down permanently. I missed the golf course at Cawder for a while and would frequently return just to play but I would rather stay down on the Ayrshire coast now and I have no end of good local golf courses from which to choose. It is a bit quieter and more relaxing – the weather is better down on the coast – and three of our children are down here now, living close to us.

I still love to go to Celtic Park. I love the memories and the rituals even though the place has changed an awful lot since my day. The dressing rooms inside the modern Celtic Park are so much better than the ones we had – so many of the dressing rooms we had in Scotland in the 1960s were in a very poor state – and inside the Celtic dressing room now the players have the choice of all sorts of fruit and sweets and drinks while they have the option of picking from three or four pairs of boots. Back in my day – and I actually do not think it was any worse for us – we had a cup of tea after a match and then we went home.

My links with the Celtic Pools also remain very much alive because at every home game I host a table in the Captain's Table restaurant and entertain representatives of Celtic Pools who are being rewarded for their doing a lot of good work for the club. I still get reps asking me if I remember coming to their doors all those years ago and asking them to continue with their work.

An even greater number of people, not only at Celtic Park but here, there and everywhere, come up and ask me almost every day in every week, what it was like to be the person who scored the winning goal in Lisbon, the golden goal that transformed Celtic from being a good, big Scottish club into one that had now broken through into serious international fame. That goal was just like any other goal really, like dozens I scored down the years: a quick touch on the ball to divert it in the right direction. I scored cleverer goals and more well-worked goals and more spectacular goals but for me, and for Celtic, this was the ultimate goal. It was the goal that rewarded all those years in which I had developed my winning touch to perfection. It was the goal that I had been born to score.

POSTSCRIPT

STEVIE CHALMERS: IN THEIR OWN WORDS

May McCambridge – nurse, Belvidere Hospital, Glasgow

'When Stevie came into the hospital he was very ill with TB meningitis. He was very quiet for a few days then became accustomed to the wild ways of the Belvidere – it was one of those wards where, because it was long term, you had to have a bit of laxity. Another boy, Eddie Cassidy, was desperately ill also and Stevie, even in his illness, made great friends with him. Eddie, sadly, did not survive.

Stevie was very funny and even though he had to undergo quite painful treatment, I never heard him complain or say very much about it. He took a lot of pain without grumbling. He was always very polite.

I think Stevie was very lucky. It was a terrible treatment that he had to undergo with injections put into the spine and spinal taps. He was very ill. You don't have TB meningitis without being very ill.

It was wonderful that he recovered but lots of patients, although they recover from that illness, are debilitated – they have pins and needles from a spinal condition or can't walk properly. So to see Stevie go on to play professional football at such a high level was special. When he scored the goal in the European Cup final, I assumed that he deserved all the praise and my family had me on about that, saying that it was only because I had been part of the team that had been responsible for him at the hospital.'

JIM CRAIG – LISBON LIONS, RIGHT-BACK

'I remember we were on our way to Russia for a European tie and, as usual, Stevie, Bobby Murdoch and me were sitting together in a row of three. We always sat together. Murdoch had a terrible habit of leaning across and looking out of the window, so I said, with some annoyance, 'Why don't you just sit at the window?' He said, 'I don't want to sit at the window; I just want to be able to lean across you and look out of the window.' So, being slightly exasperated by our seating arrangements, I asked Stevie, who was sitting in the seat by the aisle, as serenely as ever, why he always sat on the outside seat in a row of three and he said it was so he could make a bolt for it if the plane went down. It was so neatly logical; like so much about Stevie.

As a player, as a defender, I have to say that Stevie must have been a very hard man to play against because he was never still. He always moved out to the wings and back again and the other thing you must say is that when the chance to score came along, Stevie invariably took it. His scoring record is very good and if you're a striker, that matters a lot; unlike a defender, whose interventions to stop the opposition are not recorded starkly, a striker's contribution is racked up in terms of number of goals scored. Stevie was a terrific player and it is worth remembering that he was playing in an era when football – and most notably in Scotland – was on a higher plane, in terms of quality, than it is today. His goal in Lisbon was perfect – part of a move that we practised repeatedly in training and credit to Stevie that he was in the right place at the right time and that he put the ball in the net so well.

When I arrived at Celtic as a youngster, Stevie had been with the club for a few years and I found him very easy to get along with – we hit it off straightaway. We would always sit together on the bus and he always was – and is – very pleasant company, and the same can be said of Sadie, his wife, and his lovely family.'

BILLY MCNEILL – LISBON LIONS, CENTRE-HALF AND CAPTAIN

'Everybody would have loved to score the goal that Stevie got against Inter Milan in Lisbon. I used to kid him on every time I saw him by going up to him and saying, 'Chalmers – you snatched my moment of glory away from me! I wanted to score that goal.' It was all in good fun. In the European Cup final, Stevie worked the opposition persistently and never allowed them a moment's peace and his was not an easy goal – nothing is ever easy in football. Stevie just made it look easy. You're talking about scoring the winner against an Italian team with a great record in European football and a team well known for not giving the opposing team any space.

Stevie was a fine person to have around the football club. He didn't go about shouting his mouth off. He was quiet but he was positive. It didn't surprise us that he scored that goal in Lisbon because Stevie would always be likely to score if the opportunity arose. For 90 minutes, Stevie would be persistent and never think he couldn't get involved. He really put on a magnificent show in every game he played. Nobody could ever accuse him of being lazy.

Stevie was a smashing player. The energy that he put into his game on the football park and his attitude were equally incredible. Nor did he take losing well. He battled away like nobody's business. He was terrific and he loved the game. He was persistent and ran for 90 minutes and, for me, that's something that is vitally important in a football team. You need all sorts of different people in any team but, having said that, there are few teams with someone like Stevie Chalmers.'

John Clark – Lisbon Lions, sweeper

'Stevie was a quiet type of person, not one of the more boisterous people in the dressing room. He was a good professional who took great pride in what he did and a very nice man to know. There were never any problems with Stevie that I can remember, over anything, and he was rarely in trouble with referees even though he gave his full commitment to playing the game. He was the gentleman of the club.

He was a player who wouldn't give you a minute's peace on the field, he was always on top of the last defender and always on the move and if you were a defender and up against Stevie you certainly knew that a game of football lasted for 90 minutes. There are very few people like that now in the game – on the move all the time. Henrik Larsson was one of the few who showed that kind of style. At Celtic, as a defender, I often played against

Stevie in training but I never gave him a kick; he was always in my pocket.

In company, he was excellent, never a guy who liked the nightlife, he was always a family man. Players like Stevie are vital to a team. We had Jimmy Johnstone who had all the tricks, Bobby Lennox with lots of pace, Willie Wallace, who was very elusive in and around the box and Bertie Auld and Bobby Murdoch, who were clever midfield players. In that team we had a whole blend of wonderful players that was a gift to the club.

Stevie's goal in Lisbon, I would have to say, was a fluke. I always ask him if he actually touched the ball on its way into the net. No, it was actually an excellent goal-taker's goal and, as so often, Stevie was in the right place at the right time. Stevie and Tommy Gemmell are forever a part of football history because they scored the goals on the day and that is thoroughly deserved on their parts.

I left Celtic to go down to Morton because I had had a cartilage injury and for a year at Celtic Park I had struggled to obtain full fitness. Naturally, at a club like Celtic, you are likely to be displaced in the team if you are out for that long so I went to Morton to try to get playing again. Shortly afterwards, Stevie also joined up at Cappielow and as joint coaches we did quite well but being at Morton was such a big comedown from European Cup finals; and that's nothing against Morton or the players who were there. I found it hard to get motivated for matches against clubs of equal stature to Morton – the games I liked were the ones against Celtic, Rangers, Hearts, Hibs. It was hard, otherwise, to get going and I think Stevie felt similarly. I think the call of the golf course lured him away from the life of a coach.

He is still going well and he looks well. All that golf and football and fresh air as a young man has clearly helped him. I'm only sorry he has never taken up my offer of a challenge match on the golf course. I've heard he is very good at the game and a low-handicapper but for some reason he has always blanked me when I have mentioned golf. He is clearly concerned that he will meet his match.'

Tommy Gemmell – Lisbon Lions, left-back

'You could have put Stevie on Shawfield dog track – he and Bobby Lennox were flying machines. The pace that Stevie had would leave defenders lying about. You don't get many out-and-out front players who do a lot of work but it was the opposite with Stevie. He was a workhorse as well as being a good player; whose fine ball control and his making of goals for his teammates were among his other huge strengths.

He was a player who never got in any bother – the only time I saw him lose his temper was when a certain German, playing for Bayern Munich, rubbed him up the wrong way on our tour of North America in 1966 and Stevie chased him to continue their scrap on the running track. Stevie liked to think about the game but he was not as quiet as you would think. In the company of his teammates he is a particularly lively individual.

Stevie was a clever player. He would never do anything daft. He was straightforward and you got the same performance out of him in every game. He was marvellously consistent.

His goal in Lisbon is, of course, everyone's greatest memory of Stevie and it is mine too. You have got to remember that his movement before that goal was exceptional. He got into that position, to score, instinctively and although he made that goal look easy on the day, it was the result of years and years of practice; the work of a top-class striker who has done everything to improve and refine his game.

I have to say that it is wonderful that my name will forever be associated with that of Stevie Chalmers thanks to us being the two goalscorers on that momentous day in Lisbon. Before the game, you couldn't have scripted it any better in terms of how the game would go. Everybody talks about my goal because I hit it from 25 yards or so but that was for the equaliser – the most important goal was Stevie's because that was the winner. Everyone would have loved to score that goal but Stevie, entirely deservedly, was the one who did it.'

Bertie Auld – Lisbon Lions, midfielder

'The thing I always admired about Stevie was that you got the same level of performance from him in every game. Stevie was a manager's dream because when he came into Celtic Park he was always well dressed and looked immaculate and he never complained about anything. Once he was out on the field of play, though, he was a fiery competitor. He played in two or three positions across the forward line and he had tremendous composure in scoring goals. He looked after himself on the field too – if he took a bit of punishment from an opponent he would not complain about it but he would remember it. He could certainly take care of himself.

Whenever we came back from a European trip, my wife would ask me with whom I had been rooming and if it was Stevie Chalmers, she would think that was tremendous. She knew what kind of character he was, a really level-headed person, although Stevie was still always jovial and one of the boys.

Stevie was the most essential player in any team for whom he played because he was so unselfish. He would chase a lost cause and make it look good. If I hit a pass in his direction and it had been played too strongly he would make it look a whole lot better by chasing it down and getting close to the ball or even catching it. He loved the sport of football and in his leisure time kept himself fit and alert through his love of golf. He played that game with the same passion – he wanted to be a winner in both golf and football; but not at all costs.

As for his goal in Lisbon, I could have tapped that in... the ball just brushed off of him, didn't it? I always ask him whether he actually touched the ball at all. People say that our three strikers that day – Willie Wallace, Bobby Lennox and Stevie – had quiet games but that is not really true because they put in a tremendous amount of work off the ball and that is just as important as the work that is done on the ball. When the half-chance came along, Stevie was ready to take it – just as he did in scoring important winning goals in so many other matches. The difference was that in Lisbon, that twist of his boot changed the history of our club.

I later managed Stevie at Partick Thistle. I was starting out in management and it was a new experience for me so I would be quite direct with him in front of the other players in telling him I wanted more from him. The other, younger players would be looking on and wondering about me doing this to a friend, a former teammate, a Scotland cap, the man who had scored *the* winning goal and a legend in so many households; but even though my family were great friends with Stevie, Sadie and his lovely family, Stevie never looked for sympathy or favours. We would, later on, speak about the matter more quietly in private but he was always hugely respectful of my position and my authority as manager. He helped me an awful lot in that way.

He was the type of character who would encourage young players, both at Partick and, earlier, at Celtic, where he did much to help players such as Kenny Dalglish, Paul Wilson, Lou Macari. Stevie always had time for everybody: young, old, even the tea lady. He is, quite simply, a wonderful person.'

Willie Wallace – Lisbon Lions, forward

'I remember Steve as a person one could always trust and rely upon not only as a player but also in his everyday life. Steve always had a very pleasant manner and was a pleasure to work with. He has a great sense of humour and we shared many a good laugh. I did not play many games of golf with Steve but when I did, I was well and truly outclassed and I am sure that golf was another sport in which he could have been great.

As a player, Steve was very consistent. His work-rate and effort were never in question. Like all good goalscorers, Steve had the ability to put half-chances away. His style of football would fit into most teams, even today. Steve would prove to be a very difficult player for the modern defenders to handle, with his relentless work-rate. There are not many strikers today who can put the pressure on defenders as Steve could. This style and class made it much easier for players to play up front with him.

Coming from Hearts, it did not take me long to fit in beside Steve as his style of play, as I have indicated, made heaps of room for myself and the other forwards and enabled us to perform well.

As a goalscorer, Steve would rank in the top level. He could score with both head and foot and his timing and anticipation was perfect. He was also very capable of creating goals with his consistent work-rate off the ball.

Steve's goal in Lisbon will never be forgotten by any Celtic supporter. When the goal went in, there was no time to think how important this goal would become but to have the honour of this goal could not have fallen to a more deserving person. Maybe I helped him a bit by making a run to take a defender out of his way but making decoyed runs in the Celtic team at that time was done as part of our playing strategy. To me this was the strength of the 16-man playing group: no matter who played in the team, we played for each other. For me to make that run in Lisbon was probably nothing more than I would have done in many games before the Lisbon final but that run was the one that helped create history. The main thing was that Steve was able to score.

To play with Steve was a pleasure and to know his wife and family was an added bonus. I can only wish Steve continued good health and happiness for the future.'

BOBBY LENNOX – LISBON LIONS, FORWARD

'Stevie scoring the winning goal in the European Cup final is my outstanding memory of him. It was the type of goal he had scored a thousand times in training and while it might have looked as though Stevie just luckily got his toe to it, it was no surprise to any of us that Stevie had been the one to put the ball in the net. He was expert at knowing just how to get into the right spot and get that vital touch on a ball – that was the result of years of practice.

That memory stands out in particular but Stevie scored so many other excellent goals. He was a great reader of the game, he had great pace and he worked the two channels well. He was simply terrific. Stevie always gave his best. If he wasn't playing well, he still put everything into his game. He epitomised that European Cup-winning team. It was a pleasure to play with Stevie because he would continually make runs for other people and while he scored the winner in the final, he had also done an enormous amount to ensure that we got to Lisbon in the first place. When we went to Czechoslovakia for the second leg of the semi-final with Dukla Prague, Stevie was the main man in the team in the way that he played up the field on his own to help defend our lead. He played that role magnificently and although there were often four or five Czech defenders hounding him, he never stopped giving his all and taking the punishment that was doled out to him.

When I stopped playing football, I took up golf and, of the Lisbon Lions, Stevie and Ronnie Simpson were the properly good golfers. People were saying Stevie was really serious about his golf and I am more of a happy-go-lucky golfer but he is a great golfing companion and we have played in tournaments up and down the country and had great times driving all over the place to do so. I cannot get anywhere near him in terms of playing ability.

One of many good days was in Las Vegas. Stevie almost always out-drives me but this time we followed our balls down the fairway and I came to the first ball and thought it must be mine. It turned out to be Stevie's. My ball was further on – and that alone made it a memorable day. Mine must have hit a stone or something. Stevie is good fun and he helped me immensely when I took up golf around 20 years ago. On the golf course, he is just as you would expect: the etiquette has to be right and everything has to be done properly.

Stevie and Sadie have a lovely family and he is a real gentleman and not only that but he is a gentle man.'

Sir Alex Ferguson – St Johnstone, Dunfermline Athletic, Rangers, Falkirk, Ayr United, forward

'We were in Spain on holiday one year and met up with Stevie and Sadie and our families got on very well with each other. It is important to be able to put aside all the football rivalries and make sure that it never interferes with friendship. You might have been fierce rivals with someone on the field of play but when you meet them off the field you wonder if it is the same person. That was the case with Stevie and me. Bridget, my sister-in-law, was also very friendly with Sadie, Stevie's wife, as they lived close to each other in Bishopbriggs.

Stevie was the type of player who would give everything in a game – he was a bit like myself in that respect – and there is absolutely nothing wrong with being a grafter. He started late in the senior game, from Ashfield Juniors as I recall, and it is unusual for someone to come late to the game and especially to join a club such as Celtic. That bears testimony to the dedication Stevie had to his game. He was so quick as a player and he and Bobby Lennox, when together at Celtic, were the two fastest and best strikers in Scotland at the time. As a striker, it is a real skill to get in behind defenders the way that Stevie did. If you look at the make-up of any football club, it accommodates all sorts of players. At Celtic, Bobby Murdoch and Bertie Auld were great users of the ball and you need to have players such as Stevie and Bobby

Lennox, who can exploit that. Stevie was made for Celtic.

I don't want to remember his games against Rangers, when I was there! I do remember that when I was at Dunfermline, we always saw Stevie as a great threat. I remember the time I came through with Dunfermline, when Celtic were chasing the championship – it was Celtic's second-last match of the 1965–66 season. They had a full house that evening and I gave them a bit of a surprise when I scored the opening goal but with Stevie spearheading the forward line they got back on track and went on to win 2-1.

It is always a pleasure to meet Stevie. He is a first-class human being – and a great golfer too. That is all to do with having the hand-eye coordination and skill in striking a ball of the top sportsman, which he carried over from his football.

I was in Hong Kong with the Scotland touring squad when Celtic won the European Cup so I didn't see the match on television at the time and I remember it took a while for the result to come through – communications were not quite so swift as they are today. It was great that Stevie scored the winning goal and it was a reward for all the work he put in at Celtic. Some people are rewarded in the best possible way and that was Stevie's great reward.'

JIM LUMSDEN – MORTON, MIDFIELDER

'It would have been hard for anyone to work as a coach at Morton at the time Stevie joined the club. Being at that club under Hal Stewart was like a matter of survival, so the job was not ideal for a young coach such as Stevie. You could come in of a morning and find two players had been sold overnight. Hal liked to change things round a lot and to sell players on a frequent basis while Stevie had come from working with one of the greatest managers the game of football has ever seen. I would say that under Stevie we were very fit and organised but it was near impossible for him sometimes, with some of the things that Hal would say and do.

I was a young player at Morton when Stevie joined as player-coach and he used to pick me up at Bishopbriggs and drive me through to Greenock. Stevie was tremendously fit for a man in his mid-thirties – he never had an ounce of fat on him and he was so quick. He still had a turn of pace and he really knew how to play. You could tell he had been a great player. Stevie's attitude and fitness were top class and everybody looked up to him and John Clark.

In training, we would do these straight runs from one end of the park to the other and Stevie was ahead of people, even though he was in third gear. He helped me greatly, through his attitude. I was similar to him in terms of liking training to be hard and, as a coach, Stevie was not asking you to do anything he wasn't doing as well. He was fitter and quicker than anybody at the club and he was a great example of the benefits of training hard and what that could do to enable you to last in the game.'

DAVIE MCPARLAND – PARTICK THISTLE, MANAGER

'I can vividly remember Stevie from a practice game we had one summer. I had signed big Alan Hansen, aged 16, from Sauchie Juniors and we were doing pre-season training. Stevie used to harass people and put pressure on them to cause them to make mistakes and in this match, big Hansen, defending, went to hit the ball and Stevie turned side-on to him, hoping he would hit the ball off of him but Hansen just took a step to the side and evaded him. I always remember that when the players were coming off the park, Stevie came up to me to ask who the new, big fellow was. He always had an eye for a player.

I needed a bit of help at the time I signed Stevie because we had been relegated and then promoted and after being demoted I had had to move on most of my senior players to reduce costs, and had gone with young players. Now that we had returned to the top flight I had to bring in experienced guys, such as Alex Rae, Hughie Strachan and Stevie, who was a big help to me. He had a good way with people and he did a good job on the park. It was great to have a man of his experience and ability but Stevie was never in the team on reputation alone – we could not afford to carry anyone. He was a competitor, with a good attitude to life and to sport and you can't ask for anything better than that.'

John Greig – Rangers, defender and captain

'Stevie was very, very difficult as an opponent because he had great pace and I always felt that when I played against players such as Stevie and Bobby Lennox that, if they got a yard on you, you never got near them. I'm sure it is the same in the modern game. It was always good to meet Stevie at a function or with Scotland because I could see him face to face – on the field of play, the only thing I usually saw was a view of him from behind.

I think Stevie had a very good idea of the game and, as with all the other guys at Celtic, he was very lucky to have the privilege of playing under such a great manager as Jock Stein, who made the game look simple for his players.

Stevie could certainly look after himself as an opponent. He wasn't built like John Hughes but he was, to use a good old Scottish word, wiry, and he was strong. Among all the players I faced, I always admired Stevie a great deal and thought highly of him because he was like a gentleman. He had great manners and great respect for other people. He was, like all of us, desperate to win but he respected his opponents greatly. There was mutual respect among the Celtic and Rangers players – on the field we liked to beat each other, not least because there were usually at least 70,000 people screaming us on, but away from that, we were extremely companionable.

The thing I would say is that, having the respect for Celtic Football Club that I did, it didn't matter who played for them, you had to give them 100 per cent respect – in those days, to be a regular for the Celtic team or Rangers team, you had to be a very good player. When the Old Firm players joined up in Scotland squads, there was great camaraderie between us. We seemed to have a bond. I remember Stevie playing for Scotland against Brazil, the game in which he scored in the first minute.

It does not really matter how many trophies a person won as a footballer – the most important thing is still to have your health and I wish Stevie, a very special person, good health and many more years of life to come.'

FACTS AND FIGURES

Stevie's record for scoring in consecutive matches is seven, which he achieved between 11 January and 18 February 1967 by scoring against Clyde (2), St Johnstone, Hibernian, Arbroath, Airdrieonians, Ayr United (3) and Elgin City. Also between 7 January and 27 February 1961 he scored in seven matches in a row against Third Lanark, Aberdeen, Airdrieonians (2), Montrose (2), Hibernian (2), Raith Rovers and Clyde, but during that run he did not play in the away match at St Mirren.

Stevie is one of eight Celtic players to score hat-tricks in back-to-back matches for the club. His came on 2 November 1963 against East Stirlingshire (5-1 away) and the following week at home to Partick Thistle (5-3). The other players are Jimmy Quinn (twice), Henrik Larsson, Sandy McMahon, Joe McBride, Dixie Deans, Tommy McInally and Jimmy McGrory, who achieved this an incredible six times, including three hat-tricks in a row in January 1928.

In 1963–64 Stevie became only the second player to top both the Celtic goalscoring chart and the appearances list in the same season*. He played in all 52 matches that season scoring 38 goals.

The first player to achieve this was John Bell in 1899–1900; though since then Paul Wilson (1974–75), Pat McGinlay (1993–94), Henrik Larsson (1998–99, 2001–02 and 2003–04) and John Hartson (2004–05) and Gary Hooper (2011–12) have all achieved this feat.
(*Only since Scottish League started in 1890.)

Stevie is fourth on the all-time list of Celtic goalscorers with 231 goals. The only players above him are Jimmy McGrory (468), Bobby Lennox (273) and Henrik Larsson (242).

Stevie is fifth on the all-time list of players to have scored most hat-tricks for Celtic with 14. The players above him are Jimmy McGrory (55), Jimmy Quinn (20), Henrik Larsson and Bobby Lennox (both with 15).

Stevie is one of just three Celtic players ever to have scored five goals or more in a single match for Celtic on more than one occasion. He scored five against East Fife at home on 16 September 1964 in a League Cup tie which Celtic won 6-0 and on 11 September 1968 he scored another five at home to Hamilton Academical, again in the League Cup, with Celtic running out 10-0 winners. The players who share this record are Jimmy McGrory and Bobby Lennox.

Stevie is the last player to score a hat-trick in a League match between Celtic and Rangers when he netted three second-half goals on 3 January 1966 as Celtic thrashed the Ibrox club 5-1. Since then 166 League matches have been played without a hat-trick being scored.

FACTS AND FIGURES

The Lisbon Lions started just 11 competitive matches together and Stevie scored in two of them. The first time they played together was on 14 January 1967 away to St Johnstone and Stevie scored the third goal in a 4-0 win, and the only other time he scored as part of the Lions was on a certain afternoon in Lisbon later that same year.

Stevie was Celtic's first ever substitute used in a League match. On 24 September 1966 he replaced Joe McBride and scored the winner at Dens Park as Celtic beat Dundee 2-1, therefore also becoming Celtic's first ever goalscoring substitute. He was also involved in Celtic's first ever substitution in a European match when Willie Wallace came on for him away to Red Star Belgrade on 27 November 1968. The match ended in a 1-1 draw.

Stevie was Celtic's leading scorer in League matches in four separate seasons – 1959–60 (14 goals), 1960–61 (20 goals), 1963–64 (28 goals) and 1966–67 (23 goals). In 1966–67 he was the top scorer in the whole Scottish League.

He was also Celtic's leading scorer in all competitions in four seasons – 1960–61 (26 goals), 1963–64 (38 goals), 1964–65 (26 goals) and 1966–67 (36 goals).

Stevie won a total of six league titles with Celtic (1965–66, 1966–67, 1967–68, 1968–69, 1969–70 and 1970–71), three Scottish Cups (1964–65, 1966–67 and 1968–69) and four League Cups (1966–67, 1967–68, 1968–69 and 1969–70).

THE WINNING TOUCH

The 1967 European Cup final was Stevie's 10th cup final appearance for Celtic (including replays) and it was the first one he ever scored in. In the eight matches Stevie played leading up to Lisbon he failed to score and that barren run continued in the first eight matches the following season, which means in a spell of 17 games Stevie scored just one goal, and it just happened to be the most important goal in the club's history.

In eight Scottish Cup finals (including replays) Stevie scored just one goal, when he finished off the scoring as Celtic hammered Rangers 4-0 in 1968–69. It was his last Scottish Cup final appearance for the club.

In five League Cup finals (including replays) Stevie scored two goals, both in the same match in 1967–68 against Dundee, which Celtic won 5-3.

Stevie's last cup final appearance for Celtic was against St Johnstone in the 1969–70 League Cup final. Although Celtic ran out 1-0 winners, Stevie broke his leg and would only play another six games for the club.

STEVIE CHALMERS:

CAREER STATISTICS

APPEARANCES (AND SUBSTITUTE APPEARANCES) BY SEASON

	League		Scottish Cup	
1958–59	1			
1959–60	17		2	
1960–61	32		7	
1961–62	31		6	
1962–63	27		4	
1963–64	34		4	
1964–65	23		5	
1965–66	22		6	
1966–67	28	(1)	6	
1967–68	13	(4)	0	(1)
1968–69	17	(4)	5	(1)
1969–70	5			
1970–71	3	(1)		
Totals (career)	253	(10)	45	(2)

APPEARANCES (AND SUBSTITUTE APPEARANCES) BY CLUB AND LEAGUE

	1958–59	1959–60	1960–61	1961–62	1962–63	1963–6
Aberdeen		1	1	2	2	2
Airdrieonians	1	1	2	2	1	2
Ayr United		1	2			
Arbroath		1				
Clyde		1	2		2	
Cowdenbeath						
Dundee		2	2	1		2
Dundee United			2	2	2	2
Dunfermline Athletic		1	2	2	2	2
East Stirlingshire						2
Falkirk				2	2	2
Hamilton Academical						
Hearts			2	2	2	2
Hibernian		2	2	2	2	2
Kilmarnock			2	2	2	2
Morton						
Motherwell		1	2	2	2	2
Partick Thistle		2	2	2	2	2
Queen of the South						2
Raith Rovers		1	2	2	2	
Rangers			2	2	1	2
St Johnstone			2	1		2
St Mirren		1	1	2	1	2
Stirling Albion		1		1		
Third Lanark		1	2	2	2	2
Totals (by season/career)	1 (0)	17 (0)	32 (0)	31 (0)	27 (0)	34 (0

STEVIE CHALMERS: CAREER STATISTICS

League Cup		Europe		Totals (by season)	
				1	
				19	
6				45	
6				43	
1		2		34	
6		8		52	
10		4		42	
6		6		40	
9	(1)	9		52	(2)
5		2		20	(5)
3		4		29	(5)
5	(2)	2		12	(2)
		1	(1)	4	(2)
57	(3)	38	(1)	393	(16)

BY SEASON

1964–65	1965–66	1966–67	1967–68	1968–69	1969–70	1970–71	Totals (by club)	
2	1	2					13	
2		2	1 (1)	1	1		16	(1)
		2					5	
				2			3	
1	2	2	2	0 (1)		1	13	(1)
						1	1	
2	1	1 (1)		2			13	(1)
1	2	1	1	1			14	
	2	2	1	2	1		17	
							2	
1	1	2	1				11	
	1						1	
1		2	1	2			14	
2		2	1	0 (1)	1		16	(1)
2	2	1	1	2	1		17	
1	2			1		1	5	
1	2	2	1 (1)				15	(1)
1	1	2		2			16	
							2	
			1 (1)				8	(1)
1	1	1	1	0 (2)			11	(2)
2	1	1		1	1	0 (1)	11	(1)
2	2	1		1			13	
	1	2	1 (1)				6	(1)
1							10	
23 (0)	22 (0)	28 (1)	13 (4)	17 (4)	5 (0)	3 (1)	253	(10)

251

Appearances (and substitute appearances) by club and Scottish Cup

	1958–59	1959–60	1960–61	1961–62	1962–63	1963–64
Aberdeen						
Airdrieonians			1			1
Arbroath						
Clyde						
Cowdenbeath				1		
Dundee						
Dunfermline Athletic			2			
Elgin City						
Eyemouth United						1
Falkirk					1	
Hearts				1		
Hibernian			2			
Kilmarnock						
Montrose			1			
Morton				1		1
Motherwell						
Partick Thistle						
Queen's Park						
Raith Rovers			1		1	
Rangers		2			1	1
St Johnstone						
St Mirren				1	1	
Third Lanark				2		
Totals (by season/career)	0 (0)	2 (0)	7 (0)	6 (0)	4 (0)	4 (0)

League Cup

	1958–59	1959–60	1960–61	1961–62	1962–63	1963–64
Aberdeen						
Airdrieonians						
Ayr United						
Clyde						
Dundee						
Dundee United					1	
Dunfermline Athletic						
East Fife						
Hamilton Academical						
Hearts						
Hibernian				2		
Kilmarnock						2
Morton						
Motherwell						
Partick Thistle			2	2		
Queen of the South						2
Raith Rovers						
Rangers			2			2
St Johnstone				2		
St Mirren						
Third Lanark			2			
Totals (by season/career)	0 (0)	0 (0)	6 (0)	6 (0)	1 (0)	6 (0)

STEVIE CHALMERS: CAREER STATISTICS

BY SEASON

1964-65	1965-66	1966-67	1967-68	1968-69	1969-70	1970-71	Totals (by club)	
		1					1	
							2	
		1					1	
		2		2			4	
							1	
	1						1	
1	1		0	(1)			4	(1)
		1					1	
							1	
							1	
	2						3	
							2	
1							1	
							1	
				1			3	
1							1	
				0	(1)		0	(1)
1		1					2	
							2	
	2			1			7	
				1			1	
1							3	
							2	
5 (0)	**6** (0)	**6** (0)	**0** (1)	**5** (1)	**0** (0)	**0** (0)	**45** (2)	

1964-65	1965-66	1966-67	1967-68	1968-69	1969-70	1970-71	Totals (by club)	
			1		2		3	
		1			0 (1)		1	(1)
					1		1	
		2		1			3	
	1		1				2	
	2		1				4	
		2					2	
2							2	
				1			1	
2		2					4	
				1			3	
2							4	
1							1	
	2						2	
2							6	
							2	
	1				1 (1)		2	(1)
1		0 (1)	2				7	(1)
					1		3	
		2					2	
							2	
10 (0)	**6** (0)	**9** (1)	**5** (0)	**3** (0)	**5** (2)	**0** (0)	**57** (3)	

253

Appearances (and substitute appearances) by club and Europe

	1958–59	1959–60	1960–61	1961–62	1962–63	1963–64
AC Milan						
Barcelona						
Basel						2
Dynamo Kiev						
Dinamo Zagreb						2
Dukla Prague						
Go Ahead Eagles						
Internazionale						
KPV Kokkola						
Leixoes						
Liverpool						
MTK Budapest						2
Nantes						
Racing Club*						
Red Star Belgrade						
St Etienne						
Slovan Bratislava						2
Valencia					2	
Vojvodina						
Waterford						
FC Zurich						
Totals (by season/career)	0 (0)	0 (0)	0 (0)	0 (0)	2 (0)	8 (0)

* World Club Championship

STEVIE CHALMERS: CAREER STATISTICS

BY SEASON

	1964–65	1965–66	1966–67	1967–68	1968–69	1969–70	1970–71	Totals (by club)
					1			1
	2							2
						2		4
		2		1				3
								(2)
			2					2
		2						(2)
			1					1
							1	1
	2							2
		2						2
								(2)
			2					2
				1				1
					2			(2)
					1			1
								(2)
								2
			2					2
							0 (1)	0 (1)
			2					2
4 (0)	6 (0)	9 (0)	2 (0)	4 (0)	2 (0)	1 (1)	38 (1)

Appearances (and substitute appearances) by club

	League		Scottish Cup	
Rangers	11	(2)	7	
Dunfermline Athletic	17		4	(1)
Partick Thistle	16			(1)
Kilmarnock	17		1	
Hibernian	16	(1)	2	
Heart of Midlothian	14		3	
Clyde	13	(1)	4	
Airdrieonians	16	(1)	2	
Motherwell	15	(1)	1	
Dundee United	14			
St Mirren	13		3	
Aberdeen	13		1	
Dundee	13	(1)	1	
St Johnstone	11	(1)	1	
Third Lanark	10		2	
Raith Rovers	8	(1)	2	
Falkirk	11		1	
Morton	5		3	
Stirling Albion	6	(1)		
Ayr United	5			
Arbroath	3		1	
Basel				
Queen of the South	2			
Dynamo Kiev				
Barcelona				
Cowdenbeath	1		1	
Dinamo Zagreb				
Dukla Prague				
East Fife				
East Stirlingshire	2			
Go Ahead Eagles				
Hamilton Academical	1			
Leixoes				
Liverpool				
MTK Budapest				
Nantes				
Queen's Park			2	
Red Star Belgrade				
Slovan Bratislava				
Valencia				
Vojvodina				
FC Zurich				
AC Milan				
Elgin City			1	
Eyemouth United			1	
Internazionale				
KPV Kokkola				
Montrose			1	
Racing Club				
St Etienne				
Waterford				
Totals (career)	**253**	**(10)**	**45**	**(2)**

256

STEVIE CHALMERS: CAREER STATISTICS

League Cup	Europe	Totals (by club)
7 (1)		25 (3)
2		23 (1)
6		22 (1)
4		22
3		21 (1)
4		21
3		20 (1)
1 (1)		19 (2)
2		18 (1)
4		18
2		18
3		17
2		16 (1)
3		15 (1)
2		14
2 (1)		12 (2)
		12
1		9
		6 (1)
1		6
		4
	4	4
2		4
	3	3
	2	2
		2
	2	2
	2	2
2		2
		2
	2	2
1		2
	2	2
	2	2
	2	2
		2
	2	2
	2	2
	2	2
	2	2
	2	2
	1	1
		1
		1
	1	1
	1	1
		1
	1	1
	1	1
	(1)	1
57 (3)	38 (1)	393 (16)

257

APPEARANCES: MILESTONES

Full Debut:
10.3.59   v. Airdrieonians (h)   League   1-2

100th Appearance:
17.3.62   v. Airdrieonians (a)   League   0-1

200th Appearance:
26.8.64   v. Heart of Midlothian (h)   League Cup,   6-1
                                          1st Round,
                                          Group 3

300th Appearance:
3.12.66   v. Kilmarnock (a)   League   0-0

400th Appearance:
1.10.69   v. Basel (h)   European Cup,   2-0
                                          1st Round,
                                          2nd Leg

Last Appearance:
1.5.71   v. Clyde (h)   League   6-1

100th League Appearance:
27.3.63   v. Kilmarnock (a)   0-6

200th League Appearance:
17.12.66   v. Partick Thistle (h)   6-2

First Scottish Cup Appearance:
2.4.60   v. Rangers (n) Semi-final   1-1

Last Scottish Cup Appearance:
26.4.69   v. Rangers (n) Final   4-0

First League Cup Appearance:
13.8.60   v. Third Lanark (h) 1st Round,   2-0
                       Group 2

258

STEVIE CHALMERS: CAREER STATISTICS

Last League Cup Appearance:
25.10.69 v. St Johnstone (n) Final   1-0

First European Appearance:
26.9.62 v. Valencia (a)   Inter-Cities Fairs   2-4
                                Cup, 1st Round,
                                1st Leg

Last European Appearance:
21.10.70 v. Waterford (a)   European Cup,   7-0
                                2nd Round,
                                1st Leg

Cup Final Appearances

22.4.61	v. Dunfermline Athletic	Scottish Cup	0-0
26.4.61	v. Dunfermline Athletic	(replay)	0-2
15.5.63	v. Rangers	Scottish Cup	0-3
24.10.64	v. Rangers	League Cup	1-2
24.4.65	v. Dunfermline Athletic	Scottish Cup	3-2
23.4.66	v. Rangers	Scottish Cup	0-0
27.4.66	v. Rangers	(replay)	0-1
29.10.66	v. Rangers	League Cup	1-0
29.4.67	v. Aberdeen	Scottish Cup	2-0
25.5.67	v. Internazionale	European Cup	2-1 (1 goal)
28.10.67	v. Dundee	League Cup	5-3 (2 goals)
5.4.69	v. Hibernian	League Cup	6-2
26.4.69	v. Rangers	Scottish Cup	4-0 (1 goal)
25.10.69	v. St Johnstone	League Cup	1-0

When Stevie was playing, the Glasgow Cup was a serious competition but it is omitted from his career stats. His record in that competition was 8 goals in 22 appearances, playing in four winning finals.

THE WINNING TOUCH

GOALS BY CLUB
LEAGUE

	1958–59	1959–60	1960–61	1961–62	1962–63	1963–64
Aberdeen			1			2
Airdrieonians		3	2		1	1
Ayr United						
Arbroath		2				
Clyde			1		1	
Cowdenbeath						
Dundee		1	1			1
Dundee United				1	1	1
Dunfermline Athletic			1			
East Stirlingshire						6
Falkirk						3
Hamilton Academical						
Hearts					1	1
Hibernian			4			2
Kilmarnock			2	2		
Morton						
Motherwell			1	1	3	2
Partick Thistle		2	1	2		3
Queen of the South						3
Raith Rovers		2	2	1	1	
Rangers			1			1
St Johnstone			1			
St Mirren		2	1	4	3	2
Stirling Albion						
Third Lanark		2	1	1		
Totals (career)		**14**	**20**	**12**	**11**	**28**

SCOTTISH CUP

	1958–59	1959–60	1960–61	1961–62	1962–63	1963–64
Aberdeen						
Airdrieonians			1			1
Arbroath						
Clyde						
Cowdenbeath				2		
Dundee						
Dunfermline Athletic						
Elgin City						
Eyemouth United						2
Falkirk						
Hearts				1		
Hibernian			1			
Kilmarnock						
Montrose				2		
Morton						
Motherwell						
Partick Thistle						
Queen's Park						
Raith Rovers			1		1	
Rangers		1				
St Johnstone						
St Mirren						
Third Lanark				3		
Totals (career)	**0**	**1**	**5**	**6**	**1**	**3**

STEVIE CHALMERS: CAREER STATISTICS

1964–65	1965–66	1966–67	1967–68	1968–69	1969–70	1970–71	Totals (by club)
1							4
2		1			1		11
		3					3
				5			7
1		3	2			1	9
							0
	1	1		2			7
1							4
	2	1	2				6
							6
		2	2				7
	1						1
			1	1			4
1		2					9
1			1	1			7
	2					1	3
1		3	1				12
1		4					13
							3
							6
2	3						7
	2	1			1		5
1	3			2			18
		2					2
							4
12	**14**	**23**	**9**	**11**	**2**	**2**	**158**

1964–65	1965–66	1966–67	1967–68	1968–69	1969–70	1970–71	Totals (by club)
							0
							2
		1					1
				1			1
							2
	1						1
	1						1
		1					1
							2
							0
	2						3
							1
							0
							2
				1			1
1							1
							0
		1					1
							2
				1			2
				1			1
1							1
							3
2	**4**	**3**	**0**	**4**	**0**	**0**	**29**

THE WINNING TOUCH

GOALS BY CLUB
LEAGUE CUP

	1958–59	1959–60	1960–61	1961–62	1962–63	1963–64
Aberdeen						
Airdrieonians						
Ayr United						
Clyde						
Dundee						
Dundee United						
Dunfermline Athletic						
East Fife						
Hamilton Academical						
Hearts						
Hibernian					1	
Kilmarnock						
Morton						
Motherwell						
Partick Thistle						
Queen of the South						2
Raith Rovers						
Rangers			1			
St Johnstone						
St Mirren						
Third Lanark						
Totals (career)	0	0	1	1	0	2

EUROPE

	1958–59	1959–60	1960–61	1961–62	1962–63	1963–64
AC Milan						
Barcelona						
Basel						1
Dynamo Kiev						
Dinamo Zagreb						2
Dukla Prague						
Go Ahead Eagles						
Internazionale						
KPV Kokkola						
Leixoes						
Liverpool						
MTK Budapest						2
Nantes						
Racing Club*						
Red Star Belgrade						
St Etienne						
Slovan Bratislava						
Valencia						
Vojvodina						
Waterford						
FC Zurich						
Totals (career)	0	0	0	0	0	5

* World Club Championship

STEVIE CHALMERS: CAREER STATISTICS

1964–65	1965–66	1966–67	1967–68	1968–69	1969–70	1970–71	Totals (by club)
							0
							0
					1		1
		1					1
			2				2
	1						1
		2					2
5							5
				5			5
1		1					2
							1
1							1
							0
							0
3							3
							2
	1				2		3
							1
							0
		1					1
							0
10	**2**	**5**	**2**	**5**	**3**	**0**	**31**

1964–65	1965–66	1966–67	1967–68	1968–69	1969–70	1970–71	Totals (by club)
							0
							0
							1
							0
							2
							0
							0
		1					1
							0
2							2
							0
							2
		2					2
		0					0
							0
				1			1
							0
							0
		1					1
							0
		1					1
2	**0**	**5**	**0**	**1**	**0**	**0**	**13**

Total Goals by Club (all competitions)

	League	Scottish Cup	League Cup	Europe	Totals
St Mirren	18	1	1	0	20
Partick Thistle	13	0	3	0	16
Airdrieonians	11	2	0	0	13
Motherwell	12	1	0	0	13
Clyde	9	1	1	0	11
Hibernian	9	1	1	0	11
Raith Rovers	6	2	3	0	11
Rangers	7	2	1	0	10
Dundee	7	1	2	0	10
Dunfermline Athletic	6	1	2	0	9
Hearts	4	3	2	0	9
Arbroath	7	1	0	0	8
Kilmarnock	7	0	1	0	8
Falkirk	7	0	0	0	7
Third Lanark	4	3	0	0	7
East Stirlingshire	6	0	0	0	6
Hamilton Academical	1	0	5	0	6
St Johnstone	5	1	0	0	6
Dundee United	4	0	1	0	5
East Fife	0	0	5	0	5
Queen of the South	3	0	2	0	5
Aberdeen	4	0	0	0	4
Ayr United	3	0	1	0	4
Morton	3	1	0	0	4
Cowdenbeath	0	2	0	0	2
Dinamo Zagreb	0	0	0	2	2
Eyemouth United	0	2	0	0	2
Leixoes	0	0	0	2	2
Montrose	0	2	0	0	2
MTK Budapest	0	0	0	2	2
Nantes	0	0	0	2	2
Stirling Albion	2	0	0	0	2
Basel	0	0	0	1	1
Elgin City	0	1	0	0	1
Internazionale	0	0	0	1	1
Queen's Park	0	1	0	0	1
St Etienne	0	0	0	1	1
Vojvodina	0	0	0	1	1
FC Zurich	0	0	0	1	1
Totals (career)	158	29	31	13	231

STEVIE CHALMERS: CAREER STATISTICS

Total Goals by Season

	League	Scottish Cup	League Cup	Europe	Totals
1958–59	0	0	0	0	0
1959–60	14	1	0	0	15
1960–61	20	5	1	0	26
1961–62	12	6	1	0	19
1962–63	11	1	0	0	12
1963–64	28	3	2	5	38
1964–65	12	2	10	2	26
1965–66	14	4	2	0	20
1966–67	23	3	5	5	36
1967–68	9	0	2	0	11
1968–69	11	4	5	1	21
1969–70	2	0	3	0	5
1970–71	2	0	0	0	2
Totals (career)	158	29	31	13	231

Goals per Game Ratio

	Goals	Appearances	Ratio
East Stirlingshire	6	2	3.00
Hamilton Academical	6	2	3.00
East Fife	5	2	2.50
Arbroath	8	4	2.00
Eyemouth United	2	1	2.00
Montrose	2	1	2.00
Queen of the South	5	4	1.25
St Mirren	20	18	1.11
Cowdenbeath	2	2	1.00
Dinamo Zagreb	2	2	1.00
Elgin City	1	1	1.00
Internazionale	1	1	1.00
Leixoes	2	2	1.00
MTK Budapest	2	2	1.00
Nantes	2	2	1.00
St Etienne	1	1	1.00
Raith Rovers	11	12	0.92
Partick Thistle	16	22	0.73
Motherwell	13	18	0.72
Airdrieonians	13	19	0.68
Ayr United	4	6	0.67
Dundee	10	16	0.63
Falkirk	7	12	0.58
Clyde	11	20	0.55
Hibernian	11	21	0.52
Third Lanark	7	14	0.50
Queen's Park	1	2	0.50
Vojvodina	1	2	0.50
FC Zurich	1	2	0.50
Morton	4	9	0.44
Hearts	9	21	0.43

GOALS PER GAME RATIO (CONTINUED)

	Goals	Appearances	Ratio
Rangers	10	25	0.40
St Johnstone	6	15	0.40
Dunfermline Athletic	9	23	0.39
Kilmarnock	8	22	0.36
Stirling Albion	2	6	0.33
Dundee United	5	18	0.28
Basel	1	4	0.25
Aberdeen	4	17	0.24

STEVIE CHALMERS: CAREER STATISTICS

Goals: Milestones

First Goal:
19.9.59   v. Raith Rovers (a)   League   3-0

First Celtic Park Goal:
5.12.59   v. Dundee   League   2-3

100th Goal:
29.2.64   v. East Stirlingshire (h)   League   5-2
                                       (1st goal in hat-trick)

200th Goal:
30.12.67   v. Dunfermline Athletic (h) League   3-2
                                       (1st goal of two)

Last Goal:
1.5.71   v. Clyde (h)   League   6-1

100th League Goal:
25.12.65   v. Morton (h)   8-1
                                       (1st goal of two)

First Scottish Cup Goal:
2.4.60   v. Rangers (n) Semi-final   1-1

Last Scottish Cup Goal:
26.4.69   v. Rangers (n) Final   4-0

First League Cup Goal:
3.9.60   v. Rangers (h) 1st Round, Group 2   1-2

Last League Cup Goal:
13.10.69   v. Ayr United (n) Semi-final replay   2-1

First European Goal:
9.10.63   v. Basel (h) 1st Round, 2nd Leg   5-0

Last European Goal:
2.10.68   v. St Etienne (h)   4-0

Hat-Tricks

18.4.60	v. Airdrieonians (a)	League	5-2
3.11.62	v. St Mirren (a)	League	7-0
13.5.63	v. Motherwell (h)	League	6-0
2.11.63	v. East Stirlingshire (a)	League	5-1
9.11.63	v. Partick Thistle (h)	League	5-3
4.1.64	v. Falkirk (h)	League	7-0
29.2.64	v. East Stirlingshire (h)	League	5-2
22.8.64	v. Partick Thistle (a)	League Cup	5-1
16.9.64	v. East Fife (h)	League Cup	6-0 (5 goals)
3.1.66	v. Rangers (h)	League	5-1
10.12.66	v. Motherwell (h)	League	4-2
11.2.67	v. Ayr United (a)	League	5-0
11.9.68	v. Hamilton Academical (h)	League Cup	10-0 (5 goals)
9.11.68	v. Arbroath (a)	League	5-0

International Career with Scotland

Stevie made a total of 5 appearances (4 starts) for Scotland, scoring 3 goals.

3.10.64   v. Wales (a)   Home International   2-3
             (scored in 28th minute to make score 1-1)

21.10.64   v. Finland (h)   World Cup Qualifier   3-1
             (scored in 38th minute to make score 2-0)

18.6.66   v. Portugal (h)   Friendly   0-1
(as substitute)

25.6.66   v. Brazil (h)   Friendly   1-1
             (scored in 1st minute to make score 1-0)

16.11.66   v. Northern Ireland (h)   Home International/   2-1
                                           European Championships
                                           Qualifier

STEVIE CHALMERS: CAREER STATISTICS

Appearances for the Scottish League

Stevie made a total of four appearances for the Scottish League without scoring.

28.11.62	v. League of Ireland (h)	11-0
	(record win for Scottish League)	
17.3.65	v. English League (h)	2-2
7.9.66	v. League of Ireland (h)	6-0
15.3.67	v. English League (h)	0-3

Playing Career After Celtic

After leaving Celtic in 1971, Stevie signed for Morton and scored eight goals for the Greenock club in 32 League appearances. One of his first matches for Morton was at Celtic Park in the third League match of the season, which Celtic won 3-1.

He joined Partick Thistle in 1972. His record at Firhill was:

1972–73 League 18 (+2 sub appearances)	Scottish Cup 2 (+2)	5 goals
1973–74 League 20 (+2)	Scottish Cup 2 (+2)	1 goal
1974–75 League 0 (+1)		
Total: 42 (+8)		6 goals

Debut 7.10.72 v. Ayr United (a) lost 1-2; final appearance 19.4.75 v. St Johnstone (h) drew 0-0.

(Thanks to Robert W. Reid for the Partick Thistle information.)

INDEX

Abbotsinch 7
Aberdeen 38, 124, 130, 141, 191, 202, 245, 259
   see also appearance statistics
Adamslie Park 15
Airdrieonians (Airdrie) 27–30, 32–3, 38, 245, 258, 268
   see also appearance statistics
Ajax Amsterdam 107
Albion Rovers 24
Alexandra Parade canal 10
Allan, Willie 48
Amarildo 120
American Golf shop, Stirling 222
Anderson, George 202
appearance statistics
   for Celtic 250–7, 258–9
   for Morton and Partick Thistle 269
   for Scotland 268
   for Scottish League 269
Arbroath 38, 245, 268
   see also appearance statistics
Armstrong, Billy 203
Ashfield Juniors 22–4, 28–9, 33, 240
Atlas (Mexico), friendly match against 98, 100
Atlético Madrid 119
Auld, Bertie 80, 108, 130, 171, 183–4, 191, 233, 240
   and European Cup final victory 142, 149, 156, 158, 160
   as manager of Partick Thistle 210–11
   on Stevie's career 235–6
Ayr United 38, 191, 245, 267–9
   see also appearance statistics

Bader, Douglas 218
badminton, playing 220
ball, training with 88–9, 156, 201, 205
Balornock 1, 3, 11, 13–14, 21, 22
Barberac, Jacques 47–50
Barcelona, Fairs Cup match against 54, 71, 190
   see also appearance statistics
Barrowfield training ground 136
Basel 56, 179, 258, 267
   see also appearance statistics
Baxter, Jim 32, 64–5, 67, 68, 69, 119, 120, 130, 132, 223
Bayern Munich, friendly against 95–6, 98, 234
Bearsden golf course 217
Bedin, Gianfranco 146, 147, 148, 159
Beeson, Jim 19
Bell, John 246
Bellini 120
Belvidere Hospital 1–5, 20, 40, 229
Bermudan Young Men, match against 98
bias, anti-Celtic 39, 128, 132–3
Bishopbriggs 165, 186, 197, 216–17, 220–1, 226, 240, 242
Blantyre Vics 114
Bologna, friendly match against 99
bomb shelter, James Nisbet Street 10
Botany, The ('The Butney') 207, 213–14
Boyle, Jimmy 21, 25
Brackenridge, Willie 22
Brand, Ralph 53
Brazil, Scotland friendly against 59, 119–24, 236, 244, 268
Bremner, Billy 119, 121–2, 123, 188
Bridget, Sir Alex Ferguson's sister-in-law 240
Bridgeton railway station, walk to 14
Brother Gabriel 10
Brown, Bobby 127–8, 130–1
Brunswick Club, the 14–15, 21

budget constraints, Morton 200
Busby, Sir Matt 163
Byrne, Alec 36

Cadzow St Anne's 12
Cajkovski, Zlatko 96
Callaghan, Tommy 207, 225
Campsie Hills 216
Cappellini, Renato 143–4
Cappielow *see* Morton
caps, international 59–73, 117–26, 130–3, 244, 268
Captain's Table restaurant 226
career statistics 245–69
Cassidy, Eddie 229
Cawder Golf Club 216–19, 226
Cejas, Agustín 175
Celtic
   domestic and European progress under Jock Stein 97–115
   early years with 27–43, 45–58
   European Cup victory *see* European Cup: 1966–67 campaign and victory
   European Cup-Winners' Cup games for 55–6, 87, 101, 118
   Fairs Cup games for 45–50, 54–5, 63, 71, 101
   League Cup final defeat to Partick Thistle 208
   part-time signing for 23–5
   playing against for Morton 198–9, 269
   revival of under Jock Stein 75–93
   son Paul's time with 221–2
   see also Old Firm games
Celtic Pools 214–16, 226
Celtic supporters' rally (Glasgow's Royal Concert Hall) 220
Centenario Stadium (Montevideo, Uruguay), match in v. Racing Club 174–7
Central League Championship 16
centre-forward, conversion to by Jock Stein 75–6
Chalmers, Ann (daughter) 52, 71, 222
Chalmers, Betty (sister) 9
Chalmers, Carol (daughter) 43, 52, 222
Chalmers, Clare (daughter) 221–2
Chalmers, David (father) 47, 81, 166
   childhood memories of 8–9, 10–11, 12–13

   influence on Stevie's career 23, 24–5, 30, 34, 36, 183, 221
   playing career of 8, 12, 23, 34, 60, 132
Chalmers, Davie (brother) 9, 18
Chalmers, Jim (brother) 9, 42
Chalmers, Margaret (mother) 9, 13–14
Chalmers, Martin (son) 221–2
Chalmers, Maureen (sister) 9
Chalmers, Paul (son) 43, 52, 221–2
Chalmers, Sadie (née Blackenridge)
   meeting, courtship and marriage to 21–3, 36, 41
   and move to Morton 193–4
   as wife and mother 43, 165, 180, 219–21, 226, 231, 236, 238, 240
Chalmers, Stephen (son) 43, 52, 222
Charles, John ('The Gentle Giant') 66–7
Charlton, Jack 188
childhood years 9–14
chipped bone 54, 190
Christopher (grandson) 223
Clark, Bobby 124
Clark, John 122–3, 125, 161, 193–4, 198, 199, 204, 242
   on Stevie's career 232–4
club championship victories, Cawder Golf Club 218
Clyde 38, 191–2, 202, 203, 245, 258, 267
   see also appearance statistics
Clydebank 8, 12
Colchester United Reserves 20
Collins, John 120
Colrain, John 40
Connelly, George 187
consecutive matches, scoring in 245
Craig, Jim 99, 130, 142, 143–4, 149, 151, 158, 161, 181
   on Stevie's career 230–1
Craig, Joe 208, 209
CSKA Sofia 139
Cunningham, Willie 198

Dalglish, Kenny 171, 187, 237
Davidson, Vic 187
Davie, Sandy 62
Deans, Dixie 245
debut
   for Celtic's third eleven 24
   full debut, v. Airdrie 27–30, 258
Dennistoun 41, 42–3
Di Stefano, Alfredo 178
diary entries, on early performances 38

INDEX

Dinamo Zagreb 56, 104–5
   see also appearance statistics
discipline, under Jock Stein 83–4
dismissal, against Leixoes 46–50, 63–4
double fracture of leg, sustained in 1969
   League Cup final 184–7, 189–90, 192, 248
dressing rooms, Celtic 226
Duffy, Neil 23
Dukla Prague 107–13, 125, 126, 141, 239
   see also appearance statistics
Dumfries 215
Dunbartonshire Select, schools match against 14
Dundee 38, 63, 68, 70, 173–4, 176, 247–8, 259, 267
   see also appearance statistics
Dundee United 62–3
   see also appearance statistics
Dunfermline Athletic 24, 38, 57–8, 79, 85, 199, 202, 222, 241, 259, 267
   see also appearance statistics
Dunn, John 213
Dynamo Kiev 87

East Fife 61–2, 202, 246, 268
   see also appearance statistics
East Stirlingshire 245, 267–8
   see also appearance statistics
Easterhouse 43, 220
Elgin City 245
engagement, to Sadie 23
England
   v. Scotland (1967), omission from team 73, 125–30
   World Cup win 129
English League v. Scottish League matches 60–1, 269
European Cup
   1966–67 campaign and victory 101–15, 131, 135–67, 173, 177–8, 187–8 *see also* goals: European Cup match-winner
   1970 final defeat 188–9
   other games in 179, 190, 192
   see also appearance statistics
European Cup-Winners' Cup 55–6, 87, 101, 118
European match substitute, Stevie as Celtic's first 180, 247
Eusebio 160
Evans, Bobby 32, 37, 51

FA Cup, match for Newmarket Town in 20
Facchetti, Giacinto 145
Falkirk 30, 191, 198, 268
   see also appearance statistics
Fallon, John 114, 176, 203
Fallon, Sean 97, 99
Faulkner, Max 218
FC Zurich 102, 104
   see also appearance statistics
Feola, Vicente 119, 121
Ferguson, Bobby 124
Ferguson, Sir Alex 93, 198, 220
   on Stevie's career 240–1
Fernie, Willie 37
Ferrari's restaurant (Buchanan Street) 31
Feyenoord 189
Fidelis 120
final match for Celtic 191–2, 258, 269
fine, imposed following Racing Club match 175–6
Finland, World Cup qualifier against 64, 68–70, 268
Firhill *see* Partick Thistle
Fitzsimmons, Dr 36, 45
five-goal hauls 62, 181–2, 246
Forsyth, Alex 208
four-hundredth appearance 258
Friel, Benny 11

Gallagher, Charlie 49, 77, 106
Gardner, Mrs 43
Garngad 11–12
Geleta, Jan 111
Gemmell, Tommy 99, 103, 105, 108, 125, 130–1, 132, 178, 207
   and European Cup final victory 149, 151, 153, 156, 160, 161, 164, 233
   and Jock Stein 80, 97, 195
   on Stevie's career 234–5
Gerard (daughter Carol's husband) 222
Gerson 120
Gillies, Don 203
Gilmar 120
Gilzean, Alan 63, 70, 71, 72
Glasgow, childhood years in 9–14
Glasgow Celtic *see* Celtic
Glasgow Cup 259
Glasgow Select team, appearances for 14
Glavin, Ronnie 208
Glendenning, Raymond 93
Glennconner Park 12

Gloria, Otto 118, 121
goals
    European Cup final match-winner
        153–6, 157–8, 171, 183, 226, 231,
        233, 234–5, 239, 241, 248
    final goal for Celtic and the Lions 192
    five-goal hauls 62, 181–2, 246
    hat-tricks 77, 92, 181, 245, 246, 267,
        268
    in Junior international v. Ireland 23
    milestones 267
    record as Celtic's fourth-highest
        scorer 223–4
    stats 260–6, 268, 269
    v. Rangers in 1967 Scottish Cup final
        182–3
Golders Green 129
golf, love of 11, 42, 216–19, 226, 233–4,
    237, 239–40
Gosling, Dr Hilton 121
Grace, 'the Swede' 19
grandchildren 222–3
Gray, Dougie 15
Greenock 197, 205, 207, 215, 242
    see also Morton
Green's Playhouse 23
Greig, John – on Stevie's career 243–4
Guarneri, Aristide 160
gymnasium training, Celtic Park 51–2

Halme, Martti 69
Hamilton Academical 181–2, 222, 246,
    268
    see also appearance statistics
Hamilton, Alex 68
Hamilton, family roots in 9, 12, 13, 14
Hampden Park 32, 38, 40, 55, 64, 117,
    120–1, 178, 182–4, 188, 225
handicap, golf 217, 234
Hannet, Joseph 88
Hansen, Alan 208, 209, 242–3
Hansen, John 208, 209
Harper, Gary 246
Hartson, John 224–5, 246
hat-tricks 77, 92, 181, 245, 246, 267, 268
Haverhill 19
Hay, Davie 187
heart attack 219–20, 226
Hearts (Heart of Midlothian) 71, 113,
    190–1, 202, 233, 237, 258
    see also appearance statistics
Hendon House Hotel 125

Heron, Brian 203
Herrera, Helenio ('The Magician')
    114–15, 136–7, 139, 149, 157, 166–7
Hibernian 57, 79, 203, 233, 245, 259
    see also appearance statistics
High Cambuslang 4
Hilton Hotel, Glasgow 224–5
honeymoon 41
Hood, Harry 198–9
Hotel Palacio, Estoril 138, 164
Houston Hurricanes 194
Huddersfield Town 199
Hughes, John ('Yogi') 78, 104, 171, 175,
    244
hundredth appearance 258

inside-forward, playing as 19, 22–3, 34,
    75, 147, 169, 172
Inter-Cities Fairs Cup 45–50, 54–5, 63,
    71, 101
Inter Milan
    European Cup final victory against
        45, 48, 63, 114, 135–67, 231, 259
    match-winning goal against 153–6,
        157–8, 171 ,183, 226, 231, 233,
        234–5, 239, 241, 248
    see also appearance statistics
Inverness Clachnacuddin 203
Ipswich Town Reserves 20
Iron Curtain, matches behind 109–10
    see also Dukla Prague
Italy, 1966 World Cup qualifying game
    against 64–5

Jack (grandson) 223
Jairzinho 120
James Nisbet Street, tenement in 9
Jansen, Wim 189
jerseys
    Gianfranco Bedin's 159
    Pele's 59, 122, 123
Jimmy Boyle's band 21, 25
Johnstone, Jimmy ('Jinky') 56, 84, 86, 99,
    103, 108, 115, 141, 176–7, 178, 181,
    223, 233
    and European Cup final victory 148,
        153, 160
    and Jock Stein 82–3, 170
    Scotland matches 68, 126–7, 130
Juliska Stadium 110–11
    see also Dukla Prague
Junior football 12, 14, 15–17, 23, 24–5, 28

INDEX

Junior international caps
    father David's 12, 23
    Stevie's 23, 25

Kansas 97
Kelly, Bob 33, 34–6, 37, 56, 99, 164, 175–6, 177
Kelly, Johnny 36
Kelly's Hotel and Spa, Rosslare 220
Kennedy, Dr 219
Kennedy, Jim 132
Kilmacolm 13
Kilmarnock 114, 124, 258
    see also appearance statistics
Kindvall, Ove 189
Kirkintilloch golf course 217
Kirkintilloch Herald 20
Kirkintilloch Rob Roy 1, 15–17, 20, 22, 114
knighthood, failure to award to Jock Stein 163–4
KPV Kokkola 190
    see also appearance statistics

Lamb, Des 186
Lambie, John 184
Lamont, Bill 181
Lapland 190
Largs 68, 117, 124
Larsson, Henrik 224, 232, 245–6
Las Vegas 239
Laughton, Denis 203
Law, Denis 64, 65, 67, 68, 69, 71, 124–5, 130, 132
Lawrence, John 164
Lawson, Kirkie 203
leading scorer for Celtic, seasons as 50, 169, 245, 247
League Cup finals
    Celtic defeats 55, 259
    Celtic victories 29, 51, 145, 173–4, 176, 184, 188, 192, 247, 248, 259
    Partick Thistle's victory against Celtic 208
League of Ireland, Scottish League matches against 269
league titles 87, 141, 145, 188, 191–2, 247
    see also Treble, the
Leeds United 188
leg break, sustained in 1969 League Cup final 184–7, 189–90, 192, 248

Leixoes, Fairs Cup match against 45–50, 54, 63
    see also appearance statistics
Lennox, Bobby 54, 85–6, 88, 170, 172, 182, 190, 194, 221, 233–4, 240–1, 243
    dismissal against Racing Club 176
    and European Cup final victory 148–9, 159, 165–6, 236
    goals for Celtic 90, 103, 178, 181, 198, 223–4, 246
    Scotland, games for 124–5, 130
    on Stevie's career 238–40
Lisbon Lions 187, 193, 210, 230–40, 247
    final game, 191–2
    see also European Cup: 1966–67 campaign and victory
Littlehill Golf Club 11
Liverpool 107, 163, 208, 209
    Cup-Winner's Cup defeat against 87–8
    see also appearance statistics
Los Angeles 100, 117
Lumsden, Jim – on Stevie's career 241–2

Macari, Lou 171, 187, 237
MacDonald, Malky 77, 124
MacDonald, Roger 140
Maidens, honeymoon in 41
Maldon, match against 19–20
Malnomenes, Francisco 46
Manchester City 207
Manchester United 163, 208
Marine Hotel, Troon 222
marriage, to Sadie 41
Martin (grandson) 223
Martin, Norrie 182
Masopust, Josef 107
May, Alan and Eve 20, 125
Mazzola, Sandro 143, 144
McBride, Joe 88, 103, 113–14, 124, 161–2, 171, 245, 247
McCambridge, May – on Stevie's illness and recovery 229–30
McCoist, Ally 225
McColl, Ian 65, 67, 72, 118
McCulloch, Tommy 192
McGinlay, Pat 246
McGrain, Danny 99, 187
McGrory, Jimmy 8, 23–4, 33, 34–6, 50, 57, 79, 224, 245–6
McInally, Tommy 245

275

McKenzie, Dr Peter 4–5, 40–1
McLintock, Frank 126
McMahon, Sandy 245
McNab, Neil 206–7
McNeill, Billy 52, 80, 85, 97, 106, 124, 144, 161, 163
    on Stevie's career 231–2
McParland, Davie 207–9, 210
    on Stevie's career 242–3
McQuade, Denis 209–10
Mestalla Stadium 54–5
Michael (grandson) 223
milestones
    appearances 258–9
    goals 267–8
Millar, Jimmy 40, 53
Miller, George 198
Milngavie golf course 217
Mochan, Neil (Neilly) 32, 82, 99, 135
Montrose 245
Morton
    Stevie's hundredth league goal, scored against 267
    time at as player-coach 197–207, 208, 209, 233, 233, 241–2, 269
    transfer to 193–5
    see also appearance statistics
Motherwell 38, 90, 203, 268
    see also appearance statistics
MTK Budapest 56
    see also appearance statistics
Müller, Gerd 95–6, 234
Mundo Desportivo newspaper report 159–60, 162
Murdoch, Bobby 34, 56, 86, 147, 230, 233, 240
    and European Cup final victory 149, 153–4, 155, 157–8, 160, 164
    goals for Celtic 77, 125, 171
Murphy, John 202

Nantes 102–3, 104, 131
Narey, David 120
Natalie (granddaughter) 223
National Service 8, 17–20, 125
Neill, Terry 125
Newcastle United 31
Newmarket Town ('The Jockeys') 19–20
nickname, 'The Glaswegian' 9
Niven, Georgie 40
North America, 1966 tour of 95–101, 117
Northern Ireland, Home International against 71, 124–5, 268
Nottingham Forest 31, 207

O Globo newspaper report 162
off-sales business venture 207, 213–14
Old Firm games
    John Greig, on Stevie's performances in 243–4
    in League Cup finals 29, 55
    in Scottish Cup finals 55, 182–3, 225, 248, 258, 259, 267
    Stevie's first 38–41
    Stevie's goal-scoring appearances in 53–4, 76–9, 92, 246, 268
    as title decider 114–15, 141, 166
    see also appearance statistics
one-year contracts, with Celtic 42, 193
Osborne, Billy ('Sugar') 198, 201, 202
Osorio, Rodolfo 177

Pantelic, Ilija 105, 106
Partick Thistle 23, 30, 38, 199, 245, 258, 268
    transfer to and time with 207–11, 214, 236–7, 242–3, 269
    see also appearance statistics
Paul (grandson) 223
Peacock, Bertie 32, 37, 41, 51, 124
Pele 119, 120, 121–3
penalty-kicks, football writers' attempts at 131
photography, interest in 92, 100–1
Picchi, Armando 154–5, 156, 160
pitch invasion, Hampden (1980) 225
Player, Gary 218
player-coach, time as at Morton 197–207, 208, 209, 233, 241–2, 269
playing career, end of 211, 269
Portugal
    match v. Leixoes in 45–50, 63–4
    Scotland friendly against 117–19, 268
    see also European Cup: 1966–67 campaign and victory
post-playing career, overview 213–27
Prentice, John 117, 118, 119
professionalism, Stevie's 180–1
psychology, Jock Stein's mastery of 82, 91–2
Puskas, Ferenc 56

INDEX

Queen's Park 210
   see also appearance statistics
Quinn, Jimmy 77, 245–6

Racing Club 174–7
   see also appearance statistics
Radoman, Mr 221
Rae, Alex 243
RAF Stradishall 18–19, 29
Rafferty, John 180
Raith Rovers 31–3, 38, 175, 245, 267
   see also appearance statistics
Ramsey, Sir Alf 163
Rangers *see* Old Firm games
Real Madrid 114, 140, 178
Red Star Belgrade 179, 247
   see also appearance statistics
Reid, Robert W. 269
relegation struggle, Morton 202–4
retirement from game 211
Reynders, Fred 96
right-back, fielded as 99
Ritchie, Billy 53–4, 77
Rob Roy 1, 15–17, 20, 22, 114
Robertson, Jimmy 68
Robroyston Hospital 21
Rooney, Bob 46
Rough, Alan 208, 209
Royal Air Force, time in 7–8, 18–19, 29
Royal Maternity Hospital ('The Rottenrow'), Glasgow 9
Royston 11–12

San Francisco 95, 98
San Siro 189
Sarti, Giuliano 151, 160
Sauchie Juniors 242
schooling 9–10, 11–14
schools football 14
Scotland
   international appearances for 59–73, 117–26, 130–3, 244, 268
   managers of, lack of planning by 65–6
   snubbing of for 1967 friendly v. England 73, 126–30
Scotland Select friendly, v. Tottenham Hotspur 70
The Scotsman newspaper, John Rafferty article 180
Scott (grandson) 223

Scottish Cup finals
   1980 pitch invasion 225
   defeats in 55, 57–8, 259
   victories in 85, 130, 141, 145, 182, 192, 247, 248, 258, 259, 267
   see also appearance statistics
Scottish League, call-ups and appearances for 60–1, 269
Seamill Hydro 80–1, 130
Sean Connery Golf Tournament 218
selectors, SFA 59, 60, 62, 63–4, 65, 117, 131–2
Servilio 120
Shankly, Bill 163
Sharkey, Jim 29
Shevlane, Chris 202–3
signing-on fee, Celtic 31
Simpson, Ronnie 87, 128, 129, 131, 144, 152, 176, 178, 191, 218, 239
Slovan Bratislava 56
   see also appearance statistics
Somersham 20
Sorensen, Erik 202, 205
Soviet Union, Scotland friendly against 130–1, 133
Sprake, Gary 67
Springburn 20–2, 41, 220–1
St Aloysius Church (Springburn) 41
St Anthony's 12
St Etienne 179, 267
   see also appearance statistics
St Johnstone 23, 31, 70, 128, 184, 188, 192, 245, 247, 248, 259, 269
see also appearance statistics
St Mirren 30, 191, 222, 245, 268
   see also appearance statistics
St Mungo's Chapel 21
St Mungo's Primary 9–10, 12
St Paul's Hall 21
St Roch's secondary school 11–12, 22
Starks Park 31–2
Steele, Jimmy 93
Stein, Jock 177, 178, 179–80, 181, 186–7, 189, 197, 199, 203, 219, 243
   as captain of Celtic 24
   Celtic's revival under 75–93
   domestic and European progress of Celtic under 97–115
   and European Cup final victory *see* European Cup: 1966–67 campaign and victory
   Stevie's first meeting with 23

277

as part-time Scotland manager 72
post-European Cup restructuring of Celtic 169–73, 179, 187–8, 190–3, 194–5
return to Celtic as manager 57–8
Stephen (grandson) 223
Stevie Chalmers Off-Sales 207, 213–14
Stewart, Dunky 15
Stewart, Hal 194, 198, 199–201, 205–6, 241–2
Stewart, Mr 165
Stirling Albion 203
see also appearance statistics
Stobhill Hospital 21, 220
Strachan, Hughie 243
Strunc, Stanislav 108
substitute, Stevie as Celtic's first 180, 247
Suffolk, time in 7, 18–20, 125
supporter discontent, Celtic 43, 52–3
Swansea City 222
Symon, Scot 209

tactics board, Jock Stein's 81
Tate & Lyle sugar factory, Greenock 202
television, impact on the game 223
ten-nil drubbing of Hamilton Academical 181–2, 246
Texaco Cup 199
Third Lanark 38, 245, 258
see also appearance statistics
Thorup, Borge 198
three-hundredth appearance 258
tool-shop, job in 14
Tottenham Hotspur 70, 98–9, 207
Touch nursing home 4, 20
training
Celtic 88–9, 137, 156, 219
Morton 201, 204, 205–6, 242
Partick Thistle 209, 211
travel sickness 45
Treble, the 145, 181–2
Troon, move to 226
Troon, Old Course 218
Tschenscher, Kurt 143, 145–6
tuberculosis meningitis 2–5, 22, 229–30

Tully, Charlie 37, 51
Turnbull, Eddie 211
two-hundredth appearance 258

Valencia, Fairs Cup match against 54–5, 101, 259
see also appearance statistics
van Hanegem, Wim 189
Victoria (granddaughter) 223
Victoria Infirmary 184
Viktor, Ivo 107, 108
Vojvodina Novi Sad 104, 105–7
see also appearance statistics

wages 42, 43, 52, 177–8, 187–8
Wales, Home International against 62–3, 64–8, 268
Wallace, Willie ('Wispy') 108–9, 113, 171, 174, 233, 247
and European Cup final victory 148–9, 153, 236
Rob Roy, time with 114
Scotland, games for 71, 127–8, 130–1
on Stevie's career 237–8
Wallacewell Road 21
Waterford 259
Watson's, job at 16–17
White, Desmond 27, 35, 48–9, 50
White, John 70
Wilson, Davie 76
Wilson, Paul 187, 237, 246
wing, playing on 19, 33–4, 35, 75–6, 127, 169, 172
winning mentality, importance of 89–91, 210
Wolverhampton Wanderers 38
World Club Championship 135, 174–7, 254, 262
World Soccer magazine 140, 160
Worthington, Frank 199

Yeats, Ron 68
Young, Alex 118
Young, Ian 47